THE MORO WAR

HOW AMERICA BATTLED A MUSLIM INSURGENCY
IN THE PHILIPPINE JUNGLE, 1902–1913

JAMES R. ARNOLD

BLOOMSBURY PRESS
NEW YORK   BERLIN   LONDON   SYDNEY

Published by Bloomsbury Press, New York

All papers used by Bloomsbury Press are natural, recyclable products made from wood grown in well-managed forests. The manufacturing processes conform to the environmental regulations of the country of origin.

Photo credits: **National Archives (courtesy of Robert Fulton)**: pp. 6, 8, 33, 42, 53, 66, 69 top, 86, 107, 111, 124, 140, 180, 199, 211, 242; **National Archives**: pp. 11, 24–25, 37, 46, 55, 56, 63, 69 bottom, 70–71, 77, 90, 153, 167–68, 184–85, 189, 212, 263; **author's collection**: pp. 13, 45, 52; **U.S. Army Heritage and Education Center, Carlisle, Pennsylvania (courtesy of Robert Fulton)**: p. 34; **Digital Archives, Special Collections Library, University of Michigan (courtesy of Robert Fulton)**: p. 133; **Pershing Photographic Collection, Library of Congress (courtesy of Robert Fulton)**: pp. 144, 159, 229, 234.

LIBRARY OF CONGRESS CATALOGING-IN-PUBLICATION DATA

Arnold, James R.
The Moro War : how America battled a Muslim insurgency in the Philippine jungle, 1902–1913 / James R. Arnold.—1st U.S. ed.
p. cm.
Includes bibliographical references and index.
ISBN-13: 978-1-60819-024-9
ISBN-10: 1-60819-024-2
1. Philippines—History—1898–1946. 2. Muslims—Philippines—History—20th century. 3. Counterinsurgency—Philippines—History—20th century.
4. Mindanao Island (Philippines)—History, Military—20th century.
5. Sulu Archipelago (Philippines)—History, Military—20th century.
6. United States—History, Military—20th century. I. Title.

DS685.A76 2011
959.9'032—dc22
2010039113

First U.S. Edition 2011

1 3 5 7 9 10 8 6 4 2

Typeset by Westchester Book Group
Printed in the U.S.A. by Quad/Graphics, Fairfield, Pennsylvania

Contents

Maps

THE MORO WAR

ONE

A Place Called Moroland

Fishes live in the sea, as men do on land:
the great ones eat up the little ones.

Sulu proverb

THE ISLAND STEAMER CAST OFF FROM the U.S. government wharf and carefully threaded its way through Manila's bustling harbor. As it neared Cavite, the steamer passed over the shattered hulks of Rear Admiral Patricio Montojo y Pasarón's Spanish squadron. Commodore George Dewey's victory in 1898 over Montojo's hopelessly outclassed squadron had opened the way for the American occupation of the Philippines. Now it was up to a passenger aboard the steamer, Brigadier General Leonard Wood, to take the next step on the path created by Dewey's guns. Wood gave scant regard to his old Spanish foes. Renowned in Western circles as a model colonial administrator, he was eager to begin his new and exotic assignment, a posting he was sure would enhance his reputation and lead to coveted promotion. The steamer's speed increased as it entered the channel beneath the U.S. Army's convalescent camp on Corregidor Island. Then it turned south to deliver the first U.S. governor of Moro Province to his headquarters at Zamboanga on the island of Mindanao.

General Wood was an intelligent man, but he knew little more about the Philippine Islands than did his American contemporaries. If an

1

American citizen living on this August day in 1903 remembered anything about the Philippines, he recalled Dewey's words to the flag captain of the cruiser *Olympia*: "You may fire when ready, Gridley." That
celebrated command had thrust the United States into a new role as a
Pacific power with unforeseen consequences. President William McKinley sought "benign assimilation" for the people of the Philippines. Filipino nationalists violently resented being assimilated by a foreign power.
The brutal suppression of the Filipino insurgency in 1902 seemed to offer
a chance to begin anew America's first social experiment as a colonial
power in Asia. Overlooked was any notion that a decade-long war in a
place called Moroland was just beginning, and that a succession of American officers who would go on to build the army that fought in World
War I—Leonard Wood, Tasker Bliss, John Pershing—would have their
careers shaped by what took place there.

The islands of Mindanao, Palawan, and Basilan and a chain of some
369 much smaller islands of the Sulu Archipelago composed Moro Province. To the Americans, Moroland was a strange place occupied by fierce
Islamic warriors and primitive, pagan hill tribes. It was by far the largest
province in the Philippines. Moro Province's main island of Mindanao
was the second-largest island in the entire Philippines. By itself Mindanao exceeded Ireland in size. The name Mindanao came from a word
connoting "inundation by river, lake, and sea," and it was only the truth.
The island's outline looked like the worst piece of a jigsaw puzzle, a wildly
irregular coastline featuring numerous bays and estuaries separated by
bold headlands. Rivers emerged from Mindanao's uncharted interior,
sometimes flowing through broad cultivated valleys, more often shrouded
in dense jungle. Mangrove swamps and lakes filled the island's interior,
but there were mountains and high, grassy uplands as well. In the 36,000
square miles of jungle and mountain there were only about fifty miles of
road. To enter the interior one had to follow narrow trails through dense
jungle where trees eight feet in diameter grew 125 feet high in their competition for life-sustaining sunlight. Beneath these towering behemoths
thick underbrush filled every space so completely that it crowded out the
light. Even under the best conditions, wrote an American soldier, "the foliage is so dense that it is impossible to see more than 20 yards in any
direction."[1] The American soldier called this impassable brush the "boon-
docks," a corruption of the Tagalog word *bundok*.

In ancient times Asian trading vessels steered east from the mainland

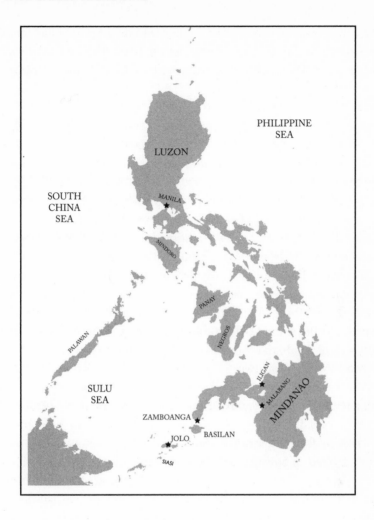

bound for the distant island of Sulu, about a hundred miles southwest of Mindanao. Sulu lay athwart the passage between the southern tip of the Philippines and Borneo. Its favorable geographic location made it an important trading center. Chinese, Indonesian, Thai, and Indian merchants converged on the island's main port of Jolo. At some dateless time, probably between the years 800 and 1000, Arab merchants arrived as well. In their wake came Islamic preachers, or *panditas*. The panditas belonged to the Shafiite sect of Sunni Islam, the prevalent sect of Southeast Asian Muslims. They taught that Mohammed was the Prophet of Allah, the Supreme Deity, who demanded the submission (*islam*) of every human being.

By 1450 a Mecca-born Arab trader named Syed Abu Bakr had founded a Muslim sultanate on Sulu. The sultan established schools for the study of Islam and created political institutions based on Islamic teachings. As the years passed, graduates spread Islam's message, first to nearby Mindanao, where the people of the Cotabato Valley converted, and then throughout the Sulu Archipelago and the southern half of Mindanao. Heretofore, the island's inhabitants had enjoyed no shared culture. Henceforth, Islam provided the only unifying bond among the thirteen or so Moro cultural-linguistic groups living in the southern Philippines. The pagan tribesmen of the hills were unmoved by Islam and continued to live their isolated lives according to their own notions.

With the exception of a few traditional customs, all Moro laws were in accordance with Islamic law, or *sharia*. Their land was *dar al-Islam,* the household of Islam. Unlike in Western tradition, there was no separation of church and state, no distinction between sacred and secular. Islam pervaded everything they did. So the Moros of Sulu and Mindanao learned that the world held two kinds of people—those who submitted to the will of Allah and those who did not—and that there could be no real peace between the two.

Moro communities organized on a clan or tribal basis. Clan size ranged from a few dozen to several thousand, and the extent of the territory they controlled varied accordingly. Regardless of the size of a clan's territory—or *rancheria,* as first the Spanish and then the Americans called it—Moro society divided according to a three-part hierarchy with the *datu* (the man of rank or noble class) at the top. A datu had patriarchal control over the inhabitants of his rancheria. Beneath the datus were the privileged class made up of free citizens. At the bottom were slaves.

Moros who lived along the coast fished, traded—an activity that profitably included slaving—and engaged in piracy. They generally observed the Sulu Seas' prime dictate: take any smaller vessel, trade with any more powerful vessel. Inland from Mindanao's coastal communities, large Moro populations settled the valley of the Rio Grande on the south coast and around Lake Lanao, a forty-square-mile body of water surrounded by unmapped volcanic mountains and isolated by primeval rain forest. The Lake Lanao Moros thus lived apart, devoted to Islam but otherwise barely conscious of any world beyond their homes. Regardless of where they lived and their outward similarity to other Filipinos, the Moros conceived of themselves as a different race. They proudly called

themselves "the People." Their sense of ethnic unity provided an enduring bond when Christian infidels from Spain arrived on their shores.

For the Spanish it was a return visit meant to avenge a crime, convert
the heathens, and add territory to the empire. Back in 1521, Fernando
de Magellan had entered an unknown region of the South Seas while
searching for a route to the Spice Islands. He came upon a chain of islands that he named the Philippines, after the Spanish king Philip II. It
proved Magellan's last discovery. Natives on the island of Cebu killed the
great explorer, leaving it up to his second in command to complete history's first circumnavigation of the globe. The Spanish returned to Cebu
in 1565 to begin a period of colonial rule that lasted until 1898 and
Dewey's decisive naval victory at Manila Bay.

Sixty-four years after the founding of Manila, the Spanish arrived
in Mindanao. On the narrow Zamboanga peninsula they found an easily
defensible position and built a fort designed to serve as a safe haven for
vessels sailing to Jolo. Zamboanga served Spain for most of the next three
hundred years as a secure base, but it was also a prison, curtailing Spanish contact with the island's interior. Indeed, Spanish soldiers ventured
inland at great risk. The danger stemmed from the basic strategic reason
they were in the Philippines. Spanish imperial policy had two goals: to
increase the Crown's territory and economic resources and to convert the
people to Catholicism. Spanish conduct was informed by more than eight
hundred years of bitter warfare against Islam. Seven hundred of those
years witnessed a death struggle for control of Spain itself as the Spanish
fought to evict the Moors (Moros, in Spanish) from the Iberian Peninsula.
This struggle, and the related Crusades, taught the Spanish to regard all
Muslims as enemies. The fact that the Moros engaged in frequent piracy
reinforced this attitude. So the Spanish colonists in the Philippines began
a series of military campaigns against the Muslim people, beginning in
1578 with an attack against the "pirate" stronghold on Jolo. Spanish firearms defeated Jolo's defenders, compelling them to beg for terms, among
which was the acknowledgment of Spanish sovereignty over the Sulu Archipelago. Then the Spanish sailed away confident that the overmatched
Moros would remain docile. In their absence, the sultan of Sulu and his
warriors assembled atop the ruins of their homes and pledged revenge
against the infidels and their Filipino auxiliaries.

Because Islam had only a tenuous toehold in the central and northern parts of the Philippine Islands, here the battle went well for the

The site of Fort Binadayan looking toward Lake Lanao.

Spanish. The Spanish expelled the Muslims from their communities in Manila and points south as far as the Mindanao-Sulu region. The great Spanish religious orders—the Jesuits, Franciscans, and Dominicans—successfully converted the Filipinos, thereby establishing what to this day remains the only Christian nation in East Asia. But in the area that the Americans would come to call Moroland the Spanish met ferocious resistance. Worldwide, throughout the age of Spanish imperial expansion, Spanish conquistadors marched to victory regardless of their opposition or the terrain, with one exception: Moroland.

Although the Moros had never formed a united state, the Spanish presence brought them together in a jihad against the invaders that persisted for 320 years. During this time, Moro society largely developed in isolation from the rest of the Philippines. With the advent of steam-powered warships, breech-loading cannon, and bolt action rifles, by the 1890s the Spanish routinely enjoyed tactical success against the Moros living along the coast. But these successes seemed to have little impact. Islam inspired Moro warriors. A typical Moro chieftain entered battle with an Arabic inscription on his turban: "We begin our task, and I know that no bullet can harm me; God and Mohammed will protect me."[2] Islam taught that death in combat against the infidel led to an afterlife in paradise. Moro pride taught the ignominy of surrender.

In 1895 Spanish governor Ramón Blanco led a campaign against the Lake Lanao Moros. His men dismantled gunboats, hauled them overland in sections from Iligan to Marahui on the north end of Lake Lanao, and reassembled them on the water. For the next three months, steam-powered gunboats armed with cannon and machine guns bombarded every lakeside settlement within range while Spanish infantry conducted punitive attacks. The lake Moros had no answer to this overwhelming display of mobility and firepower. Yet these victories too failed to establish Spanish sovereignty. In the midst of brutal but ultimately unsuccessful efforts to pacify the Moros, the Spanish tried another approach by transplanting thousands of Christianized Filipinos from their homes in the north to Mindanao. The strategy was not without appeal for the Filipinos. Land was scarce in the north. In Mindanao they could simply take it from the inhabitants. Yet it was far from a risk-free land grab. A typical Moro raid in the 1890s against a settlement in Iligan killed twenty Christianized Filipinos and carried off twenty-four captives to serve as slaves. Still, by the dawn of the twentieth century about 40,000 Christianized Filipinos lived on Mindanao. Their presence failed to quell resistance from the island's 275,000 Moros. However, centuries of violent struggle along with deliberate Spanish efforts to foster religious antagonism between Catholic converts and the Moros did produce one enduring legacy: a bitter enmity between the two groups.

Blithely unaware of the history that had shaped Moro society, and supremely confident in the virtues of their own ideals, the Americans came to Moroland in 1899.

AMERICAN SOVEREIGNTY OVER Moroland flowed from the war-ending negotiation with Spain, the 1898 Treaty of Paris. By its terms, the Americans acquired the Philippines and the Moros acquired a new Christian colonial master. A nettlesome detail was the fact that Spain had never managed to conquer the Moros. Moreover, when the Spanish withdrew their garrisons, the Moros logically concluded that they had won. Moro datus cheerfully resumed their traditional habits, namely, engaging in ancestral blood feuds, cattle and slave stealing, and piracy, and the countryside reverted to a state of lawlessness. This was Moroland on the eve of the American arrival: a feudal society where the powerful ruled by the might of the sharp, steel-edged *kris* and outlaw bands ravaged the weak.

At the time of first contact, the United States was preoccupied with its struggle against Filipino insurgents under the command of Emilio Aguinaldo. American leaders concentrated resources to conquer the main island of Luzon. When they gazed south they contemplated estimates based on the advice of Spanish officers suggesting that defeating the warlike Moros would require a hundred thousand men. This was an obviously impossible number. Consequently, in order to avoid diverting forces from the fight against Aguinaldo, Brigadier General John C. Bates received the mission of negotiating with the Moros. The most powerful Moro leader appeared to be the sultan of Sulu, Jamal-ul Kiram II. Sketchy American intelligence estimated that the sultan had a standing army of twenty-six thousand men. In fact, the sultan commanded his immediate bodyguard and little else. Bates and his superiors had no idea that Jamal-ul Kiram II was ruler in name only.

Back in 1878 the sultan had negotiated a treaty with the Spanish. Bates's offer was less favorable, so the sultan balked. But there were internal divisions among the members of his ruling council. Three of his senior advisers feared another futile bloodletting if the sultan resisted the Americans. They eventually persuaded Jamal-ul Kiram II, against his personal preference, to sign the treaty on August 20, 1899. The

Sultan Jamal-ul Kiram II arrives to sign the Bates Agreement.

United States obtained similar, although unwritten, agreements with other Muslim chiefs on Mindanao and Basilan. According to the terms of the Bates Agreement, the Moros acknowledged American sovereignty over the Sulu Archipelago. In return, the United States pledged not to meddle with the "rights and dignities" of the sultan and his ruling datus, or chiefs. Most significantly, the United States said it would not interfere with Moro religious customs. The agreement forbade the import of firearms and war matériel. The sultan agreed to work to suppress piracy. The sultan's courts would deal with Moro-on-Moro crimes, while the U.S. justice system dealt with Moro crimes against non-Moros. Slaves were to have the right to purchase their freedom. For the immediate future, foreigners would request permission from the sultan to travel into the interior. But the agreement optimistically noted that this procedure would prove unnecessary as the Moros and the Americans became better acquainted. The fifteenth and last article established monthly salaries for the sultan and his lieutenants, a key consideration given that the sultan enjoyed a lavish lifestyle complete with occasional visits to the fleshpots of Singapore.

Unknown at the time of signing were significant translation errors between the English and the Tausug versions of the text. The Tausug, or Moro, version made no mention of American sovereignty.[3] Consequently, both sides attained what they wanted. The Americans believed that the Moros had promised to remain peaceful while acknowledging their sovereignty. In their view, their relationship with the Moros was like that between the U.S. government and the American Indians; like the Indians, the Moros were living on territory owned by the United States. Moreover, neither Bates nor any other American understood how little power the sultan actually exercised. Moro leaders, on the other hand, believed that they had negotiated a live-and-let-live arrangement that kept the Americans out of their internal affairs. The thirty-year-old sultan entered the treaty in good faith with the understanding that he would be able to continue his rule essentially unchanged. Furthermore, the sultan thought that the agreement could be altered only through the mutual consent of the two parties. In addition, he did not know that the Americans regarded this piece of paper as merely a temporary expediency to be revisited once they suppressed the Filipino insurrection.

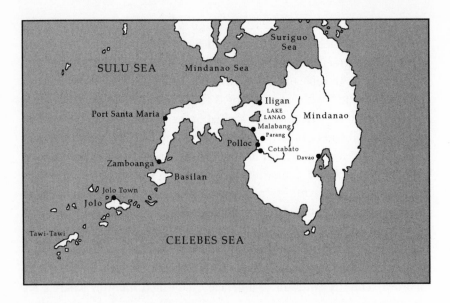

FOR LITTLE GOOD reason beyond the perceived need to show the flag, the U.S. Army entered Moroland in 1899 to occupy selected towns and forts formerly occupied by the Spanish. Company-size infantry and cavalry detachments established garrisons on the western and southern coasts of Mindanao, including the major ports and towns—Zamboanga, Cotabato, Polloc, Parang, Davao—without firing a shot. Likewise, the Americans spread across the Sulu Archipelago, garrisoning the principal port of Jolo as well as the remote port of Siasi at the archipelago's far southern end. By the next year the army presence rose to twenty-six hundred men, still a tiny number for such a huge area. However, even a small American military presence, inserted into the midst of an utterly alien culture, made for uneasy relations with the Moros.

Indeed, a Moro warrior's very appearance and demeanor struck Americans as barbaric. They carried a variety of edged weapons in addition to the ubiquitous swordlike kris, and they wore turbans, loose jackets, and either ankle-length trousers or silk sarongs. But it was the colors that caught the eye: loud combinations of solids and stripes in reds and yellows accented by shades of blue, green, and brown. Every important male Moro had teeth stained black and lips turned bright red, consequences of chewing betel nut. Their haughty body language, reinforced

Moro with badge of manhood, a kris secured in his sash.

by betel nuts' stimulative properties, conveyed a message of serious intent. This sense of self-importance seemed imprinted into the Moro character. Even minor datus came to meetings with small entourages of bodyguards and servants, including the ubiquitous betel nut bearer. Almost everything about them was odd to Americans. Their strange habit of walking beneath the shade of an umbrella made them appear ridiculous in American eyes, but in the Moro view it conferred status. A minor datu had one umbrella bearer, an important datu two, and if the bearer carried a green umbrella, it meant that the datu was a holy man who had completed the pilgrimage to Mecca.

William A. Kobbe was the first officer assigned to command the American garrisons in Moroland. Although there were periodic conflicts arising from Moro attacks against Filipinos, in general relations between the Americans and the Moros remained peaceful. Soldiers from the main garrison at Zamboanga wandered twenty miles into the countryside, unarmed, without fear. The situation was so calm that officers did not even establish sentinels and outposts. Consequently, most of Kobbe's time was spent dealing with heaps of paperwork. A pleasant interruption in the routine came on August 20, 1900, when he attended a ceremony arranged by two prestigious Moro leaders, the datus Piang and Ali. Piang granted Kobbe the highest honors; his followers fired musket and cannon salutes, beat drums, and waved flags. Piang's harem was present, several hundred "gorgeously dressed . . . very comely" young women wearing skimpy sarongs that revealed their breasts and legs.[4] The entertainment consisted of feasting, dancing, and song. For Kobbe the day was simply a pleasant diversion. He did not perceive that Piang would turn out to be the most progressive, pro-American Moro leader on Mindanao.

Kobbe's ambivalence about whether to stay the night—the comely la-dies were on offer, but the thing in itself was clearly wrong—mirrored the attitude of his country. At no time during its occupation of the Phil-ippines was the United States completely comfortable with its imperial role. To alleviate its troubled conscience it created a civilian governing body known as the Philippine Commission. The first head of the com-mission was William Howard Taft. The Taft Commission visited Jolo in May 1901. The *New York Times* reported that the heretofore optimistic commission found the situation depressing, with the Moros in violation of several of the provisions of the Bates Agreement: "They showed no desire for anything different from their old way of giving easygoing al-legiance to their nearest datus and to the Sultan; paying to them their trifling poll tax, and when convicted of theft, a not uncommon occur-rence, stealing more in order to pay their fines and avoid being sold into slavery. Close acquaintance with the barbaric backwardness of these people was an object lesson to the commission."[5]

A probing *Times* reporter talked with Moro leaders and American army officers who commanded the four companies assigned to garrison Jolo. The Moros expressed a desire for a more regular municipal govern-ment. The Americans claimed that the preservation of civil government on the island was an impossibility since the only law the datus seemed to recognize was the Koran, which they freely interpreted according to their individual interests. The officers complained that the Bates Agree-ment hampered their efforts to accomplish tasks such as eradicating piracy, and predicted that it would have to be abrogated before civil government could come to Moroland. However, with their military resources absorbed with fighting the Filipino insurgents to the north, from 1899 to 1903 the Americans avoided interference with Moro politics and the Moro internal economy.

During this period, the American army viewed its mission as keeping the Moros peaceful without antagonizing them. This involved suppressing piracy, trying to limit the slave trade (though not abolish it for fear of causing a war), and trying to keep internecine conflicts from getting out of hand. The officers who commanded the many remote garrisons had immense responsibility and near absolute power because their word was backed by the firepower of the American soldier. When responding to criminal acts of violence, particularly those directed against American soldiers, they served as sheriff, judge, jury, and executioner. In all these roles they could not escape from the prevailing prejudice, learned from the Spanish and from Filipinos, that "the Moro was a religious fanatic who believed that the more Christians he killed the more maidens he would have in paradise after his death."[6]

Some American officers built excellent relations with the Moros. But even they could only begin to fathom Moro culture and experience. Captain Sydney Cloman commanded the southernmost garrison in the entire Philippines. On July 4, he arranged a festival to which he invited all the local datus. Part of the entertainment was a series of athletic competitions. None of them seemed particularly to interest the Moros until

Typical fishing village perched above the water near Siasi.

the tug-of-war. The Moros asked if they could compete. They stripped to the waist, still wearing their knives in the belts, and announced themselves ready. The ensuing tug-of-war almost led to open bloodshed when the losers tried to reclaim victory with their krises. As Cloman ruefully recalled, "I was not aware at that time of the jealousies and ancient feuds, of forays that had never been forgotten, of island fishing grounds that had been encroached upon, of chiefs that had tried to extend their authority over adjacent islands and of the bloody wars that such things had caused."[7]

The core problem was that American relationships with the Moros were between men, not nations. It took time for a handful of sensitive American officers to recognize this critical distinction. Unlike the Americans with their unquestioning fealty to their government, the Moros owed their allegiance to their family, village, subtribe, and tribe, a hierarchy manifestly observed in that order. The Moros had acquired from Islam the conviction "my brother and me against my cousin; my cousin and me against the outsider."

Driven by progressive notions in vogue at home, the American soldiers set about improving Moro society. They excelled at engineering tasks, and so here they focused their labors. They built bridges, roads, and wharves, all of which provided economic benefits. American military doctors offered modern medical care. American administrators introduced public health and sanitation regulations in the towns. They opened schools and invited the locals to attend. They also imposed customs regulations and levied taxes. All of these changes challenged Moro culture. Moreover, the arrival of American surveying expeditions deep into the hinterland, places where the Spanish had never ventured, alarmed the Moros.

In sum, most Moros resented the American effort to civilize them. Individual leaders worried that the American presence would erode their personal authority and enslave their people. Their response was predictable. Ever since the arrival of the Spanish, the Moros' first concern had always been to preserve their distinct Muslim community (*ummah*) within a nation dominated by Christians—first Spanish, then American—who wanted to impose the prerogatives of state control. They would resist such control with the same means that had allowed them to live the life they had known for unchanged centuries. Their resistance posed an unprecedented challenge for the American army: how to defeat an Islamic insurgency on its home soil.

TWO

First Contacts

*They are an essentially different people from us in thought, word and
action and their religion will be a serious bar to any efforts towards
Christian civilization. So long as Mohammedanism prevails,
Anglo-Saxon civilization will make slow headway.*

—General Samuel Sumner, 1903

MOROLAND'S TIME OF HARMONY PROVED short-lived. Quite simply, the
more the Americans and the Moros mixed, the more their essential differences stood out. Brigadier General George W. Davis, the commander
of the Department of Mindanao-Jolo and de facto governor of Moroland,
was far more inclined than most American officers to accept the Moros
as they were, and reported that the American notion of a regulated liberty
was a hopelessly irrelevant, unknown, and unknowable concept to the
Moros: "It is a proud boast of the Mussulman [Muslim] that a people
who live in accordance with the teachings of the prophet [the Koran]
have no need for other codes, constitutions, charters, and bills of rights,
for they say that a rule to regulate every possible human action or rem-
edy every wrong or injustice is to be found in the inspired writings of
Mohammed, as recorded in the Koran."[1]

According to the Bates Agreement, the Americans were supposed to
let the Moros govern their own internal affairs. This required considerable restraint because Americans found Moro judicial practices based

on sharia odious. Men faced amputation of an arm for a second conviction of theft, yet men of the privileged class who murdered a slave escaped
with a small fine. Moro women were second-class citizens, compelled to
endure barbaric punishments for a variety of offenses. The written rule of
law specified how many strokes of the lash a woman faced for committing
different crimes. In the case of adultery she was "to be buried up the chest
and stoned with medium-sized stones."[2] The more the Americans learned
about Moro history and culture, the less they liked.

The Moros heartily reciprocated the American dislike. One of the few
attitudes the two shared was a confidence that their way was the right
way and that a foreign-imposed alternative was strange at best and more
often insultingly offensive. In fundamental contrast to American notions,
Moro ethics did not conceive of a crime against the state. Restitution for
criminal injury was something to be worked out between victim and
perpetrator. If the victim died, then restitution became the task of his
blood relations. The payment of monetary considerations to the victim
if he survived, or to his blood relations if he did not, fully satisfied Moro
justice. In the event of theft of cattle, slaves, or other personal property,
the victim had the privilege to make reprisals in lieu of monetary restitution. If people died in the ensuing reprisals, it was not murder but
rather justified killing. When leading families grew tired of the cycle of
violence, they would get together and in their own way balance losses
and gains in order to bring peace. Nominally the Moros governed themselves by the laws of Islam and the sacred Koran. In reality they followed
the law of the kris. Thus, if the Moro view of ethics and justice was foreign to Americans, the reverse was also true.

The transformation of the attitudes held by Major Owen J. Sweet, the
district commander at Jolo, occurred among almost all American authorities. At first Sweet thought that the natives' study of the Koran offered a useful tool for the United States to exercise "enlightened control."
As the months passed and contact between the two cultures brought
mutual disillusionment, Sweet concluded that he had no confidence in
the Moros and no longer trusted them. He reported that 90 percent of
the Moro people would cheerfully renounce their allegiance to their datus and swear allegiance to the United States. But the traditional leaders
held sway and "they will promise anything in the shape of reforms but
these are never carried out."[3]

More important, experience revealed a fundamental dichotomy: The

U.S. Army had the limited goal of bringing about compliance with the Bates Agreement. But in a more general sense it conceived its mission as maintaining order. However, conflict among Moro factions and tribes predated the American arrival and did not change once the army garrisoned its various posts. Army officers were uncomfortably aware of the intra-Moro raids, piracy, and occasional pitched battles taking place around them, yet the Bates Agreement stipulated a policy of noninterference. From an American perspective, this was an intolerable arrangement. Sweet and fellow officers concluded that additional progress was impossible under the constraints of the Bates Agreement. In their view, the United States needed to take complete control of the islands. Thus, they advocated the abrogation of the Bates Agreement so the United States could introduce internal order and civilization. In Sweet's view this could be accomplished only by persistent force to dominate the Sulu Moros. As Sweet's successor put it, the U.S. government expected him to "civilize one hundred thousand Moros, with a bloody record of hundreds of years, and the only power conferred on me for the purpose was that of moral suasion."[4]

CAPTAIN SYDNEY A. CLOMAN experienced the limits of moral suasion. Cloman commanded the southernmost garrison in the entire Philippines, at Bongao in the low-lying, fever-ridden Tawi-Tawi Islands. His mission was to suppress pirates. A small Spanish garrison had occupied Bongao but never ventured far inland, preferring to remain inside the safety of their stone fort. Cloman opted for a much more active presence and moved his men throughout the island chain. On some of the smaller islands, the children had never before seen a white face. He conceived that he and his men enjoyed good relations with the Moros, so when five of his soldiers asked permission to go pig hunting, Cloman said to go ahead. His only regret was that an attack of malaria prevented him from joining them. The soldiers sailed to a nearby island, where they were joined by a large sailing canoe carrying ten natives. The Moros helped them establish camp. As night fell, Corporal Leonard J. Mygatt went to the beach for a swim, leaving his four comrades playing cards around the fire. Card play always seemed to delight the Moros. The corporal's last view was of cheerful Moros squatting behind the Americans and watching the game unfold. The sounds of shots and screams interrupted his swim. He heard the noise of men running to the beach and hid among the rocks. The Moros searched for a while and then departed.

The corporal returned to camp to behold a terrible scene. At a given signal the Moros had drawn their knives and tried to behead the card players. Mygatt saw that his sergeant was dead and his other three comrades badly wounded. One had a terrible gash in his skull whence his brains oozed. A second soldier had a hatchet sunk into his back. A third had his head half severed from his neck. The Moros had stolen the party's firearms before departing. A night of horror ensued as Mygatt and his wounded comrades helplessly awaited the return of the Moros.

In the morning, Mygatt managed to load the boat, push it across the reef, and set off for Bongao. The wind was unfavorable, so he had to row the twenty-two miles. One man succumbed during this voyage. By virtue of heroic effort the boat hove into view off Bongao with its cargo of two dead, two unconscious, and Mygatt, who had reached the limit of his endurance and was almost incoherent. The garrison brought them to shore, and a jolt of whiskey revived Mygatt sufficiently to give Cloman a brief account before he passed out.

The attack had come out of the blue. Cloman did not know if it was an isolated instance of killing for rifles and loot or part of an organized campaign against the American garrison. Accordingly, he embargoed the port to prevent news from spreading and put the most powerful local leader, Datu Tanton, under arrest. Then he organized a punitive expedition. A lack of boats limited the size of his expedition to forty men. They would set off the next morning. However, the entire garrison wanted to go, and some even spent the night rigging several dilapidated catamarans so they could accompany the expedition.

The improvised fleet landed at the village nearest to where the murders had occurred. Cloman issued simple orders: permit anyone to enter the village but shoot anyone who tried to leave. Cloman then interviewed the village's three chiefs: "They said they were not implicated in the murders in any way. This was believable. They said they did not know who was guilty, and in fact had never heard of the affair until I told them. I knew this to be a lie. In the intimate life of a Malay tribe, it would be impossible to keep the chiefs in ignorance of such an important event."[5]

Cloman was not yet ready to employ extreme measures. Instead he ordered every villager to strip to the waist and come out unarmed. Mygatt's ability to identify the perpetrators was hazy because to him they all looked similar. Nonetheless, he fingered several suspects. Cloman was fairly certain that the guilty men would have remained hidden in the village. He sent his men to search, and they used their rifle butts to herd together twenty more suspects. Cloman then threatened the chiefs with death unless they turned in the guilty men. The chiefs identified the perpetrators, and Cloman had the alleged killers tied to stakes in preparation for execution the next day. All night Cloman interviewed the suspects in order to answer the most important question: Why? He obtained no satisfactory answer. The Moros' explanation "always came down to the fact the soldiers were in their power and could be killed," so therefore they were.[6]

According to Cloman's memoirs, in the morning the suspects were untied in order to serve them breakfast and load them into the boats to return to Bongao. They made "a desperate break for liberty" and during the ensuing melee all were killed. Whether this is what actually transpired is unknowable. The claim that prisoners were killed while trying to escape has been a useful dodge for summary punishment throughout military history. However, it satisfied Cloman's superiors. The annual report of the lieutenant general commanding the army repeated this claim: "Captain Cloman went to the scene of the murder . . . with 45 men, took possession of their village and killed the murderers endeavoring to escape."[7]

News of this incident leaked to the American press. Anti-imperialist newspapers printed elaborate accounts including vicious cartoons showing Cloman killing innocent natives. Cloman wrote: "Among these deluded 'humanitarians' the treacherous murder of a splendid American caused no remark other than that 'he should not have been there,' while the news of the death of the murderer aroused shrieks of rage and resentment."[8] The newspaper attention brought him a great deal of mail, some laudatory, some critical. He retained his sense of balance. One day two letters arrived: one an ardent letter from a young lady in St. Louis, who demanded a picture of her "dream-man" right away, the other a cartoon from a Boston paper depicting him as a degenerate, ferocious killer with a misshapen skull and gorilla-like face. Cloman sent the young lady this portrait of her "dream-man" and thereby preserved his bachelor-hood for several more years.[9]

THE AMERICAN MIND broadly divided Moro Province into two parts: Mindanao and Jolo (the Americans quickly came to call the entire island of Sulu by the name of its principal port, Jolo) and everything else in the Sulu Archipelago. The attack against Captain Cloman's hunting party turned out to be an isolated crime in the Sulu Archipelago, not a coordinated outbreak against American rule. However, as mutual tensions stretched all relations, American authorities became alarmed about what might be taking place within the mysterious interior of Mindanao.

Led by officers whose formative experience had come during the Indian Wars, American military leaders considered Moroland to be like a huge Indian reservation populated by savage tribes ruled by warrior chieftains. This attitude pervaded all command levels, starting at the top with Secretary of War Elihu Root. Root saw a close analogy between government relations with the Indians and relations with the Moros. This led him to conclude that rather than attempt to impose American or Philippine government directly on individual Moros, the United States should allow the existing Moro tribal structure to continue. The Moros would be wards of the American state and treated as "domestic, dependent Indians."[10]

The practical implications of this policy became apparent when authorities consulted a map of Mindanao and saw a vast uncharted interior. Here about eighty thousand Moros, inhabiting some four hundred separate rancherias, lived in a world apart. Along the shores of Lake Lanao, 2,200 feet above sea level, nature had allowed them to develop in isolation. A belt of thick jungle, some twenty to thirty miles wide, separated the lake Moros from the coast. During the era of Spanish control, Moro columns had followed a network of narrow trails to raid the coast and then retire to their secure fastness about the lake. Natural geography limited Western forces, with their much greater logistical requirements, to two approaches to reach the lake: from Iligan, on Mindanao's north coast, and from Malabang, on the south coast. For over four centuries the lake Moros had been masters of their own fate. They had never been subdued by the Spanish and saw no reason to accept American rule now.

The commander of the Department of the Philippines, the Civil War veteran Major General Adna Chaffee, had scant knowledge about Moro history and attitudes. He naively thought that if the Moros could be brought to understand that the Americans did not intend to interfere with Moro customs and religion, then a patient policy of introducing Moroland to the benefits of benign assimilation would triumph. Why Chaffee held this sanguine viewpoint is difficult to understand. The Christian Filipinos had not particularly appreciated benign assimilation until compelled by a ruthless combination of military might, concentration camps, and starvation. Now the United States would employ the same approach with a warrior people who practiced Islam. Untroubled by such reflections, the department commander, General Davis, agreed with Chaffee's strategy. In September 1901 he dispatched a middle-aged cavalry captain named John J. Pershing as an emissary to the Lake Moro datus. It proved the turning point in Pershing's career.

On October 2, 1749, a man named Frederick Pfoershing arrived in Philadelphia. Religious persecution had driven him from his native Alsace. He was an indentured laborer, exchanging the cost of his transatlantic passage for labor as a weaver and wheelwright. After discharging his obligation ahead of schedule, he headed west with a new wife and the naturalized American name of Pershing. One of his descendants, John Frederick Pershing, fetched up in Missouri, and there, on September 13, 1860, John Joseph Pershing was born. Seven months later came the Civil War.

Like the nation as a whole, and particularly the border states, the war divided the Pershing family. John F. Pershing held strong abolitionist views. The house alongside the Hannibal and St. Joseph railroad where he lived and worked flew a Stars and Stripes. When rebel sympathizers demanded he lower it, he threatened to shoot the first man who touched the flag. Pershing's wife, a spirited women who hailed from Tennessee, sided with her native South. But the couple was united in their fierce protection of what was theirs, and this attitude almost cost the elder Pershing his life.

By the summer of 1864, through hard work and shrewd investment, the Pershings owned a prosperous general store in the small town of Laclede, Missouri. Although far away from where the war was being decided, Missouri remained the scene of bitter guerrilla warfare that often descended to sheer banditry. On a June day, the notorious rebel chieftain Captain Clifton Holtclaw led his men into town. Pershing knew what to expect. As Holtclaw's troopers approached his store, he went for his shotgun, only to recall that he had unloaded it that morning because three-year-old John, who had already displayed a keen interest in firearms, was playing in the store. Pershing locked the safe, grabbed John and his gun, and left through the back door as the guerrillas came in the front.

Pershing hurried along the alley to his home, where his wife told him that two raiders had just left. He handed young John to his wife, loaded his gun, and strode angrily to the front door. Out in the town square, Captain Holtclaw was busy haranguing a crowd of cowed civilians while his men looted homes and stores. Pershing raised his shotgun, but there was his wife at his side, begging him not to fire—it was a useless gesture that would merely deprive the young boy of his father. Reluctantly Pershing complied, and watched as the guerrillas completed their work and departed. An otherwise insignificant incident in the larger scheme of war had caused the deaths of two civilians and removed from the townspeople perhaps three thousand dollars' worth of goods and property. However, the raid on Laclede marked the introduction of a future general of the Armies of the United States to guerrilla warfare.

Nine years later the Panic of 1873 caught the Pershing family financially overextended. The elder Pershing told his thirteen-year-old son that the family's hopes for sending him to college were gone. Instead, the boy would have to take work as a farmhand to help support the family while his father set out as a traveling salesman. Thereafter the boy farmed during daylight hours and spent the evenings studying by lamplight. He later said that although these were difficult times, he learned a great deal about the practical side of life.

Although poorly educated by formal standards, the younger Pershing found work as a teacher, first at the Negro school, then at a white school in Prairie Mound. He ruefully reported that he probably learned more than any of his pupils, particularly lessons about how to manage others. While saving his money in hopes of eventually becoming a lawyer, he entered Kirksville Normal School for the spring term of 1879. In the fall of 1881 he saw a newspaper announcement that a competitive examination would be held at Trenton, Missouri, to select one cadet for the

United States Military Academy at West Point. Although Pershing had little notion of being a soldier, he liked the idea of a free education.

At West Point, Pershing's hard work and self-reliance allowed him to overcome his academic deficiencies. He steadily rose in merit to become class president his first year, senior corporal his second, and senior sergeant his third, culminating in the most distinguished rank, senior captain of the class of 1886. Thereafter, as was the case with most West Pointers who graduated into an essentially peacetime army, his career stalled. He participated in several Indian campaigns and then fought in Cuba with the 10th Cavalry Regiment, a black regiment commanded by white officers. A Civil War combat veteran, Frank Baldwin, observed his conduct at the Battle of San Juan and wrote Pershing, "You were the coolest and bravest man I ever saw under fire in my life."[11] Pershing again distinguished himself in the war against the Filipino insurgents, emerging from that war as a forty-one-year-old captain with no particular prospects for future advancement. Given a backwater assignment in Mindanao, Pershing spent time studying carefully the land and its people. He became the resident authority on Moroland, so naturally when General Davis assumed department command, he leaned on Pershing's expertise: "Pershing, as you are the only man left here who knows anything about the Moros, I'm sending you to Iligan . . . Do everything possible to get in touch with the Moros of central Mindanao and make friends of them."[12]

The assignment thrilled Pershing. As a mere captain, he was honored to assume command of a force made up of two cavalry troops and three infantry companies. Such a command normally went to a more senior officer. Moreover, the port of Iligan lay at the start of one of only two trails that formed troops could travel to approach Lake Lanao. The chance to be the first American officer to make contact with the lake Moros promised excitement and opportunity.

THE UNITED STATES ARMY traditionally had enjoyed the lead role in exploring America's western frontier. The army's mission was not only to subdue the natives but also to open the way to future settlers and miners. The same policy applied to Mindanao. Troops stationed in the vicinity of unexplored regions had the job of exploring the uncharted interior. They were to study the topography, make maps, collect soil samples, and

Captain John Pershing, Mindanao, 1903.

report on the numbers and condition of the inhabitants. As the Americans pushed inland they entered the region controlled by the Lake Lanao Moros. In turn, the attitude of these Moros was informed both by decades of conflict and by a recent encounter.

Long before the Americans arrived in Moroland, a blood feud raged between the lake Moros and the people of the nearby Cotabato Valley, a region dominated by Datu Piang. Unaware of this background, on April 29, 1900, Lieutenant Colonel L.M. Brett, Thirty-first Infantry, U.S. Volunteers, led twenty-six men accompanied by one hundred of Piang's Moros to demand satisfaction for a recent raid against Piang's people. A Spanish officer warned Brett not to take Piang's men, but Brett disregarded his advice. Brett's command found the Moros inside a small Spanish blockhouse near the beach where the Americans landed. Brett met with a minor datu named Amirul to initiate negotiations to allow the Americans to search the blockhouse. With negotiations at an impasse, Brett said that Amirul had three minutes to comply or else. When

Pershing and Moro datus.

the deadline came, Brett impetuously turned to order his men to charge the blockhouse. Who fired the first shot remained clouded in mystery. Some said it was one of Piang's sixty Moros who had firearms. Others said that the shot came from near the blockhouse. By the time the smoke had cleared, Amirul and fourteen of his warriors were dead. To the lake Moros, the only fact that mattered was that the Americans had come near their territory accompanied by Piang's warriors and killed one of theirs. This fact colored all future relations between the American troops and the lake Moros.

Brett's commanding officer, William Kobbe, considered the entire affair a "fiasco."[13] He had warned Brett to exercise discretion, and in Kobbe's opinion Brett had failed. Thereafter, the Americans and lake Moros met at two large councils. The Americans explained their intent to explore the lake region; the lake Moros expressed their lingering bitterness about the death of Amirul and demanded satisfaction for this outrage.

So matters stood when Captain Pershing came to Iligan. Pershing thrust himself into this unpromising environment with energy and insight. For the next five months he held lengthy meetings with Moro datus. He acquired enough of the Moro language so that he could deliver the everyday conversational niceties. At considerable personal risk he ventured inland into uncharted regions to attend conferences with Moro leaders. His bravery and forthrightness, as well as his willingness to learn the language, impressed many datus. Pershing, in turn, began to perceive that the Moros held a far from universal view of Americans. Their attitudes varied from village to village and ranged from friendly to hostile. Pershing summarized the challenge ahead: "The Moro is of a peculiar make-up as to character, though the reason is plain when it is considered, first, that he is a savage; second, that he is a Malay; and, third, that he is a Mohammedan. The almost infinite combination of superstitions, prejudices, and suspicions blended into his character make him a difficult person to handle until fully understood."[14] Pershing also candidly reported that the lake Moros were sullen and dangerous.

At first Chaffee dismissed Pershing's report. Chaffee attributed Moro attitudes to a misunderstanding probably caused by Pershing's misbehaving cavalry troopers. Then, in March 1902, the Lake Lanao Moros killed their first American soldiers.

THREE

The Battle of Bayan

*The Filipino insurrection was mild compared to the difficulties
we had with the Moros.*

—Benny Foulois

WHEN THE FIRST DAYS OF MARCH 1902 came to Mindanao, American soldiers moved outside their camps' perimeter without fear. They hunted, fished, bathed, or simply marveled at the exotic scenery. So it was on March 9 when Private Frank Morris left Parang, a port on Mindanao's south coast, to take a walk. Someone killed him, although who could not be positively established. It was a portent of things to come.

Three days later an eighteen-man cavalry detachment set out from Parang to scout a trail heading north to Lake Lanao. They sent friendly runners ahead to inform the lake Moros about their intentions. The troopers made slow progress through the jungle, covering about thirty miles in three days. On the third day, while riding through the jungle on a narrow trail, suddenly and without warning a large band of concealed Moros opened fire. It was a perfect deadfall. The troopers could neither advance nor retreat along the trail. In near panic, they abandoned their horses and fled into the jungle, leaving behind the body of one fallen comrade.

Unaware of this encounter, on March 30, two privates were walking outside the port of Malabang, located across Mindanao's narrow waist from Parang on the north coast. Six Moros approached them. The soldiers had no reason to fear them. Heretofore the garrison had enjoyed good relations with the locals, and these six gave every indication of being friendly as well. Suddenly they attacked, hacking one American to death with their *bolos* and taking the rifle of the other who dropped his weapon as he fled. The post's commanding officer investigated. Datu Piang's Moros, who were still on friendly terms with the Americans, told him that there was no question that the assailants came from the south shore of Lake Lanao. The officer looked at his sketchy map and saw that the village of Bayan was the largest inhabited place in this region.

At the higher levels of command, the murder of two, and possibly three, soldiers and the theft of at least twenty-one cavalry horses and mules presented an unacceptable affront to American sovereignty. At least this was the opinion of Colonel Frank D. Baldwin, the commander of the Twenty-seventh Infantry. Among the galaxy of American fighting men, Baldwin occupied a rarefied place: a living soldier who had earned two Congressional Medals of Honor. He won his first in 1864 fighting with Sherman's army outside of Atlanta, where he had led a counterattack through withering fire, entered the Confederate trenches, and personally captured two officers and the unit's colors before returning with his prizes to Union lines. Ten years later Baldwin participated in a campaign to recapture two white girls being held captive by Indians. When his two companies unexpectedly encountered a much larger Indian force at McClellan's Creek, Texas, Baldwin had to make an immediate decision that could make or break his career. He knew if he waited for reinforcements to even the odds, the Indians would escape with their captives. Consequently, he disregarded the odds and charged, thereby freeing the two girls. His gallant conduct won him a second Medal of Honor, making Baldwin one of only nineteen servicemen in American history to be twice awarded the Medal of Honor. During the Philippine Insurrection, Baldwin campaigned in the insurgent heartland in southern Luzon. Under the command of that war's hard man, General J. Franklin Bell, Baldwin displayed toughness and zeal while carrying out Bell's instructions to make civilians who supported the insurgents feel "the full hardship of War."[1] For a soldier with this background, there was only one legitimate response to Moro behavior: a stern military reprisal.

Baldwin received permission to organize a punitive expedition. He would base his force at the port of Malabang, on Mindanao's south coast, and then follow the natural invasion corridor along the Mataling

River to Lake Lanao. While his troops assembled, he sent an Afghan-born imam to explain to the lake Moros why the Americans were preparing a punitive expedition. The Afghan carried the message that it was necessary for the Moros to deliver up the murderers and return the stolen livestock or face the consequences.

The lake Moros greeted the Afghan as an American stooge. Their datus told him that the Americans were a proselytizing people intent on converting Moros from Islam and enslaving their people. The Afghan responded that in the nearby Cotabato Valley, Moros had benefited from the American presence. The Americans were interested neither in converting the Cotabato Moros nor in taking their possessions. But in the lake Moros' view, the Afghan was an unreliable, discredited envoy. If Baldwin or his superiors had bothered to learn about local Moro sensibilities and the history of recent Moro blood feuds, they would have easily understood the lake Moros' attitude. The Afghan's daughter was one of Datu Ali's wives. Ali, in turn, was the most powerful presence in the Cotabato region and a man whose father-in-law was the detested Piang. Piang's men had accompanied Lieutenant Colonel Brett's soldiers in the fateful encounter with Amirul back in 1900, the encounter that the lake Moros vividly recalled had led to Amirul's death. Consequently, the lake Moros scornfully rejected the Afghan's appeals. The Americans heard in this rejection defiance. Because of their ignorance of the long history of internecine Moro feuding, the Americans had no idea that they hardly could have chosen a worse ambassador to carry their message of peace.

The lake Moros' rejection of the peace overture satisfied the neat American sense of fair chance. But still the department commander, Major General Chaffee, tried again, this time arranging a two-day meeting with an assortment of Moro leaders. Some of the Moro participants were overtly pro-American, others simply pragmatic. Only a handful were actually lake Moros, but those few continued to stress that the killing of Amirul by the Cotabato Moros under the command of American officers was a grievance that had to be addressed before anything else. So the scene was set: the Americans had several recent murders firmly on their mind, while the Moros demanded satisfaction for an older grievance.

Chaffee concluded the meeting by sending a letter to the datus who continued to resist American authority. Addressed to the Moros of Lake Lanao, the letter began: "Under the treaty of Paris between Spain and the United States, executed in the year 1899, the Philippine Islands, including the island of Mindanao, were ceded by Spain to the United States, together with all the rights and responsibilities of complete sovereignty."[2] Chaffee issued an ultimatum that they had two weeks to surrender the murderers and horse thieves or suffer the consequences. He assured nonoffending Moros that the Americans had no intention of harming them. In American minds, Chaffee's letter was a sincere appeal for the peaceful resolution of a crime.

The letter's recipients viewed it otherwise. They had never heard of something called Paris. Regardless, they logically asked how it was possible that Spain, a country that had been unable to conquer their lands, could cede their territory to anyone. To most datus, Chaffee's letter was an arrogant attempt at taking something from them by diplomacy that the Americans could not take by force. There was not the remotest chance that they would accept Chaffee's terms. The sultan of Bayan sent an unpromising response in which he asserted, among other things, that he did not recognize American sovereignty and instead paid homage exclusively to the sultan of Turkey! However, at the express insistence of President Roosevelt, who, having just finished the war against the Filipino insurgents, did not want a new war, Baldwin received strict orders to avoid hostile actions until the two-week grace period ended.

While waiting for the Moro reply, Baldwin gathered supplies and set soldiers to work improving the trail running from Malabang to Lake Lanao. His command consisted of the Twenty-fifth Battery Light Artillery with four mountain guns and seven companies of the Twenty-seventh Infantry. This total of twelve hundred men was about one quarter of the entire strength of the Seventh Separate Brigade. Hundreds of Moros from the Cotabato River valley volunteered to join Baldwin's expedition. They had a score to settle and were happy to march side by side with infidels to settle that score. However, neither Baldwin nor his superior, General Davis, trusted these allies, and so they declined the offer.

Maintaining a supply line from the coast to Lake Lanao was a difficult proposition. The existing paths through the jungle were mere foot trails blocked by fallen trees, ditches, and large holes. The toiling American infantry who worked to widen the paths quickly learned that axes and saws made little impression against thick, towering tropical hardwoods. Baldwin abandoned his notion to build a wagon trail and decided to use Moro bearers instead. All proceeded smoothly until the bearers learned

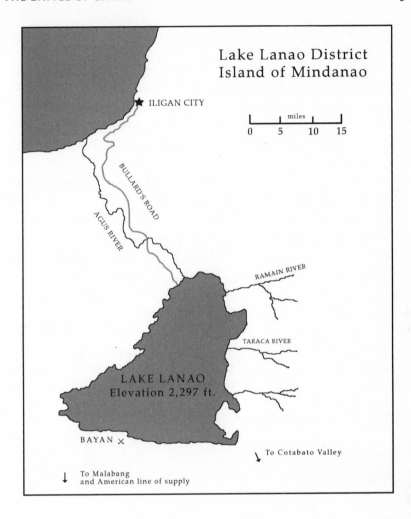

Lake Lanao District
Island of Mindanao

★ ILIGAN CITY

miles

0   5   10   15

BULLARD'S ROAD

AGUS RIVER

RAMAIN RIVER

TARACA RIVER

LAKE LANAO
Elevation 2,297 ft.

BAYAN ✕

To Cotabato Valley

To Malabang
and American line of supply

that the principal American ration was canned pork. In horror they cast down their burdens and deserted en masse. They wanted nothing to do with people who "eat the devil."[3] Henceforth the soldiers lived on what they could carry. This major hiccup in American logistical planning reduced the field ration for the fighting soldiers at the front of the trail to two meals a day. Operating on reduced rations, it took the Americans almost seventeen days to improve the thirty-two-mile trail to Lake Lanao. The unbalanced diet of coffee, hardtack, and bacon played havoc with the soldiers' bowels. Dysentery began to sap their strength.

On the first day of May 1902, Baldwin's expedition established a camp about two miles from Bayan and issued a final ultimatum giving the sultan of Bayan twenty-four hours to hand over the murderers. During the night and morning of May 1, the Moros sniped at the American camp but the Americans did not reply, pending a formal response to the ultimatum. The next day brought more of the same, except this time a larger body of Moro riflemen approached the camp and opened fire. Baldwin sent two squads out from camp to drive off the snipers.

The ultimatum expired at noon. The issue of who would hold supremacy in the Lake Lanao region, the Americans or the Moros, would be tried in battle. Fifteen minutes later Baldwin's command sortied from their camp. It would be the first combat for most of the regiment's men. They marched toward a Moro fort on Lempessen hill occupied by the sultan of Bayan's ally, the datu of Binadayan. It was a strong earthwork located on the highest ground in the area and defended by some two hundred to three hundred Moro warriors. Companies F and H moved through sporadic long-range fire to the base of the hill about a hundred yards beneath the fort. After recovering their breath, the infantry advanced another fifty yards, fixed bayonets, cheered, and charged. The Moros abandoned Fort Binadayan in the face of this intrepid charge. Only one American was wounded during this phase of the battle. Although the fort was now virtually undefended, gaining entrance proved

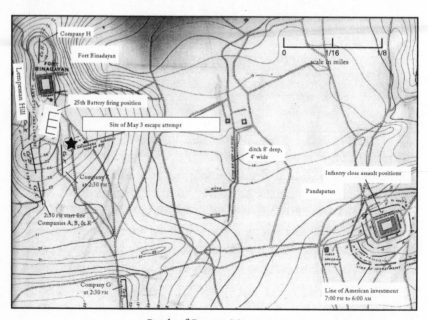

Battle of Bayan, May 1902.

Twenty-seventh Infantry marching toward Bayan.

extraordinarily difficult. In order to scale the ten-foot-high earthen wall, soldiers had to help each other climb, some making bridges with their backs, others climbing atop their comrades' shoulders. This difficulty was a warning of things to come.

About a thousand yards away, a second Moro strongpoint, which the Americans called Fort Pandapatan, crowned a steep hill. Red battle flags flew over Pandapatan, and here the sultan of Bayan concentrated his personal force of about 450 warriors along with 150 reinforcements—some volunteers, others sent by sympathetic neighboring rulers. Company G descended into the valley that separated the two forts and was driven to ground by heavy Moro fire four hundred yards short of Pandapatan. In response, the Twenty-fifth Battery unlimbered its four mountain guns on Lempessen hill and opened fire against Pandapatan. Because Pandapatan stood about eighty feet lower than Lempessen hill, the mountain guns were able to rake its interior with accurate shell fire. At 2:30 P.M., Baldwin ordered his infantry to capture Pandapatan.

Companies F, G, and E descended into the valley and climbed the steep slope toward Pandapatan. That the artillery fire had been less successful than expected became apparent when again the Moros opened heavy fire. The defenders were barely visible but seemed to be concentrated in the trenches and pits in front of the fort. Baldwin committed a fourth infantry company to support the assault. The soldiers had to cross three trench lines filled with Moros. There was nothing for it but to clear the ditches one by one in a series of vicious hand-to-hand combats.

One of the first officers into the ditch was Baldwin's engineering officer, Lieutenant H. L. Wigmore. Wigmore had asked for permission to join the assault and then hurried forward to accompany the infantry. Since the Civil War, revolvers had replaced swords as combat weapons. American officers practiced sword drill for exercise alone and wore their blades largely for ceremonial purposes. Wigmore provided an amazing exception. He fought several desperate personal combats pitting his sword against Moro krises and emerged victorious. His performance subsequently earned a brevet promotion.

Also among the combatants was twenty-two-year-old second lieutenant Hugh A. Drum. The diminutive Drum—he stood only five foot six at full stretch—had left college to enter the newly formed Twenty-seventh Infantry Regiment via a special provision made by President McKinley for the direct commission of men whose fathers had been killed in the

Lieutenant Hugh A. Drum.

Spanish-American War. As was the case for almost all the infantry, this fight was Drum's first exposure to combat. Drum saw a Moro rise from a trench with a long sword in his hand. As the krisman's arm began to descend toward the head of an unsuspecting sergeant, Drum fired his pistol. His shot struck the warrior in the head. After dispatching the surviving Moros, Drum and his comrades pressed ahead toward Pandapatan.

By 4:00 P.M. the infantry had cleared the outlying trenches and surrounded the fort. They descended into the moat beneath Pandapatan's ten-foot-high wall. The Moros had planted sharp bamboo stakes into the parapet walls and covered them with thorn brush. Loopholes pierced the walls every three or four feet. While standing in the moat, the Americans were exposed to fire from both the parapet embrasures and specially cut firing portals that pierced the walls themselves. Soldiers discovered that they could not scale the wall in the face of this intense Moro fire. American riflemen worked to suppress the Moro fire, and a tremendous firefight ensued. Hugh Drum tried to scale the wall. As he was scrambling upward a Moro emerged atop the parapet and prepared to slash at the vulnerable Drum. Just as he began his downward swing, Lieutenant Frank Bickham raised his Krag-Jörgensen rifle and shot the Moro. The Moro toppled backward, his sword grazing Drum's hand as he fell.

Unable to scale the wall, Drum and Sergeant William Kelleher stood shoulder to shoulder to make a platform onto which climbed Corporal John Ward. Ward opened fire against anyone who exposed himself inside the fort. As soon as Ward emptied one magazine, soldiers passed him another rifle with a fresh magazine. For thirty minutes he continued firing from his exposed perch. Meanwhile, in the ditch below, the two men standing on either side of Drum were hit by Moro fire. Although completely exposed to enemy fire, Ward remained untouched. His bravery earned him a nomination for the Medal of Honor.

In spite of such displays of valor, the attackers were stalled. Soldiers began running out of ammunition. They searched the wounded for fresh magazines. Baldwin saw them wavering and sent his adjutant with the message to hold their positions with the bayonet and to tell them that scaling ladders would arrive soon. In mounting desperation, Lieutenant Thomas A. Vicars led Company F against Pandapatan's main gate. Vicars lost his life in the failed attempt. His second in command, Lieutenant William Jossman, fell with a serious wound, as did several enlisted men. The company's first sergeant, Christian Pederson, rallied the leaderless unit as they recoiled from the well-defended gate.

The men of the Twenty-seventh Infantry were in the awkward position that confronts brave men thrust into an unsustainable assault. They could not advance farther because the promised ladders failed to materialize, but they refused to retreat. They stubbornly held on until nightfall before finally retiring a short distance. Baldwin ordered Companies F and G to retire to Fort Binadayan because they had suffered severely, but in the darkness it proved impossible to carry out this order. Consequently, five companies maintained a cordon around the fort until dawn the next morning.

During the assault, the Americans lost one officer and nine enlisted men killed and three officers and thirty-seven enlisted men wounded. The attack had failed because of Baldwin's blunders. There had been ample time to study the Moro position. A proper reconnaissance would have revealed the need for scaling ladders as well as dynamite to mine the walls. These necessary tools were available, having been deposited seven miles away at an outpost along Baldwin's line of communication. Instead, Baldwin had impetuously attacked without proper preparation and suffered a costly rebuff.

That night Baldwin's soldiers huddled miserably beneath a pelting rain that flooded their trenches. They had left their gear back in camp, so they were without their blankets and blouses. It was a very dark night, only occasionally illuminated by flashing strokes of lightning. The decision to retire from Pandapatan's walls came so late that the wounded could not be moved back to shelter; the carrying parties who tried plunged into unseen pitfalls and trenches before finally giving up. Consequently, medical officers treated the wounded at two improvised field hospitals just outside the fort's effective range. Meanwhile, the soldiers in reserve began fabricating scaling ladders. Around 3:00 A.M. Baldwin learned that his assault companies were almost out of ammunition. That he had not learned this vital information earlier was additional proof of his command failures. But no one questioned the courage of this two-time Medal of Honor winner. Baldwin issued orders to make the attempt with bayonets alone. Reportedly the colonel himself intended to lead the dawn assault.

May 2, 1902, had been a terrifying introduction to combat. No one who experienced the fight in the ditches outside Fort Pandapatan could

Two surviving Moro prisoners after the Battle of Bayan.
A posed photo to depict the fact that
some of the defenders possessed firearms.

help being shaken by the experience. Hugh Drum had behaved courageously, but now, as he huddled in his flooded trench he sought reassurance by fingering a little gold locket his Indiana fiancée had given him
just before he departed for the Philippines. That, plus recollections of
his mother's religious faith, helped Drum retain his composure. During the hours of darkness there was one abortive Moro sortie that the
investing force easily repulsed. However, there were shouts and cries
and shots from Pandapatan all night, often answered by Moros outside
the siege lines. It was unnerving for the Americans to sense that they
were caught between two fires.

At dawn the Americans were surprised to see the red battle flags
replaced by four white flags flying over the fort. Unbeknownst to the attackers, the Moros had suffered such terrible losses that they decided to
concede. A parley led to a surrender of eighty-three survivors. The Americans thankfully occupied the fort at 6:00 A.M. They did not know that a
handful of diehards remained inside Pandapatan. Suddenly two warriors
emerged to make a desperate dash for the gate seemingly without regard
for their own safety, slashing with their krises at all whom they encountered, Moro and American alike. The startled soldiers killed the pair, who
turned out to be the sultan of Bayan and his chief lieutenant.

Then the Americans herded eighty-three prisoners back to Lempessen hill, and here too Moro conduct surprised them. They appeared completely tranquil for the remainder of the morning as General Davis arrived on the field and interviewed them. Around 1:00 P.M. the prisoners rushed the guards in a well-organized escape attempt. The prisoners worked as a team to open a gap in the chain of sentinels that encircled them. While one group overpowered a guard and secured his rifle, another individual grappled with the adjacent guard. Although this Moro died, he occupied the soldier's attention long enough to allow the prisoners time to make their bid for freedom. The Americans killed thirty-five fleeing prisoners and recaptured nine others. Thirty-nine Moros escaped. Davis later asserted that he had hoped to release the prisoners as a sign of American magnanimity. Instead, the incident proved a discreditable massacre, adding to the estimated total of four hundred to five hundred Moros who perished during the battle.

The Battle of Bayan was the first major combat of the Moro War. As such, it provided lessons for the perceptive observer. Veterans of the Indian Wars and the Philippine Insurrection had learned that speed of attack was everything. It was very hard to bring to battle the Plains Indians or the Filipino guerrillas. Doing so routinely took days or weeks of relentless pursuit while the enemy used the terrain masterfully to evade contact. When encountered, officers had but a fleeting opportunity. Hesitation allowed the enemy to escape. Consequently, the tactic of choice was the immediate, all-out charge.

The Americans would learn that this approach was not necessary against the Moros. Once they took a stand in a fortified enclosure, or *cotta*, and flew their battle flags, they were going to fight until overwhelmed. They might make a tactical retreat to a nearby better position, as when the datu of Binadayan abandoned his cotta on Lempessen hill to join the sultan of Bayan at Fort Pandapatan, but they would almost never retreat from the field. This meant that the Americans could employ a methodical approach using their vastly superior firepower. It would prove to be a tactic for which the Moros had no answer.

The Battle of Bayan was the Twenty-seventh Infantry's first exposure to combat. It cost the lives of one officer and seven enlisted men, with four officers and forty-one enlisted men wounded. Three of the wounded died within three days. The gravely wounded Lieutenant Jossman lingered until July 25 before dying. Although the cost had been steep, it

was an undeniable victory. The storming of Pandapatan, the fight between kris and Krag, entered regimental lore and became part of the
regimental song. The Twenty-seventh Infantry would celebrate May 2,
1902, as its regimental birthday.

The battle also proved exceptionally meaningful to Lieutenant Hugh
Drum. His conspicuous courage attracted the favorable attention of
Colonel Baldwin. Baldwin promoted Drum to brevet captain and recommended him for the Silver Star. In the future, Drum would rise
far, coming up just short of the supreme position attained by his rival,
George C. Marshall, when World War II began. None of the many honors Drum later earned pleased him as much as this citation for valor in
the ditches beneath Fort Pandapatan.

The sense of a job well done extended all the way to the White House.
On May 5, 1902, President Theodore Roosevelt cabled his congratulations and thanks "for the splendid courage and fidelity which have
again carried our flag to victory."[4]

Across the lake from where the battle had taken place, Captain Jack
Pershing held a different view. Four years earlier Baldwin had praised
Pershing's combat courage. Now Pershing saw this famous hero in a
less flattering light: "Colonel Baldwin wanted to shoot the Moros first
and give them the olive branch afterwards."[5]

FOUR

The Rise of Jack Pershing

*We must not forget that power is the only function of
government that they respect, and the time may come when force
must again be used.*

—General George W. Davis, 1902

THE DAY AFTER THE CAPTURE OF Fort Pandapatan, the Americans built
Camp Vicars, named after the young lieutenant who had died while assaulting Pandapatan's main gate. Camp Vicars sat on a rise about a thousand yards from the Moro forts. Located near an excellent spring, it would
grow to become the army's major post to control the Moros along Lake
Lanao's southern shore.

On May 12, General Chaffee visited Camp Vicars. He issued instructions to General Davis regarding the future conduct of the garrison and
Colonel Baldwin. Chaffee forbade soldiers from trespassing on Moro
property, engaging in sharp trading practices, or attacking the Moros unless Davis authorized a new expedition. Chaffee's efforts to rein in Baldwin seemed a tacit rebuke of his bloody campaign. Chaffee sincerely, if
naively, summarized his policy: "Having given the Moros a severe and,
it is believed, salutary lesson as a result of their treachery, defiance of
United States authority, General Chaffee now wishes them to feel that
our purposes are peaceful, that their personal welfare and material prosperity are objects of solicitude at all times, and they can rely absolutely on

our protection."[1] Chaffee regretted that the United States had been compelled to resort to "harsh measures" but concluded that the bloodshed
was necessary to establish and maintain peace. The garrison of Camp
Vicars did not view their duty as that of peacekeepers. They knew they
lived on the edge of a wild, dangerous frontier where ambush and assas-
sination could strike at any time.

American policy confused the lake Moros and their neighbors. They
wondered why, having just won an overwhelming victory at Bayan, the
Americans did not continue their campaign and attack nearby rancherias that remained defiant. When a Moro datu held the upper hand, he
used his advantage to inflict more physical or economic pain on his
enemy. The Moros saw American military restraint as weakness. The
Moro understanding of Mohammed's life story taught that a party engaged in diplomacy merely to buy time to recover from setback. Thus,
Chaffee's return to diplomacy reinforced the Moro perception of American weakness.

DURING THE TIME Baldwin had campaigned against the sultan of Bayan,
Captain Pershing remained at Iligan. Back in early April Davis had told
Pershing that his duty was to keep the Moros on the north side of the
lake quiet so Baldwin could pursue his campaign on the opposite shore.
Accordingly, in late April Pershing convened a council with Moro leaders.
They were upset and excited because of the rumors about Baldwin's
buildup across the lake. Pershing patiently addressed their concerns,
carefully explaining that America did not intend a general war against
the Moros. Rather, Baldwin's expedition was against the bad Moros. Good
Moros would be left alone to pursue their lawful and peaceful occupa-
tions. Of course, many of the pursuits the Moros considered lawful and
normal—slavery, piracy, cattle theft from one's ancestral foes—the
Americans judged as crimes. But Pershing tactfully persuaded most of
the Moros who attended the conference to stay in their cottas and ignore
Baldwin's campaign. A handful of firebrands did cross the lake to join
the sultan of Bayan's doomed defense, and they did not return.

Thereafter, Davis weighed Pershing's diplomatic accomplishments
versus Baldwin's military accomplishments and concluded that Baldwin
was the wrong man for the job. Davis explained that Pershing had the
physical and mental energy necessary to endure long meetings with the

Men of the Twenty-seventh Infantry line up for payday at Camp Vicars, 1902.

Moros. The traditional long deliberations that the Moros expected required an American who also had patience; one who could make nuanced
decisions when confronted with "fanatical, semi-savages."[2] Accordingly,
Davis advised the War Department that the commander at Camp Vicars
required surpassing talents because he stood at the end of the spear of
American power. Davis offered his support for the War Department's
intention to promote the hero of Pandapatan. He then allowed Baldwin
to be transferred and sent Pershing to Camp Vicars to take charge.
Nominally, Pershing was Baldwin's intelligence officer; in reality he
commanded the most turbulent outpost in Moroland. Davis had brilliantly evaluated the situation and then played the army bureaucracy
with great skill to ensure that the War Department placed the right man
in command at Camp Vicars.

Camp Vicars was a command worthy of a colonel. In an army accustomed to strict adherence to the privileges of seniority, everyone assumed
that a high-ranking officer would take command. Instead, Captain Pershing's arrival engendered great jealousy from his fellow officers. For
once the War Department recognized genius at work and ignored the
complaints. It even came up with the useful dodge of sending reinforc-
ing units to Camp Vicars while detailing those units' commanders to
staff jobs in Manila so that they would not outrank Pershing. In this
fashion Pershing accumulated a miniature army. Among them was
Second Lieutenant Benny Foulois.

The call for volunteers to fight against Spain found high-school-
dropout Foulois working for his father's plumbing business. A martial

spirit flowed in the family. Foulois's father had fought in the French army during the Franco-Prussian War. In 1898, Foulois slipped his older brother's birth certificate out of the family Bible, packed his kit, and rode his bicycle from his Connecticut home to New York City. His brother's birth certificate and the recruiter's wink and nod at his not quite five-foot-six-inch frame allowed him to meet the army's age and height requirements. Promoted to lance corporal, Foulois served with an engineer unit in Puerto Rico. It did not see combat, but disease claimed thirty-eight of forty noncommissioned officers. Sick with malaria, Foulois mustered out of the service, but his restless nature did not adjust well to civilian life. "The town of Washington, Connecticut, had shrunk a lot in the seven months I had been gone," he explained.[3] When he learned that a company of regulars was forming for service in the Philippines to fight Filipino insurgents, Foulois reenlisted, this time using his own birth certificate.

Foulois proved a natural soldier. His first combat experience came at close quarters when concealed Filipino guerrillas opened fire. Foulois stood up in the tall jungle grass to see better, immediately had his hat shot off, perceived six guerrillas firing from a trench, and calmly returned the fire. That night he proudly recorded his first kill by notching a mark in his rifle butt. His subsequent combat experience against the Filipinos allowed him to carve five more notches. Foulois's exemplary conduct led to his promotion to second lieutenant. He was one of the 1,135 new officers commissioned on February 2, 1901, joining a list of notables that included a Virginia Military Institute graduate named George C. Marshall and a barrier-breaking black man, Benjamin O. Davis, who, like Foulois, rose from the ranks.

Assigned to Mindanao, Foulois commanded Company D, Seventeenth Infantry. As was the case in the battle against Philippine *insurrectos*, the fight against the Moros was a young officer's war. The demands of leading a patrol through dense jungle in a hot, humid environment eliminated the physically unfit. The amount of mental energy required to command a small outpost in the hinterland weeded out aging dullards. Assigned to the port of Cotabato, Foulois learned that his responsibilities expanded beyond company command to include inspector of customs, collector of internal revenue, captain of the port, city treasurer, chief of police, and fire chief. The paperwork alone associated with his civil duties was staggering.

In his capacity of fire chief, Foulois received his first "wound." To

combat rampant venereal disease, the battalion commander had established a clean brothel staffed by imported Japanese prostitutes. One
night a fire broke out in the girls' quarters and Foulois, as fire chief,
rushed to the scene to organize a bucket brigade. While he was standing
on the blazing roof, a jet of flame shot out and blistered his hand. The
scars remained for the rest of his life. Thereafter, whenever anyone at a
party asked how he got his scarred hand, he always truthfully answered,
"In a government whore-house fire in the Philippines in 1902."[4] Foulois
found that his interrogator never asked a follow-up question.

Foulois's ready wit served him well as he worked to pacify nearby
rancherias. Within the small community that was the regular army in
the Philippines, every officer had heard about Captain Pershing's unusual approach to pacification. Foulois "decided to try the Pershing approach to Dato Piang." He led a patrol up the Mindanao River into the
area Piang dominated. He established an outpost and strung a telephone line back to base. Then he summoned Datu Piang and his retinue to a meeting. Although Piang was deeply suspicious, his curiosity
got the better of him. He and Foulois conferred and then Foulois offered to show the Moro leader something he had never seen while the
Spanish were there. He telephoned the base and told Piang to listen
while a Moro on the other end talked with him. "Piang heard the voice
on the receiver, and immediately dropped it as if it had scorched him.
He burst outside to see where the man was. When he couldn't find him,
he was wide-eyed with amazement."[5] To complete the spell, Foulois
played a wax record on his Thomas Edison–designed Ediphone. Piang
had just experienced three astonishing events: the Americans had displayed superior courage by venturing into his rancheria, a place the Spanish had never entered; the Americans had made their voices travel great
distances; and they had played music without instruments. Foulois's
performance helped convince Piang that the Americans were vastly
more powerful than the Spanish. He became Foulois's friend and would
remain an influential ally during the entire Moro War.

Soon thereafter, Foulois and the Seventeenth Infantry were ordered
to join Pershing at Camp Vicars. Foulois did not think that the lake
Moros would pose a significant threat. He wrote his mother, "We don't
anticipate much trouble from these Moros as they have very few firearms, and are a cowardly lot of savages."[6] Had Foulois spoken with the
veterans of Bayan, he would have realized that he was only half right.

Henry Savage Landor's drawing of a lantaka
used to defend Bacolod.

Having fought one pitched battle at Bayan against the Moros, the Americans had acquired a good idea of their capacities as fighting men. Moros were clearly adroit with edged weapons and apparently less capable with firearms. Most of their shoulder arms had been obtained from the Spanish in battle, by theft, or by illicit trade. Their firearms ranged from obsolete muskets to more modern Remington rifles. A combination of purchase and theft had brought them Snyder rifles from British North Borneo. However, both the Remingtons and the Snyders were one generation behind the Krag-Jörgensens carried by the U.S. infantry. More important, a chronic ammunition shortage limited Moro rifle practice. Consequently, they were not skilled marksmen. They also showed a notable tendency to open fire ineffectually from too great a distance. To enhance their firepower and help defend their cottas, the Moros obtained in trade with the Chinese or manufactured themselves small-caliber bronze swivel guns called *lantakas*. As had been shown in the ditch beneath Pandapatan, at point-blank range the lantaka's shotgun-like discharges of packed slugs could be deadly. The Moros also had an assortment of antique cannon either captured from the Spanish or procured by pirate attacks against merchantmen who had dared sail the Sulu Seas.

Throughout their war against the Americans, Moro warriors tried to increase their firepower. With the U.S. Navy effectively isolating them from outside supply, they had to rely on the U.S. Army. They willingly

Moro edged weapons. From top to bottom: barong, kampilan, kris.

took huge risks to steal arms. They stalked sentries, patiently waited for their chance, and then aimed their first blow at the arm holding the rifle, either severing it completely or inflicting enough pain to compel the hapless American to drop his weapon. The Moro seized the weapon and ran, proudly carrying a trophy that affirmed his manhood. Ammunition was scarce and also highly valued. A datu considered twelve cartridges fair trade for one wife. Faced with such temptation, renegade civilian traders, including Americans, conducted black market exchanges. The Moros also gleaned abandoned ammunition from American camps and even sent pearl divers plunging into the depths of Lake Lanao to retrieve munitions that the Spanish had jettisoned when they abandoned their inland forts. However, none of these measures provided sufficient firearms and ammunition. Consequently, warriors had to rely upon their traditional edged weapons.

Every male adult past the age of childhood wore a blade. To appear unarmed in public was a sign of disgrace or indicated that one was a slave. Practice from an early age taught the Moro warrior to wield his edged weapons skillfully. The kris was about twenty inches, akin to a short sword by Western standards, and was well balanced, featuring a double-edged steel blade. Warriors used the kris to slash rather than thrust. They carried a variety of other edged weapons in addition to the ubiquitous kris. The traditional weapon of choice for the men of Mindanao was the *kampilan,* a single-edged war sword up to forty inches in length carried in a special breakaway scabbard. A peaceful-seeming Moro could turn into a fanatical assailant in a twinkling of an eye merely by striking the kampilan while it was still in the scabbard to cut the binding holding the two halves together, thereby freeing the weapon. The ensuing two-handed stroke was deadly, cleaving through skull and bone before a startled victim had time to react. The Moros were also adept with the *barong,* a short, leaf-shape bladed knife usually sixteen to eighteen inches long. Single-edged and deliberately forged to be heavy, the barong was a superb chopping weapon. Easily concealed beneath a warrior's robes, in one flashing stroke the razor-sharp barong could slice off a head before the victim realized his peril.

In pitched battle, the Moros carried a collection of krises, kampilans, and barongs, as well as spears, and wore "vivid turbans and carabao [water buffalo] armor and even shirts of mail" along with iron or brass helmets.[7] Thus attired, they entered battle like inspired warriors, but warriors from the feudal age. One American veteran described them as "a combination of Moor, Malay, tiger, wildcat, skunk, and nitroglycerine."[8] In sum, and in contradiction to Foulois's naive assertion, the Moro warrior was anything but a coward.

WHILE YOUNG BENNY FOULOIS was serving his country as fire chief and befriending Datu Piang, Pershing was busy forging relationships with the lake Moros. In marked contrast to Baldwin, he treated them as human beings. He daily spent hours receiving their delegations and mingled socially with them. Observers often saw Pershing squatting on the ground conversing with important Moro leaders, a quid of tobacco firmly in his cheek, while the datu chewed on his betel nuts. He encouraged his officers to show the Moros a common humanity, and it was during this time that he met Hugh Drum. Drum had shown strategic skill by besting all comers at chess. Pershing pitted Drum against a chess-playing datu and Drum won a five-game match three to two. His victory solidified the datu's respect and marked one more small advance toward a pacified Moroland. To further this goal, Pershing invited Camp Vicars's Moro neighbors to attend a July 4, 1902, festival. Some seven hundred Moros obliged.

As time passed, what became known as the Pershing touch achieved promising results as lake datus entered American lines to establish friendly relations. But Pershing knew that many others still refused to acknowledge American sovereignty. He also understood why: "The Moro considers himself the rightful owner of the country he has inhabited for generations" regardless of certain concessions he may have made first to Spain and then the United States. "This assumed lordship, acknowledged from time immemorial by surrounding peoples and tribes, has become so deep-rooted in his mind that he resents the slightest indication of encroachment or interference."[9]

Around Lake Lanao, none resented American interference more than the sultan of Maciu. The Maciu Moros claimed an ancient lineage dating back at least to the thirteenth century. Among a prideful people, they stood near the summit. Having never been conquered, they easily persuaded themselves that Pershing's diplomacy masked weakness. Their warriors began probing Camp Vicars in July and August 1902, beating gongs, shouting defiance, and taunting the American guards with mocking laughter. The lack of American response encouraged them to escalate.

August 12, 1902, dawned unusually dark as lake fog shrouded the ground. Because there had been no actual attacks against Camp Vicars's sentinels, the three-man outpost commanded by Sergeant Foley may have relaxed its guard. If so, it proved a fatal error. Unbeknownst to them, a dozen men had been stealthily crawling through the underbrush toward their post. Suddenly they rose from the ground and charged. Before the soldiers could react the Moros were on them, slashing with sword and spear. The alarm brought soldiers rushing to their relief, but it was too late. Sergeant Foley and Private Carey were dead, Private Van Dorn crippled with wounds. Henceforth, the sentries of Camp Vicars had orders that they did not need to call out the usual "Halt. Who goes there?" before firing at anyone moving at night.

Moro sniping attacks continued, and raiders repeatedly cut the telegraph line to Malabang. No white person could travel the Malabang road without a strong escort. By the beginning of September 1902, American losses at Camp Vicars had climbed to four killed and twelve wounded. Among the killed was the gallant Sergeant Pederson, the soldier who had replaced the fallen Lieutenant Vicars and rallied the wavering men in front of Pandapatan's main gate.

Elsewhere on Mindanao, the drumbeat of violence also intensified. It was hard for the Americans to detect a pattern in all of this, but quite often the offending Moros seemed to come from Bacolod or nearby cottas allied with the sultan of Bacolod. But the most hostile element, or so friendly Moros claimed, lived east of Camp Vicars and gave allegiance to Sultan Uali of Butig.

This situation was clearly intolerable. Pershing believed that overall his efforts at pacification were making "material progress" but that he had to administer "a good sound drubbing" to solidify the gains.[10] He did not think it mattered much where this punishment took place, and he also thought that one lesson would be enough. So Pershing received permission to conduct a punitive expedition against Sultan Uali. His orders still required him to try to negotiate with the Moros, but if they rebuffed his peaceful overtures he was to use force. The command consisted of one cavalry troop, four infantry companies, a two-gun mountain howitzer section, a field mortar, and a medical detachment. Along with staff officers the force numbered about 550 men.

Having made the decision to act, Pershing ordered his command to rise shortly after midnight on September 18, eat a hasty breakfast, and march east along the lakeshore toward Butig. Ten picked men from each infantry company served as scouts. The expedition followed a trail along a narrow, wooded ridge until coming within sight of Lake Butig. The scouts saw two forts blocking the trail and observed armed Moros moving in and out of them. Since he was nominally there to forge "friendly relations," Pershing did not want to fire the first shot. Instead, he deployed two of his infantry companies to face the larger fort and ordered the two Maxim-Nordenfelt 75 mm mountain howitzers commanded by Captain William S. McNair to unlimber.[11] Suddenly the Moros opened fire from a fringe of timber. This was what the Americans had been waiting for. The marksmen serving as scouts returned the fire. Their accurate long-range fire surprised the Moros because they had no idea that they were vulnerable at distances as far as five hundred yards. This unpleasant experience began to impart the hard lesson that the Americans could kill as far as they could see.

The Moro defensive position appeared formidable. The large fort loomed over the narrowest part of the trail. Three hundred yards away,

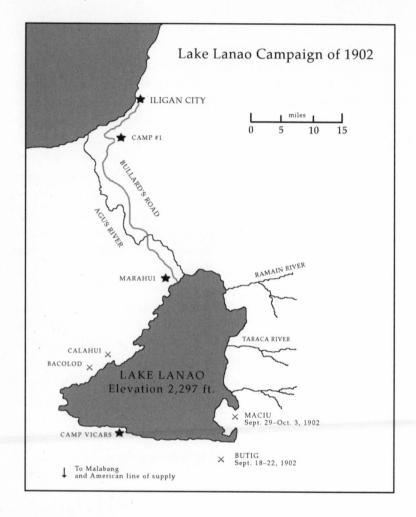

Lake Lanao Campaign of 1902

ILIGAN CITY

CAMP #1

miles
0   5   10   15

BULLARD'S ROAD

AGUS RIVER

RAMAIN RIVER

MARAHUI

TARACA RIVER

CALAHUI ✕
BACOLOD ✕

LAKE LANAO
Elevation 2,297 ft.

✕ MACIU
Sept. 29–Oct. 3, 1902

CAMP VICARS ★

✕ BUTIG
Sept. 18–22, 1902

↓ To Malabang
and American line of supply

a smaller fortification was located so as to provide flanking fire against anyone who attacked the main fortification. Red Moro war banners flew atop both forts. McNair's howitzers opened fire against the smaller fort. Accurate shelling reduced it to rubble. The high-angle shells searched out the safeholds inside the fort. The Moros had never experienced such a shelling. The shrapnel drove them out into the open, where American rifle fire cut them down. Then the howitzers were trained against the main fort. Again the shells pulverized the mud-and-bamboo fortification. When the defenders' return fire slackened, Pershing ordered an infantry probe. Company C advanced against the sultan of Butig's stronghold, but the defenders fled before they were overrun. Although the

Americans managed to capture several more outlying forts, the rain-swollen swamps protecting the main settlement proved impassable on this day. The baffling terrain, with its network of narrow trails through swamp and jungle, proved more of an obstacle than the Moros. Although Pershing's command had suffered no casualties, the soldiers were nearing exhaustion. Consequently, Pershing ordered his men to retire to a defensive laager and prepare for the morrow.

The next morning a well-coordinated march brushed aside all opposition and overran a series of hostile cottas. Usually the inhabitants fled before the Americans arrived. Inside the cottas the Americans found glowing cooking fires adjacent to well-constructed dwelling places. They burned the houses and storage buildings with their seasonal food supplies of rice, cocoa, and coffee. For officers such as Pershing who were veterans of the Indian Wars, this was standard procedure. Food destruction had worked against the Plains Indians because they were nomads living on a subsistence economy. In contrast, the Moros intensively farmed the same plots during a tropical year-round growing season and could readily replenish their stockpiles.

Although his troops had destroyed what they could destroy and suffered no losses, Pershing suspected that the Americans had inflicted few losses on the enemy. However, the punitive expedition seemed to be having an effect. Now that the inhabitants saw what they confronted, Moro sympathizers who were eager to save their cottas from fire and destruction began entering the American camp. They spoke often and at length, but the quality of their intelligence was uneven. Furthermore, it proved difficult for a large American force stealthily to approach a Moro stronghold. For example, the sultan of Lumbayanague met with Pershing and "after some hesitation" acknowledged that some of his men had fought against the Americans the previous autumn. He guided the column to the home of "Dato Imam, who he said was the guilty dato, but Imam and his people had escaped."[12]

Pershing spent the next two days trying to find a practical route to advance against his main objective, Maciu. He eventually decided that it could not be done with the forces at hand. Reluctantly he ordered a return to Camp Vicars. Throughout military history, many first independent commands fail. The first major military event in George Washington's career was his surrender of Fort Necessity. In his first field battle in the American Revolution he badly botched the defense of New York City and

Pershing on campaign along Lake Lanao.

might have lost the war if the British had been led by more aggressive leaders. Robert E. Lee failed badly in western Virginia during his first independent command. Pershing's performance was not nearly so bad. On the credit side, when he realized that he was insufficiently prepared he prudently ordered a retreat. Many other officers confronting the same situation would have sacrificed their soldiers in order to burnish their own reputations. Also, there were no American losses, while friendly Moros reported that the various forces arrayed against the Americans had suffered thirty killed. On the debit side, the expedition had been plagued by a lack of engineering tools. The inability to build a passable trail that could serve as a line of supply severely curtailed the length of time the expedition could remain in the field. Consequently, the expedition had not accomplished nearly as much as Pershing intended.

Pershing learned from this experience and did not make the same mistake again. Everything that should have been done before the first expedition was done in preparation for the second campaign. An engineering detachment joined the expedition. A seventy-five-mule pack train carried the tools necessary to build bridges and boats, including ample saws and axes. McNair's artillery had proven invaluable, so Pershing reinforced the gun teams, bringing the artillery captain's command up to eighty-eight men, and loaded the mules with ample high explosive and shrapnel rounds. He trimmed one company from the infantry force in order to reduce the logistical burden, leaving him with three infantry companies with a total of 229 men. Each soldier carried two hundred rounds of ammunition. Lastly, Pershing exchanged a fresh, sixty-two-man cavalry troop for the worn-out troop that had gone out the first time. On September 28, 1902, just ten days after the start of the first expedition, the column set off to sort out the sultan of Maciu.

Since the Americans had last been in this area, the Moros had built a small earthwork faced with stone to defend the place where they anticipated the Americans would cross an arm of Lake Lanao. Pershing ordered a reconnaissance to find a different line of approach. The patrol returned with the news that the Moros had felled trees across the only alternative trail. For the next several days the Americans laboriously cleared trails to permit an advance against Maciu. Each patrol met resistance from Moro snipers, but Moro rifle fire was poorly aimed and inflicted few losses.

Benny Foulois commanded an infantry detail charged with building a bridge across a ravine. Although Foulois knew that the engineering manual called for four-inch logs, he ordered his men to fell trees twice as thick. While they were fitting the logs into place, a tall, lean rider appeared. As befitted a grizzled cavalry trooper, Pershing was well known to spice his words with curses appropriate to the time, place, and intelligence of his listener. He asked what Foulois was building a **** bridge for, a siege train? Showing the ready wit and spunk for which he would become famous, Foulois replied, "Yes, sir, if that's what you want. I just don't want to have to come back here a second time and build it again."[13]

Pershing would recall this exchange fifteen years later when both men were generals in France. At that time Foulois would be in charge

Twenty-fifth Field Artillery Battery with 75 mm mountain guns.

of building the army's fledgling air force, and Pershing told him to employ the same philosophy that had guided his bridge building in Moroland "because we don't want to have to come back here a second time and
build it again."[14]

On September 30, the expedition advanced to a ridge overlooking
Maciu. From a range of only three hundred yards, McNair's mountain
guns poured fire into the cottas. As the defenders fled, Pershing advanced two infantry companies. Their rapid and accurate fire cut down
scores of fleeing Moros. That evening Pershing sent a written ultimatum to nearby cottas. A Moro messenger returned with the response
that the local datus had read the letter and would be waiting with two
hundred men to defend against all comers. Such defiance in the face of
great odds was utterly characteristic of the Moro warrior mentality.

The next day Pershing again arranged a methodical advance on Maciu,
relying on long-range fire to crush resistance. The mountain guns and
riflemen quickly achieved fire superiority, driving the Moros from exposed positions on the cotta's walls. The infantry advanced to within 150
yards of the enemy position. The Moros answered the ensuing bombardment with war cries, beating drums, and prayers chanted by their
religious leaders. Although the Americans could not see clearly the effect of their fire, translators told Pershing that the chants rising above
the din of battle came from Moro panditas offering prayers for the
wounded and slain. In spite of their tactical dominance, the Americans
could not see a clear path to assault the cotta. A brave lieutenant scouted
the approaches and reported that the fortification featured twenty-foot-
high vertical walls impossible to scale without ladders. Rather than risk
unnecessary losses, Pershing opted for siege tactics.

At dusk Pershing advanced his lines to within one hundred yards of
the cotta. Although separated from the enemy only by the length of a
football field, close investment proved impossible because of the fifteen-
foot-high cogon grass that bordered the Moro fortification. Moreover,
countless deep, narrow ditches scored the ground in front of the cotta
walls. Fearing that these ditches might provide the Moros with avenues
to attack, Pershing ordered fires lit between the American lines and the
cotta to illuminate any Moros who tried either to attack or to flee. From
inside the cotta came continual song and prayer indicating that the enemy remained in force. Pershing was untroubled. As he later reported,
"It was not thought possible for the Moros to escape."[15] Around 3:00 A.M.

Soldiers in cogon grass.

came a Moro sortie. It was repulsed at the cost of several Moro dead. It was probably a diversion to allow the majority of the Moros to escape, because at dawn the amazed Americans found that the Moros had abandoned the cotta and somehow escaped through their siege lines.

When Pershing inspected the deserted cotta, he found a network of tunnels extending outward that had allowed the garrison safe passage beneath the American lines. After inspecting the cotta, Pershing ordered it destroyed. Suddenly a suicidal warrior sprung from the cogon grass and attacked the nearest American, Private R. G. Macheth, slashing his left arm badly with his kampilan and inflicting a terrible wound. Although startled, Macheth's comrades intervened and fired at the assailant. As was so often the case, it took repeated hits to stop him. When the smoke cleared the Americans examined all the dead. They discovered one of the most tenacious foes of the American presence in Moroland, Sultan Cabugatan, lying amid his warriors, his body covered with seven wounds. Cabugatan's death ended the campaign.

The victory over the Moros living around Maciu had consequences, although they were not as great as Pershing's superior claimed. General Davis made a conventional military evaluation of the balance of forces and reported to Washington that the lake Moros had now repeatedly witnessed American martial superiority and were resigned to the new

Carrying the wounded from Maciu, October 2, 1903.

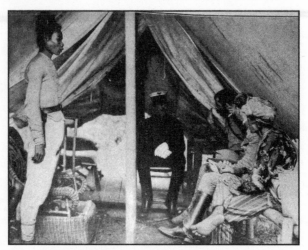

General Nelson Miles (seated, facing camera)
in Pershing's tent at Camp Vicars.

order. Indeed, after Pershing's expedition, Camp Vicars's line of communication remained secure and sniping attacks against the camp ceased. But, as events proved, this was far from Lake Moro acquiescence to American rule.

In mid-November 1902, Pershing had the great pleasure of playing host to Lieutenant General Nelson A. Miles, the venerable commander of the entire army. President Roosevelt had sent his "brave peacock," a reference to Miles's fondness for excessive uniform display, to the Philippines to remove him from Washington so that Secretary of War Elihu Root could carry out major reforms in the army's command structure. While in Manila, Miles had already created a stir by condemning the army's torture of prisoners in order to extract intelligence. In contrast to his displeasure about events to the north, Miles arrived at Camp Vicars in fine fettle. He had spent the past few days reunited with Chaffee and Davis, two fellow Civil War veterans, and time had passed agreeably as they reminisced about their glory days. Miles had also enjoyed the ride through the "beautiful and picturesque country" surrounding Camp Vicars. As Miles gazed out at his audience of young soldiers, he recalled meeting their commander back in Arizona some twenty years ago and told the soldiers that his hopes for Pershing had come true and that they were fortunate to have such "an intelligent, judicious, and able commanding officer." The old general complimented the soldiers for their fortitude and patience dealing with the Moros, noting that they had well maintained the character of the American army. In a veiled reference to army misconduct on Luzon and Samar, Miles concluded by noting that he had heard no reports of "cruelty or injustice by this command" and praised the soldiers' humane conduct "in this remote and dark region of country."[16]

FIVE

The Conquest Begins

The Moros know little even of the Mohammedan religion . . . but he does know that Mohammed conducted a holy war against Christians and, following this example, he generally looks upon it as a meritorious thing to kill and rob Christians.

—John Pershing, 1908

Major Bullard Builds a Road

IN 1867 A SIX-YEAR-OLD ALABAMA BOY named Billy Bullard persuaded his parents to let him change his name to Robert Lee Bullard in honor of the great Confederate general. Bullard graduated from West Point in 1885. Ironically the Civil War veteran who handed him his diploma, Commanding General of the Army Phil Sheridan, had once been among the most hated men in the Confederacy. Thereafter, like most of his classmates, Bullard looked for opportunities for promotion. In the Spanish-American War, the fastest route was to serve as an officer in a volunteer unit. Accordingly, Bullard became brevet major of the Third Alabama Volunteers, an African American unit. Although the regiment never engaged in combat, Bullard received accolades for his leadership skills and sensitive handling of racial issues. His empathy for the disadvantaged seemed to flow from a well-developed chip on his shoulder, a sense that authorities discriminated against him because he was a poor boy born in the South. Bullard next served in the Philippines as colonel of a volunteer regiment. He taught his men innovative tactics to combat Filipino insurgents, a performance that added to his luster before he rejoined the regular U.S. Army.

Major Robert Lee Bullard returned to Manila after the Battle of Bayan. At age forty-two, Bullard well understood the army's pace of promotion. It made for a disheartening future in which merit was less important than seniority. To acquire higher rank and higher pay one merely had to hold out longer than one's peers. The only alternative was to distinguish oneself in combat, and the best chance for that was obviously Moroland. Accordingly, Bullard lobbied headquarters in Manila until General Davis relented. Meanwhile, he read everything he could find about Moro customs and language. At the end of September 1902, Bullard and the Third Battalion of the Twenty-eighth Infantry transferred to Mindanao.

All colonial powers operating in remote, undeveloped regions confront logistical difficulties. The America solution for Mindanao was the same one the Romans would have chosen: build a road. The Spanish had tried this approach and made a serviceable wagon track, but they lacked the resources to complete and maintain it. The Americans figured that they could do better. A road connecting the port of Iligan on Mindanao's north coast and Marahui on the northern end of Lake Lanao would solve a host of logistical problems. Such a road would follow one of the two natural invasion corridors leading to Lake Lanao. Mule trains and horse-drawn wagons could carry supplies to Marahui, from where boats could transport them to any other American outpost on Lake Lanao. A dependable line of supply based on the Iligan–Marahui–Lake Lanao route would greatly assist the garrison of Camp Vicars in their efforts to pacify the lake Moros. Bullard's battalion received the assignment of building the road.

The port of Iligan presented few attractions to Bullard and his men. A small Spanish fort dominated the harbor. Some six thousand people inhabited the dilapidated town, which consisted of wooden or adobe buildings with grass roofs. The buildings lined unpaved streets that were alternately dusty or muddy depending on the season. A thatch-roofed Catholic church decorated with garishly painted figures overlooked a central plaza that featured a peeling wooden bandstand and a large glass mosaic formed by inverted beer bottles inserted into the ground by some of the three thousand bored but artistic Spanish soldiers who had been assigned guard duty on the trail from Iligan to Marahui. A single U.S. infantry company had replaced the Spanish. However, in the wake of the Battle of Bayan, eight hundred fighting men—including two cavalry troops, six infantry companies, two companies of Philippine Scouts, and an assortment of civilian clerks and teamsters—occupied Iligan at the time Bullard's battalion disembarked. To the Indian Wars veterans among them, the entire scene evoked memories of the ramshackle garrison forts in the American West. And like those garrisons, there was little for the men to do inside the security perimeter, while unknowable dangers lurked outside.

The battalion's six officers and 344 enlisted men established a tent camp outside the port and went to work. At first work progressed well, as the battalion followed the grade of a Spanish railroad, another of the island's many unfinished Spanish infrastructure projects. About three miles inland, the route departed from the flat coastal land and entered the rain forest. An arduous work regime of felling giant trees, creating a roadbed one shovel load at a time, and dynamiting everything that resisted hand tools reduced the pace of progress. Disease, heat exhaustion, and malingering compelled Bullard to alter his hard-charging approach. He instituted a new program of starting work at sunrise and halting before noon so that the balance of the day could be spent recovering. This regimen restored morale but failed to advance the road at the pace Bullard desired.

But slowly the jungle yielded to persistence and dynamite. Simultaneously, Bullard made surprising progress with his second assignment: convincing the Moros who lived near the road to allow the work to progress peacefully. Bullard utilized a special fund to pay Moro laborers and spread the word that paying work was available. For three months the Moros avoided contact with the American soldiers while a handful of warriors tested American camp security. It was an explosive situation partially defused by Bullard's ability to speak conversational Moro. Consequently, when a formal Moro delegation finally visited the American camp, Bullard was able personally to negotiate with them. Because he had studied Moro culture, Bullard observed the protocol of talking at length about tangential issues before addressing the heart of the matter.

Thus, Bullard learned that a cholera epidemic had recently swept through the region. The Moros knew nothing about this killing disease except its outcome. Bullard explained how to boil water to rid it of cholera's evil spirits and distributed quinine to help the sick. Discussion eventually shifted to the matters that most concerned the Moros: guns, food, and money. Bullard innocently asked why the Moros needed guns since the soldiers had not attacked them. Food and money could be obtained in exchange for work on the road. The road, in turn, would make it much easier for the inland Moros to bring their produce to market. By negotiating in a manner that the Moros could recognize and understand—exceptionally rare conduct for a white person—Bullard persuaded the datus that American intentions were good. As one datu remarked, Bullard must be a white Moro sent by Allah to help his brothers on Mindanao.

Thereafter, the first Moro laborers appeared to begin work. Eventually some three thousand contributed uneven but still useful labor. As the road penetrated the interior, Bullard's battalion moved its camp inland and established Camp Pantar, a little more than halfway to the lake. Here, in the spring of 1903, rumors of the buildup of American forces across the lake disturbed the Moros. Bullard learned that Pershing was preparing a punitive expedition against the powerful sultan of Bacolod. Bullard protested to headquarters in Manila on two grounds: Pershing's plan would endanger the progress he had made with the Moros in his region; moreover, he thought his own unit deserved the combat assignment. But Bullard had run afoul of his commander, General Samuel Sumner, which was why his battalion was relegated to construction duty. Moreover, Sumner was an old cavalryman, so it was natural that he give the choice combat assignment to fellow cavalry officer Pershing instead of the foot sloggers. Stuck in what he correctly understood to be a backwater assignment, Bullard jealously observed from afar Pershing's next dramatic campaign.

The Battle of Bacolod

The commander of the Division of the Philippines, Major General George Davis, harbored great regret for how the U.S. Army had pacified the American Indians. Davis believed that the pacification was a record of neglect, deceit, and wanton slaughter. He tried mightily to avoid a repeat in Moroland. Yet Moro conduct frustrated him. He believed with his entire heart that the U.S. government and the army had provided "abundant proofs" of its benign intent. Above all, Davis believed in the sanctity of American prestige. The Moros needed to learn that they could not molest American troops as they passed along roads and trails. Furthermore, they had to learn that they could not "with impunity brandish their weapons and fly war flags in our faces."[1] Unfortunately for all concerned, as 1902 came to an end, this is exactly what the Moros began doing.

Americans such as Davis, Pershing, and Bullard had come to Moroland equipped with a combination of ideals and prejudices that influenced how they approached their mission of civilizing the Moros. The Moros, on the other hand, saw the American occupation as merely the arrival of a new set of infidels who, like the Spanish, seemed bent on changing their traditions and culture. They viewed routine American activities with deep suspicion, particularly when the U.S. Navy embarked on a program of surveying the port of Jolo. Surveying teams erected tripods and flags on prominent heights around the port in order to make measurements. This activity coincided with a severe outbreak of cholera. Some Moros concluded that the Americans had planted the tripods and flags to cause the epidemic. Others believed that the surveying activity was in preparation for seizing land. In February 1903 Moros fired shots at a navy vessel engaged in surveying activity. Later an angry Moro mob chased a naval surveying party back to their boats.

Tension increased as American authorities began conducting a census. Rumors spread among the Moro communities that this was a first step toward taxation and land seizure. In sum, the entire panoply of American activities—surveying, census taking, movement of troops, and road construction, all activities that Americans associated with benign social progress—were viewed very differently by the Moros. To them it was all too reminiscent of Spanish behavior and represented a dire threat to their culture.

In General Sumner's mind, increased Moro resistance not only threatened everything that had been accomplished so far but also appeared to be close to plunging Mindanao and Jolo into a state of anarchy. Consequently, when Pershing proposed a new expedition, Sumner readily agreed. Examining his maps, Sumner saw that American exploring expeditions had traversed most of the shore of Lake Lanao. But a gap remained, an uncharted twenty-mile section of the eastern shore.

General Samuel Sumner (seated on left) in Pershing's tent at Camp Vicars meeting with datu and retinue.

This was the territory dominated by the sultan of Bacolod, among the most hostile remaining Moro leaders. Sumner ordered Pershing to march through this unexplored region. As before, if hostile Moros tried to oppose him, then Pershing could take necessary measures to subjugate them.

Pershing departed Camp Vicars on April 5, 1903. Because he anticipated serious resistance, he had strengthened his command to include three troops of the Fifteenth Cavalry, four companies of the Twenty-seventh Infantry, two Vickers-Maxim 75 mm mountain guns, and two 3.6-inch field mortars. Each soldier carried four days' rations and, because of the fear of cholera, special equipment to boil water. Unusually for a military that loathed journalists, a British correspondent for the *London Mail*, A. Henry Savage Landor, accompanied the expedition.

Landor was one of those memorable characters who combined Victorian hauteur with pluck and a thirst for knowledge and fame—although not necessarily in that order—and populated the world's remote regions at the dawn of the new century. The son of a celebrated poet and writer,

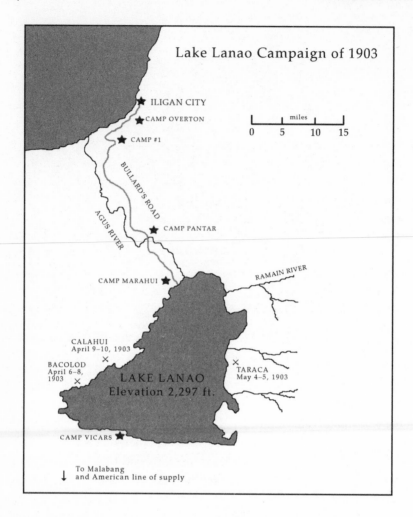

Landor seamlessly made the transition from Italian-trained painter to Tibetan explorer without skipping a beat, in spite of suffering captivity and torture at the hands of Tibetan tribesmen. Credited with the discovery of the mouth of the Indus River, Landor found that his fame gained him access to the world's powerful and famous, including Czar Nicholas II and Queen Victoria. His charm and self-promotional ability easily won over American military officers, so it was natural that while nominally embarked upon a study of Philippine anthropology, Landor joined Pershing's expedition.

The column departed Camp Vicars at 7:00 A.M. Its march paralleled the lakeshore so the soldiers saw the reassuring sight of four large

Moro boats, manned by U.S. troops, keeping pace with the column. The boats' task was to maintain contact with base in the event the column required help. There was no question that expedition was entering enemy territory, as it soon encountered attacks from unseen snipers. The column halted a few miles short of Bacolod to make camp. The officer of the day established a picket line to provide security. This was anything but a routine detail. That night a cat-footed Moro krisman stalked an American sentry outpost. He emerged from the underbrush only six feet away before the sentinels knew he was there. Before escaping unharmed, the Moro seriously cut up two cavalry troopers. They were the expedition's first casualties.

At 4:30 A.M., April 6, 1903, reveille sounded. Pershing had issued detailed orders, so food was ready and canteens filled with safe water boiled the night before. Two hours after reveille the expedition resumed its march toward Bacolod. Bacolod stood on a prominent ridge that rose from the shore of Lake Lanao. The sultan had been fortifying this impressive earthwork for more than a year. On its three landward faces, twelve-foot-high earthen walls overlooked a ditch thirty-five feet wide and forty feet deep. At its base the stone-faced wall was fifteen feet thick. The parapet was loopholed for rifle fire and featured embrasures, cannon, and lantakas. An earth berm ran along the fort's exterior perimeter. The Moros had dug combat bunkers and bomb shelters beneath this berm. A bamboo roof reinforced with earth provided overhead shelter. As expected, numerous red battle flags flew above the cotta. Henry Savage Landor described the scene: "We could faintly hear the distant fanatical yells of the natives, chanting their war-songs, and suddenly along the shores of the lake glittered in the sun hundreds of brandished *kris* and *campilan* blades. It was an invitation—a challenge to come on."[2]

A fighting trench supported by rifle pits extended north from the fort's northwest corner along Bacolod ridge. The initial American objective was to clear the ridge and force the Moros back inside the fort. The Americans came to the first significant obstruction, a deep defensive ditch about five hundred yards from the fort. A heavy rain set in, which slowed the pace of advance. While the pair of 3.6-inch field mortars provided long-range covering fire, the leading infantry company opened into skirmish order and advanced down the ridge toward the fort. The Moros replied with heavy fire from lantakas and small arms. The infantry crossed the ditch, closed to a range of three hundred yards, and partially

The march to Bacolod. Captain Pershing on left pointing.
Just off camera to Pershing's left is Henry Savage Landor.

invested the fort. McNair's section of mountain artillery opened fire, while the infantry extended their flanks toward the lake to complete the blockade. Darkness came with the usual tropic suddenness and the troops hunkered down for the night.

The next morning patrols discovered another large fort toward Calahui, and here too the war flags were flying. Had the Moro way of war featured aggressive mobile operations, troops issuing from Calahui would have presented a major threat. But Pershing was confident that he could methodically reduce Bacolod before attending to Calahui. Moreover, the direction of the American advance fooled the defenders. They had concentrated their cannon and lantakas to resist an assault from the south or southwest; instead the attackers came from the opposite direction. Consequently, to the surprise of the Americans, a flag of truce appeared above Bacolod with the Panandungan, the chief counselor for the Bacolod Moros, requesting terms of surrender. Pershing replied that nothing but unconditional terms would be accepted. The Panandungan wanted his men to retain their arms and remain in the fort. During the time the interpreters conducted the parley, the Panandungan stood on the parapet hurling insults about the craven Americans who refused to close like men and fight hand-to-hand. With no room for compromise between these opposing positions, the fighting resumed.

The shelling continued until nightfall. Coming from a range of nine hundred yards, the American artillery guns collapsed the walls and destroyed the embrasures and portholes along the fort's north and east faces. A shell toppled the tripod mast flying a huge seven-pointed battle flag. The Moros immediately hoisted a new banner, but it too promptly fell to the accurate shellfire. Periodically the Panandungan reappeared on the parapet to wave his sword. But other than such individual acts of defiance, the defenders had no response to the intense bombardment.

After leaving a screen of pickets surrounding Fort Bacolod, the soldiers retired to their camp for food and rest. Here they encountered foes more deadly than Moro rifle practice: drinking water contaminated with microbes causing a particularly virulent strain of dysentery, as well as those causing typhoid fever and cholera. Although the soldiers conscientiously boiled their drinking and cooking water, the first cases of disease emerged only two days into the campaign, with the first fatality occurring on April 7. The American preoccupation with good sanitation bemused the British adventurer Henry Savage Landor. He insisted that it was a silly practice with a fresh source of water so close at hand. For the duration of the campaign he and a handful of followers drank unboiled Lake Lanao water and, as he archly noted in his memoirs, all avoided the camp diseases that raged through the American ranks.

Not yet alarmed by his soldiers' declining health, Pershing contemplated what to do next. Although showing substantial damage, Bacolod still appeared imposing. In hopes of sparing everyone the horrors of an assault, the next morning Pershing responded to the appearance of a child on the parapet waving a flag of truce by agreeing to another parley. Again, neither he nor the Panandungan yielded, so there was nothing to do but organize a storming column.

In preparation for the final assault, working parties approached the edge of a forty-foot-deep dry moat that protected Bacolod. The artillery fire had been so effective that even at close range the sporadic Moro fire was little more than a nuisance. Soldiers spanned the moat with an improvised bamboo bridge. Then they partially filled in the moat with cut timber to pad the fall of any soldier shot off the bridge. Soldiers lined the edge of the moat to deliver an intense covering fire while the storming party charged across the bamboo planks. Cavalry Sergeant G. Marik led the way but went down when a rifle slug struck his ankle. The third man over, Sergeant Samuel Hafer, had his right arm severely cut by a kris-wielding Moro and his left arm destroyed by a gunshot wound. The fourth man over, Lieutenant George C. Shaw, received a gunshot wound in the hand. Suddenly the bridge collapsed, dropping several men into the moat. Thereafter, the Americans had to use the bridge like a scaling ladder to clamber, one at a time, up the walls of Bacolod.

Pershing reported that the attackers "crossed to the berm and sprang upon the parapet, encountering Moros in hand-to-hand combat, who rushed with *kampilans* and *krises* from the berm galleries and interior of the fort to meet them. Three men were wounded almost instantly, but short work was made of the remaining Moros, who in all parts of the fort continued to fight desperately to the death."[3]

Pershing's terse account fails to capture fully the horrors of Bacolod. When the storming party entered the fort they were met by hordes of desperate Moro warriors who emerged from bombproofs and tunnels. It was a kill-or-be-killed melee pitting kris and kampilan against bayonet and rifle butt. Chaplain George Rice was among the first to enter the fort. He wanted to record the scene with his Brownie camera—a simple, boxy, handheld device introduced by Eastman Kodak only three years earlier—and almost died in the attempt when the Panandungan appeared from a covered passage and charged with his kris. Rice managed to dodge the attack. The Panandungan turned to attack surgeon Lieutenant R. Patterson, who was kneeling to attend the mutilated Sergeant Hafer. Patterson, a big, strong man, lashed out with his fist and struck the Panandungan in the chest, thus buying time for nearby comrades to kill the Moro leader.

One group of Moros occupied a bombproof. To descend underground through the door meant certain combat in confined quarters, the kind of fighting at which the Moros excelled. Consequently, the Americans fired their rifles through the bombproof's other aperture, but this did not seem to quell resistance. Voices from those concealed underground shouted defiance. The Americans had risked their lives to storm the fort, and their fighting blood was up. Soldiers gathered dried grass, planks, and anything else that would burn, piled it atop the bombproof, and set it afire. Landor described what took place: "Amid hurrahs the fort was now ablaze and we retired across the trench to await events. The powder magazine blew up and with it went the solid roof of the fort, the flames

*American infantry delivering suppressive fire
with their Krags against Bacolod.*

Rice's photo of Bacolod's massive ditch.

Rice's photo, five minutes after charge, showing Americans examining fallen defenders.

A Lake Lanao datu coming to surrender to Pershing.

Dead Moros at Bacolod.

shot up, and a tall, gloomy black column of smoke. That was the end of impregnable Bacolod."[4]

Nine prominent Moro leaders and another 60 to 120 warriors died during the fighting, most of them victims of the artillery bombardment. American combat losses numbered one killed and fourteen wounded.

Despite the expanding outbreak of cholera, which eventually killed six soldiers and two civilian packers, after the fall of Bacolod Pershing set out toward Marahui. For once he lost control of the column. Men straggled; others departed the line of march to sightsee. Pack animals broke free and scattered. By late afternoon the column had marched only three miles across undulating terrain. Into view came Fort Calahui, its parapets crowded with strutting warriors. Calahui resembled Bacolod in that it stood on the lake end of a ridge. Steep slopes descended to the water on the fort's east and south. A forty-foot-deep wet moat protected the fort's west face. Towering above the fort was a wooden totem carved to resemble an immense bird. A red battle flag with a blue border flew in the center of the fort. There was still enough daylight left for an artillery bombardment and a one-company reconnaissance in force. While McNair's methodical bombardment slowly pulverized the fort, the infantry advanced in skirmish order to the edge of the moat. Then came darkness, and the Americans retired into camp.

Scouts told Pershing that it appeared many defenders were escaping aboard native canoes called *vintas* to nearby islands. To encourage the flight, Pershing ordered his artillery to continue its bombardment. The next day brought confirmation of the encouraging intelligence when Pershing beheld an American flag flying over the fort. The artillery ceased fire and a child emerged from Calahui carrying a Stars and Stripes. Protracted negotiations ensued, but when the American artillery resumed fire, this time aiming at the portholes from which issued intermittent return fire, the Moros yielded and evacuated the fort. The important Moro leader Datu Ampuan surrendered. Since the datu willingly pledged an oath of allegiance to the United States, Pershing released him immediately in the hope that this would set an example. Datu Ampuan reported that many warriors and their leaders had indeed escaped by boat, although some twenty-three warriors had died from the bombardment. Pershing quickly inspected Calahui and then ordered the fort to be blown up.

Pershing rested his command the next day. During the day he met with numerous Moro leaders from the surrounding territory. Many had been subjects of the sultan of Bacolod. Others had been allied with the sultan for reasons ranging from self-preservation to economic benefit. Clearly, the easy destruction of Bacolod and Calahui, the strongest forts on Lake Lanao, had made a powerful impression. The Moros gave Pershing strong expressions of friendship and goodwill while promising not to oppose the American march regardless of where it went.

But dangers remained, as evidenced by an ambush that afternoon when four kampilan-armed Moros sprung from behind some large boulders and attacked the pack train's escort. Three soldiers were terribly cut up, one of whom died within an hour. A lieutenant had a very close call when his .38 revolver failed to stop his assailant and then he stumbled to avoid a sword slash. His attacker leapt atop him and the two men grappled in the dirt. With his gloved hand the lieutenant pushed the Moro's blade away and then beat in his face with the butt of his revolver. This series of blows stunned his assailant and bought time for help to arrive and kill the Moro. Like so many such affairs, it was all over in seconds, with four Moros killed and an equal number of Americans wounded, one mortally.

The expedition continued its circuit along the western shore of Lake Lanao and reached Major Bullard's outpost at Camp Pantar on April 12. Moro datus visited Pershing's camp to welcome the victor and pledge

their loyalty to the United States. The enormous shift in Moro senti-
ment particularly impressed Bullard. Whereas before the Bacolod campaign he had been skeptical and jealous of Pershing, now he sensed that
he was in the presence of a special leader. He confided to his diary: "The
more I see of this unusual work the more I know that few men are fit to
manage it, and the more I am of the opinion that General Davis did
right to keep Pershing in charge of these Moros instead of placing in
charge some fool officer who ignorantly supposed that he could come
and in an off-hand manner manage these savages."[5]

After resting for a day, the column retraced its steps on the return
march to Camp Vicars. Whereas the outward march had been plagued
by the threat of sniper attack and ambush, the return march was a triumphant parade as hordes of Moros escorted the victors homeward.
Pershing proudly reported to Davis that the expedition had been more
successful than he had anticipated. The success of his handpicked ap-
pointee gratified Davis, who saw in Pershing's conduct the correct balance of military might and diplomacy.

On May 2, Pershing set off from Camp Vicars on another expedition to
complete his circuit of the lake. This time he chose to march along Lake
Lanao's eastern shore. Several influential Moros accompanied the expedition and, by pointing to the example of Bacolod, managed to persuade the
local datus that opposition to the Americans was futile. Consequently,
the march initially proceeded without impediment, but on the third day
the column entered the Taraca watershed and the rancheria controlled by
Datu Ampuan-Agaus. The Taraca Moros had been early converts to Islam. Prideful even by Moro standards, they refused all peaceful overtures
from the infidels. Pershing's column came to a hostile cotta known as
Fort Pitacus and found it "literally covered with war flags."[6] Pershing followed what by now was the standard procedure: The infantry advanced to
invest closely the enemy position, while the artillery methodically bombarded the Moro fort. Then came the infantry storming columns.

Lieutenant George C. Shaw had the assignment of clearing a belt of
timber from where Moro riflemen were delivering enfilade fire across
the approaches to Fort Pitacus. Hidden within the trees were numerous
small fortifications and a large village. Based on the volume of fire, Pershing sensed that Shaw was confronting something difficult and sent Troop
E of the Fifteenth Cavalry to reinforce him. Together, the dismounted
cavalry troop and Shaw's infantry company stormed a large village and

nearby cottas, capturing thirty-six cannon and killing a staggering total of about 250 Moros.

Shaw's fighting blood was up. Ahead he saw two war flags still flying above Pitacus. Yet it appeared that the artillery had done its work well, because the fort had fallen silent. Shaw led his men to the fort's eastern face. Expecting no opposition, they set their scaling ladders and began climbing. When the infantry reached the top of the wall, Moro riflemen, heretofore concealed within the fort, opened a withering fire. Shaw held his position atop the walls of Pitacus while Moro bullets killed Corporal Samuel Schwartz and wounded several more soldiers who had followed Shaw up the ladder. Shaw was no stranger to enemy fire, having been wounded the previous autumn. But this situation was far more desperate.

From across the Taraca River Pershing could see the fighting and hear the cacophony of battle in Moroland: the booming of artillery, the crack of rifle fire, the clanging of Moro gongs, the guttural cheers of the American fighting men, the answering shrieks of the Moro warriors. Pershing witnessed Lieutenant Shaw at the top of his scaling ladder waving his campaign hat to encourage his men, then saw the soldiers near Shaw topple from Moro fire. Shaw remained, firing his revolver until reinforcements arrived, a performance that would prompt Pershing to recommend him for the Medal of Honor. Shaw's Medal of Honor citation laconically related what the lieutenant had done: "For distinguished gallantry in leading the assault and, under a heavy fire from the enemy, maintaining alone his position on the parapet after the first three men who followed him there had been killed or wounded, until a foothold was gained by others and the capture of the place assured."[7]

Pershing had again captured a Moro stronghold defended by inveterate foes who suffered enormous losses. Among the slain was the sultan of Pitacus. Moreover, Pershing's patient tactical approach had won at the cost of only two killed and six wounded. His battle tactics contrasted favorably with those employed by Colonel Baldwin the previous year. At Bayan, Bacolod, and elsewhere, the Moros had fought as they always had, using tactics that worked against each other and had also worked against the Spanish. At Bayan, the Moros had repulsed Baldwin's first assault. Confronted with the same challenge that Baldwin had faced, Pershing's command swept the field with relative ease. His tactical approach pointed the way forward for American operations in Moroland.

After the storming of Pitacus, the remainder of the march proceeded without incident. Five years later Pershing recalled what had been accomplished by his march around the lake: "American troops entered the heart of the Moro country and stripped the Malay lords of Mindanao of the prestige of hundreds of years."[8] At the time, few Americans paid much attention to the price the Moros paid during Pershing's campaigns. A headline in the *Manila American* read, BACOLOD MOROS SLAUGHTERED WITH KRAGS. The anti-imperialist press in the United States was still focused on examining American atrocities during the Philippine Insurrection and did not pick up on this story. Pershing's campaign would prove the last one to escape scrutiny from the anti-imperialist movement.

Pershing's leadership vindicated General Davis's inspired decision to install Captain Pershing in the most important command in Moroland. Davis enthusiastically claimed that the expedition was the first time that white men had ever marched around Lake Lanao. He lavishly praised Pershing: "He has displayed rare good judgement, infinite patience in dealing with these suspicious people, wise foresight in preparing for every emergency and contingency, and, finally, when nothing remained but to crush the resistance, to so dispose his force as to accomplish the result with the least possible loss."[9]

By May 1903, Pershing had seemingly conquered Moroland at a cost of fewer than twenty dead from all causes. But his health had broken: Fever, diarrhea, and weight loss sapped his renowned energy. It was time to head home for rest and recovery. After newspapers and magazines reported on Pershing's exploits, he became a popular hero in the United States. Chaplain George Rice's photographs, taken with his Brownie camera, of the Battle of Bacolod appeared in a booklet sold at the 1904 St. Louis World's Fair. Pershing visited the fair and signed autographs for an adoring public. Three years after Captain Pershing left the Philippines, President Roosevelt promoted him to brigadier general, jumping him over 862 more senior officers. Quite simply, the campaign around Lake Lanao made Jack Pershing.

SIX

"A Model Administrator"

*There is no doubt about the American being the most generous and
kind-hearted fellow living, but his experience of Eastern natives is
still somewhat crude. With the tenderest intentions in the world, he
unfortunately bitterly offends folks who do not understand his
ultra-democratic ideas nor his rapid commercial notions.*

—A. Henry Savage Landor, 1904

WITHIN THE HIERARCHY OF COMMAND positions in the U.S. Army, the
Division of the Philippines stood like the last base camp beneath the
summit of a towering mountain. An officer who achieved command of
the Division of the Philippines had a very good chance of ascending to
the head of the entire army. General Adna Chaffee commanded the division until October 1902. Chaffee believed that military might alone
would not solve the Moro problem. Whatever solution his country imposed, Chaffee believed, there would have to be some accommodation
to Moro customs and religion. Such accommodation required special
tact. A military man who combined colonial administrative experience
with combat experience would be ideal. To give this hypothetical ideal
candidate the best chance for success, Chaffee recommended merging
the civil and military governorship of Moroland under one hat. Before
Chaffee could see how these administrative changes worked out he was
transferred back to the United States, eventually becoming army chief

of staff in 1904, the only man ever to enter the army as a private and rise to its top position.

After Chaffee left the Philippines, the ideal candidate to serve as civil and military governor of Moroland unexpectedly became available. His name was Leonard Wood. By outward appearance and demeanor, Wood was a soldier's soldier. Medium height, broadly built, plain to the point of homeliness, he did not look like a person who could inspire, yet he possessed a force of personality, a natural leadership that impelled soldiers to follow him. As a child growing up around Buzzard's Bay, Massachusetts, Wood delighted in outdoor pursuits, happily spending his time hunting, fishing, and sailing. Then and thereafter he prided himself on being physically fit. His father was a medical doctor who wanted his son to follow in his footsteps. Accordingly, when his father died, Wood resolved to honor his request and entered Harvard Medical School in 1880. He completed his academic work in three years and, in lieu of acquiring his degree, took a competitive examination that earned him a position at Boston City Hospital.

At first, work as a junior intern seemed to be a life-changing experience. Assigned to a poor section of the city, Wood discovered misery, crime, and suffering straight out of the pages of Charles Dickens's bleakest novels. As he pondered the circumstances that formed lives in Boston's slums, Wood wrote to a former teacher that what he witnessed "rather shakes up a fellow's settled ideas." His work among the poor forged surprising bonds: "I have no finer friends in the world than among some of the worst people in the city."[1]

General Leonard Wood.

In addition to displaying an apparent special empathy for the disadvantaged, Wood exhibited a more enduring characteristic: an intolerance of authority. The terms of his internship specified in detail what he could and could not do. Wood routinely ignored them. While refusing to sit in his assigned seat or fraternizing with nurses were judged minor infractions, his failure to accept the rule that stated that no interns perform operations proved too much for hospital authorities. Wood argued that in his capacity as an emergency intern he had no time to request special permission but rather had to do what needed doing. Authorities disagreed, first placing him on probation and then, a month later, after Wood had disobeyed again by performing an emergency skin graft, dismissing him from the hospital. A dismissal at this point in his career meant that he would never be allowed to serve again on a hospital staff. A second major path to a medical career, assisting a practicing physician, was also most likely closed.

Having attended medical school but failed to earn a degree, and having worked as a medical intern but failed to live by the rules, Wood turned to a third option, military service. Again his conduct proved irregular. He expected to enter at the rank of first lieutenant, noting with satisfaction that this was one grade higher than a newly graduated West Pointer. The pay was reasonable, prospects for promotion good. Having told friends and teachers about his decision, Wood learned that he had ignored one niggling detail: the War Department could not appoint him until a vacancy emerged. Instead, the army offered him an immediate position as a contract surgeon outside of the regular military hierarchy, at half a regular surgeon's pay rate with no promises for the future. Lacking any other professional option, Wood accepted.

An active life on the Arizona frontier suited the twenty-five-year-old Wood, allowing him to continue his boyhood pursuits with gusto. Better yet, from a career standpoint it gave him the opportunity to participate in the Geronimo campaign in 1886. The Apaches had proven themselves to be among the army's toughest opponents until a skilled general and even better administrator, General George Crook, assumed command of the Department of Arizona and brought peace. Crook took a real interest in Indian welfare, which put him outside of prevailing attitudes. Indeed, when Crook departed Arizona, a self-serving collection of politicians and businessmen moved the Apaches from desirable land onto the unhealthy San Carlos reservation. Here Geronimo, with a small band of disgruntled warriors, recommenced raiding and killing. For the next ten months the U.S. Army futilely stalked the fabled Apache chieftain through the Arizona mountains and along the border with Mexico. Then a hard man, Nelson Miles, replaced Crook.

Miles ordered any of his patrols that cut the Indians' trail to follow the track and pursue as long as physically possible. Simultaneously, he erected a chain of signal stations throughout the Southwest so that as soon as a patrol found Geronimo's track, the intelligence could be spread to all commands so they could converge to trap the Apaches. Miles's hope was that unrelenting pressure would eventually run Geronimo to ground.

Although a mere contract physician and not a military-educated officer, Wood distinguished himself during the campaign. Wood and officers of the Fourth Cavalry proposed to Miles that they form a select hunting party of American soldiers, scientifically chosen for their endurance. Guided by Indian trackers, supported by a mobile supply train using pack mules, this select group ought to be able to match Indian endurance. In the end, the American pursuit did wear down the Apaches. Then a former commander of the Apache Scouts demonstrated excellent diplomatic skill and persuaded Geronimo and Natchez, the Chiricahua Apaches' hereditary chief, to surrender.

The diplomatic aspect of the victory made no impression on contract surgeon Wood. During the campaign he had won modest renown for carrying dispatches through the wild country along the Mexican border infested with outlaws and Apaches. He exhibited tremendous stamina while searching for the elusive Apaches and displayed initiative by taking command of a demoralized, leaderless infantry detachment and restoring it to respectability. This was commendable conduct, but hardly worth the Congressional Medal of Honor he later received in 1898 for this service. The explanation lay in the fact that he revealed another aspect of his character during the Geronimo campaign: a deep understanding of how to play army politics. As then second lieutenant Robert Bullard, a young officer who played an even smaller role in the campaign—Bullard's contribution was to "command" two support wagons and serve with the force that escorted Geronimo to the train that took him to his prison cell in Florida—observed, Wood displayed a proven capacity to "retain the close friendship of important men who were fighting one another with the utmost hostility."[2]

As the years passed, Wood expanded his circle of influential mentors.

It hurt not at all that he served as President William McKinley's personal physician. Another of his close friends was an assistant secretary of the navy named Theodore Roosevelt. When war with Spain came, Wood sought a combat command. His political connections led to his appointment as the commander of the First Volunteer Cavalry (Rough Riders) with Theodore Roosevelt as his second in command. Thereafter, there was some question of precisely what Colonel Wood did during the fighting in Cuba besides exhibiting courage. An eyewitness described him at the combat of Las Guásimas on June 24, 1898: "No man has ever made a finer spectacle in battle than he did that day. He went well in advance of his own men . . . I shall never forget how he looked as he stood there with his face burned to a brown, which was almost like that of the Khaki uniform he wore. His sandy mustache, too, had been grizzled by the sun until it fitted into the general harmony of tone, and he stood there brave and strong, like a statue in light bronze. The Cuban grass reached almost to his waist. There was not a breath of air, and yet the grass about him moved, once, slowly, as if a breeze was blowing. At first I had no right idea of what had caused this, but presently the thought came to my mind that it might be bullets. And then I realized that Colonel Wood, forming, with his horse, the most conspicuous item in the view before the Spaniards, was naturally the target for all the bullets they could shoot. It was the effect of volleys fired from Spanish trenches and from the bush across the valley that made the grass wave about his feet. I realized it slowly. He knew it from the start."[3]

Indeed, although he stood unperturbed beneath a hail of Mauser bullets, Wood did little else. When asked about his conduct, he acknowledged that he was leaving the tactical decisions up to his subordinates while contemplating his decision to forgo a prior offer of a $100,000 life insurance policy! His contributions to the celebrated charge up San Juan Hill provided the stuff of later controversy. However, coupled with his powerful connections, his military service in Cuba proved enough to overcome his lowly place in an army shackled by adherence to the seniority system. President McKinley appointed him a brigadier general, a startling vault over more than five hundred senior officers.

By that time Wood had further distinguished himself, first as military governor of Santiago and then military governor of the entire island of Cuba. He truly shone in this capacity, reverting to his first avocation as he dealt with sanitation and public health emergencies. In Santiago, he applied common sense and iron determination to reverse decades of neglect and indolence that had created seemingly intractable public health and sanitation problems. Wood personally inspected bakeries, ordering shuttered those that failed to meet cleanliness standards. He conscripted laborers regardless of their social class and set them to work draining pestilent cisterns one bucket at a time and repairing leaking water mains. He ordered accumulated garbage and offal removed from the streets. Because corrupt church burial fees precluded all except the wealthiest from burying the dead, and grave sites in the churchyard were rented, most people had no choice but to abandon their dead wherever was convenient. To the dismay of the church and delight of most everyone else, Wood ordered the priests to perform burial services without pay. When the priests objected, he silenced them with the threat of street cleaning detail. He did all this even though he did not think much of the Cuban people, labeling them "stupid and downtrodden" and observing that they were utterly resistant to hard work unless forcefully compelled.[4]

Wood also applied himself to long-term solutions by instituting a number of social and educational reforms, including the then novel notion that Cuban children should be educated by other Cubans instead of by Spanish-appointed clergy. His sweeping political measures generated particular admiration. Operating under the belief that American-controlled municipal government could not succeed without the consent of the governed, he gave the Cuban people unprecedented political freedoms. Wood departed the island in 1902. His administrative accomplishments earned him the thanks of many Cubans, including the grateful people of Santiago, who named a street after him. Other prominent observers agreed. Lord Cromer, Great Britain's administrator of Egypt, told his Foreign Office that there was only one other man in the world capable of doing his job, and that man was Leonard Wood. Secretary of War Elihu Root stated in the War Department's annual report for 1902, "I know of no chapter in American history more satisfactory than that which will record the conduct of the military government of Cuba. The credit for it is due, first of all, to Brigadier-General Leonard Wood . . . Military Governor of the Island."[5]

During his Cuban service, Wood forged additional relationships that greatly benefited his career. Not only were they with the influential men at the top—McKinley, Root, Senator Henry Cabot Lodge, Roosevelt—but

Wood also attracted members of a new generation of army officers, the so-called armed progressives. They saw Wood as perfectly suited for the army's growing role on the world stage. He exhibited the diplomatic and administrative talents of a model colonial administrator: firm, professional, capable but not hidebound, impelled by great ideals. His admirers included Colonel Tasker Bliss, who served as collector of customs in Cuba; Colonel Hugh Scott, who served as Wood's chief of staff; and Lieutenant Frank McCoy.

Wood first met McCoy in Cuba on the slopes of Kettle Hill, where the pivotal combat of the July 1, 1898, Battle of San Juan Heights took place. Wood noticed the young officer bleeding from a leg wound inflicted by a Spanish sniper. He paused to apply a dressing before moving on with the Rough Riders. Wood next encountered McCoy after the war ended. McCoy commanded a small detail escorting Wood during one of his Cuban inspection tours. The party came to a swollen river ford and debated whether it was passable. McCoy impetuously rode his horse into the current and crossed to the far side. His youthful energy so appealed to Wood that he invited him onto his staff. Moreover, in contrast to his relationship with most West Point–educated men, with whom he was acutely aware of his lack of military training, Wood felt relaxed and comfortable with McCoy. McCoy did not have the rigidity of the typical West Point graduate and never conveyed the air of belonging to an elite caste. The two got along famously. Within three months, the very capable McCoy was director of finances for all of Cuba.

While attracting the armed progressives, Wood ran afoul of many senior army officers. They simply could not stand the notion that a mere doctor whose military command service amounted to eight weeks as colonel of a volunteer regiment should be promoted ahead of career military men of vast experience. Wood's personality gave his foes ammunition. Tasker Bliss observed that Wood held strong opinions and was disinclined to accept advice or criticism. Chaffee briefly served as Wood's chief of staff while Wood was military governor of Cuba. While some of Wood's attributes favorably impressed Chaffee, he penned a caveat: Wood was "a quick thinker, a hard worker, but this does not necessarily imply that he is a correct thinker always."[6] Chaffee believed that Wood needed steady men on his staff to challenge his thinking but instead surrounded himself with sycophants who shared Wood's belief that he was embarked on a great mission and that he was infallible. As a growing chorus of senior military officers complained about Wood, Theodore Roosevelt leapt to the defense of his old commanding officer, writing a magazine article entitled "General Leonard Wood: A Model American Military Administrator."[7]

Beneath this veneer of accomplishment two ugly tumors were growing. One was increasing resentment of old guard army officers who begrudged his meteoric rise. They did not like the fact that Wood had received the Congressional Medal of Honor even though at the time he had neither been a serving officer nor seen combat. They rued the day that a man with no formal military training and the briefest of line experience could be made a brigadier general in the regular army. The celebrated Civil War general James Wilson caustically referred to Wood when he congratulated the naval cadets at Annapolis for their choice to join a branch of the service "which did not make doctors into admirals."[8]

Such resentment reached a peak when Wood became the next brigadier general up for promotion to two-star rank. Eligibility for such promotions was a strict matter of seniority, a system criticized by reform-minded officers as placing antiquated generals of limited intelligence in important posts from which they never resigned and in which they were exempt from court-martial. In addition, the Senate had to give its approval. The ensuing confirmation hearings gave Wood's army enemies and Roosevelt's political opponents a stage to criticize in painstaking detail Wood's entire career.

Roosevelt had been vice president when an assassin's bullet killed President McKinley in September 1901. As he completed McKinley's term, Roosevelt resolved to run on his own. His rival for the Republican presidential nomination, Senator Mark Hanna, used the controversy surrounding Wood to orchestrate an intense personal attack against the former contract surgeon. The anti-administration press gleefully joined in. One of the less vicious cartoons showed Hanna emerging from the narrow end of a giant tuba labeled "Gen. Wood's Military Record." Hanna had a lantern in his hand and a puzzled look on his face, the message being that inside Wood's large reputation there was nothing to be found. For four months witnesses testified about Wood's conduct during the Spanish-American War, seemingly bringing into question whether he had ever done anything more than circulate somewhere in the rear

while others shed their blood. It was mostly untrue and completely un-
fair, but it allowed the anti-administration press to publicize anti-
Roosevelt opinions.

Wood was partially shielded from the worst of their vindictive lies
because Roosevelt hustled him out of the country before the hearings began. Quite simply, Roosevelt knew that the former colonel of the Rough
Riders would be unable to control his temper in the face of repeated personal attack. So Roosevelt sent Wood to the Philippines to govern the
troublesome Moro Province, assuring his old friend that as soon as the
whole matter blew over he would promote Wood to the plum command of
heading the entire Division of the Philippines. However, the controversy,
and particularly seeing his reputation tarnished, apparently changed
Wood. He complained to Roosevelt that press scrutiny made public service unappealing, noting, "I am so heartily tired of the systematic campaign of lying and misrepresentation that I feel I made a mistake in
requesting service in the Philippines."[9]

There was another cause for Wood's despondency and cynicism: a
brain tumor lodged in his skull had begun to grow unchecked.

SEVEN

The New Governor
Takes Charge

*They are able to produce rice, sugar cane, coffee, corn, cattle,
beautiful woven fabrics . . . and give surprising proofs of their
ingenuity and industry. A race of men who are capable of doing all
this and who possess many manly qualities, should be kept alive and
not shot down in war. They should be aided and encouraged and
taught how to improve their own natural and social condition,
and benefit us at the same time.*

—General George W. Davis, 1902

THE PORT OF ZAMBOANGA WAS A "gem-like post beside the sea . . . a
little Paradise," recalled an officer's wife, Rita Wherry Hines.[1] The Malays who had first landed here named it Jambangan, "land of flowers."[2] It
had often been the scene of conflict, featuring Moro attacks against the
Spanish, a bombardment by a Dutch fleet in 1646, and a British attack
in 1798. The Americans who came to occupy the two-story house formerly occupied by the Spanish commandant knew nothing about this
history. The house conveniently sat near the tip of Zamboanga Peninsula. From the front veranda, one looked inland toward Zamboanga's
town center with its whitewashed old Spanish buildings dating back to
about the time the Pilgrims landed at Plymouth. Scarlet-blossomed fire

trees bordered Zamboanga's central square. From the town center, mangrove swamps and rice paddies extended outward to the green foothills of a mountain range whose peaks stood four thousand feet tall.

But it was the superb view from the back lawn that everyone remembered. After walking beneath the palm and almond trees that provided shade for an expansive but impeccably manicured tropical garden, one reached the seawall. The near view was of pristine coral beaches. Gazing south over a sparkling blue sea, one saw in the middle distance the Greater and Lesser Santa Cruz Islands. On the horizon was Basilan, beyond which, well out of view, lay Jolo of ill repute, the remainder of the Sulu Archipelago, and British Borneo. Caressed by a nearly constant sea breeze and located outside the typhoon belt, Zamboanga possessed a refreshing climate that made it one of the most desirable stations in all the Philippines. In this house Spanish generals Ramón Blanco and Valeriano Weyler had lived while trying to accomplish the same job now assumed by Moroland's first American military governor, Leonard Wood.

Wood assumed command of a province on the cusp of a dramatic change. The period of American noninterference in Moro internal affairs was coming to an end, to be replaced by direct American control. To facilitate that control, the Americans divided Moro Province into five districts: Zamboanga, Lanao, Cotabato, Davao, and Sulu. They organized provincial and district governments headed by American army

Provincial governor's residence, Zamboanga.

officers, with the staff drawn almost exclusively from the 65,000 "civilized" residents of Moroland. This select group included Christian Filipinos, Chinese, and a handful of Europeans, Asians, and Americans. With this structure in place, Wood set to work to change the culture of the province's 300,000 Moro inhabitants and 100,000 pagans.[3] He introduced Western concepts of justice and outlawed slavery. He encouraged Filipino Christians from the north to move to Moroland. To pay for physical improvements such as new public schools and roads, and in order to teach the Moros the meaning of government, he imposed and collected taxes. From an American viewpoint, all these measures were consistent with President McKinley's 1899 statement that "the Philippines are ours, not to exploit but to develop, to civilize, to educate, to train in the science of self-government."

The Moro leaders saw all of this in a very different light. Never in their history had they been compelled to pay a general tax. They correctly viewed Wood's policies as direct attacks against social and political customs that dated back to the arrival of Islam. American-imposed provincial and district government administrators held the power that they once had held. American public schools undermined existing Moro religious schools. Taxes were a drain pure and simple. Worse, giving Moro land to Christian settlers stole their most valuable asset while threatening traditional practices of ancestral landholding. In sum, the creation of Moro Province meant the supremacy of infidel customs and law over Islamic customs and law, and Moro leaders resented it.

Unconcerned with Moro opinions, Wood forged ahead. He had inherited a reasonably favorable situation created by Pershing's hard work. However, eager to acquire combat experience to discredit his critics and gain future promotion, Wood showed little interest in Pershing's slow, methodical approach. To begin, Wood undertook a whirlwind tour of Moroland. Accompanying him was his devoted aide, Frank McCoy. They traveled to exotic locales that stirred Wood's hunter instincts. Along the beaches, naive flocks of white snipe, pigeons, and assorted waterfowl provided unmissable targets. From the coast near Iligan, Wood traveled along the road that Bullard's men and their Moro laborers had built. Gigantic trees rose through the jungle, draped in hanging vines and multicolored orchids. From the jungle canopy came the calls of songbirds and parrots, while overhead, monkeys seemed to track their progress as they swung from tree to tree. McCoy described the scenery as "one of those exuberant cocoanut, boa-constrictors, monkeys-leaping-from-tree-to-tree forests which we used to read about" in boys' adventure books.[4] The general arrived at Marahui to witness why dealing with the Moros required a special touch.

HAVING COMPLETED HIS road all the way to Lake Lanao, Bullard took charge of the lakeside garrison at Marahui. The Lake Lanao Moros had cultivated the ground to the east and west, so the vista presented a peaceful scene of carefully tended rice paddies interspersed with cultivated groves of banana, coconut, and date. The garrison was on generally good terms with these people. Yet Bullard experienced daily reminders of the fragility of relations with the Moros. One day a hotheaded officer quarreled with a Moro, and the situation quickly grew explosive. Bullard's intercession barely defused it. Afterward, he wrote that he felt like "breaking that officer" but knew he could not show him up in front of the Moros.[5] It took Bullard two weeks to smooth out the trouble following this momentary loss of American temper.

Then, on August 11, 1903, a fresh challenge emerged when the newly appointed governor of Moroland came riding up the Iligan road to inspect his command. Bullard had arranged a formal reception to impress his new commander. However, just before Wood's arrival a vigilant sentry had detected a Moro acting suspiciously. The encounter ended with the sentry clubbing the Moro with his rifle butt. This Moro turned out to be a minor datu whom Bullard had been trying to convince to accept the American presence. To retrieve the situation, Bullard had his battalion stand at attention and fire a salute. This was the scene Wood and McCoy beheld as they arrived at Marahui. Alongside the soldiers were peaceful datus, each with his entourage of bodyguards and slaves, each holding an American flag given to him by Bullard. The Alabama officer's easy familiarity with Moro leaders impressed Wood. As McCoy wrote, Bullard "is Sultan of Sultans."[6] Before Wood boarded a launch to take him across Lake Lanao, the two officers discussed strategy. Bullard advised two policies: to punish those who had been bad, and "to get the good will of Moros by gifts (in accordance with Moro customs) to heal the sore hearts of those who in our fights have lost friends."[7] In his diary that night Bullard noted that Wood enthusiastically endorsed his first suggestion while totally ignoring his second.

It did not take a penetrating mind to perceive that Wood intended to

change radically American strategy. As Wood continued his tour, he left the forty-two-year-old Bullard confronting an ethical choice with life-changing implications for him personally and for the Lake Lanao Moros. Predisposed by personality to doubt anyone's capacity to perceive his true merit, but ambitious nonetheless, Bullard keenly felt his career prospects receding. To date, Bullard had diligently applied himself to peaceful pacification, made notable progress, yet received neither acknowledgment nor praise from higher authority. The only other American officer who had earned a local reputation for his civil work in Mindanao was Pershing. However, not until Pershing conducted the punitive campaign against the Bacolod Moros did he earn official recog nition in Washington along with a prestigious stateside assignmen The lesson was clear: The army rewarded those who distinguishe themselves in combat far more than those who ably performed pac cation duties. Moreover, the new department commander enjoyed pc erful connections in the capital, and Wood had clearly explained preference for aggressive action. So Robert Bullard was tempted, an he fell, asking for and soon receiving permission to begin punitiv tacks against rancherias known to harbor Moro "criminals."

While Bullard searched his conscience, Wood continued his to the Lake Lanao country. He took practical note of the region's ecor potential but mostly focused on the inhabitants themselves. They d impress him. Their apparent hostile, warlike manner reminded I Geronimo's Apache warriors. One significant difference was the habit of concentrating in fixed locations. Everywhere Wood trav saw the imposing-looking cottas, the Moro fortifications built o works topped with sharpened bamboo stakes surrounded by Wood's tour persuaded him that his predecessors had for too lc looking at the province through a magnifying glass and thus hac on distracting details about such matters as tribal rivalries and nomic competition. Wood's broader view brought the Moro situ proper focus, he felt. From this vantage point, Wood conclude naive Moro mind required a simple, patriarchal government. T needed to learn that the territory belonged to the United St; army. Then the benefits of peace would flow. It did not occur t the Spanish had tried this policy for three hundred years.

Wood informed President Roosevelt that he intended to e restraint but that he anticipated the need to give the Moros a

Jolo datus, 1899; hard men accustomed to unquestioned autonomy.

He explained that his plan was to make the lesson so shocking that there would not be the need for another. Wood may or may not have believed that one exemplary punishment would be sufficient. Certainly if he had taken the time for even a cursory study of Moro history, he would seen that Moro identity was based on resistance to outside control.

Twelve days into his governorship, Wood demonstrated how he intended to govern. Along Mindanao's coast a Moro band had chased off a customs inspector. In response, Wood assembled fifteen soldiers, a Gatling gun, and one of Colt's rapid-fire guns, and set off to teach the savages proper obeisance to American authority. The show of force sufficiently cowed the Moros and no violence ensued, which did not suit Wood's purpose at all. He returned to Zamboanga, assembled a considerably larger force, and set off for Jolo to challenge what he hoped would be a fiercer foe.

MAJOR HUGH SCOTT served as the district governor of Jolo. In American minds the inhabitants were the "most turbulent of all the Moros," presenting the greatest challenge to American rule.[8] They were the descendants of a once dominant people who had grown rich and powerful by controlling the nearby sea-lanes through which flowed a lucrative trade. In the recent past, Jolo's pirates had raided far afield, spreading

carnage and terror. The Spanish occupation had restricted but not ended their activities.

Unlike many Americans, Scott grew to like and respect many aspects of Moro culture. Along with Bullard and Pershing, he learned to practice a special brand of personal diplomacy that frequently placed his own life at risk while defusing numerous explosive confrontations. His judgment was tested when a Moro named Biroa murdered another Moro just outside of the port of Jolo and compounded his crime by kidnapping a young Moro girl. According to the terms of the Bates Agreement, such intra-Moro conflict was not supposed to concern the Americans. However, Scott's predecessor had intervened and demanded that the sultan of Sulu arrest Biroa, thereby elevating a minor matter into a test case of American authority.

This was a type of challenge that even the best colonial administrators dreaded, a confrontation that needed to be defused before it became a surpassing issue of national prestige. Three days into his governorship, Scott pondered what to do. He decided to keep pressing the sultan to arrest Biroa until the sultan either accomplished the task or asked the Americans to do it for him. Through a deft combination of persuasion and threat, Scott convinced the sultan to send a powerful Moro datu, Panglima Indinan, to go after Biroa. Indinan found Biroa holed up in his father's cotta, a fortification perched on the knife-edge of a mountain with vertical sides five hundred feet high. Indinan negotiated the release of the kidnapped girl and retired to his own home.

There matters stood for a while until Scott decided to visit Indinan. Having learned where he was likely to find the datu, Scott used a naval vessel to land on a beach near Indinan's home. Leaving his escort of five sailors to guard the launch, Scott, several other officers, and an interpreter approached what appeared to be an empty house supported on stilts. They climbed the bamboo ladder and, just as his intelligence had predicted, found Indinan. They also unexpectedly found his bodyguard, some fifty heavily armed Moros, hiding in silence in the hopes the Americans would overlook them.

After some preliminary greetings, Scott brazenly sat down next to Indinan and said, "Indinan, they tell me that you are the biggest thief in Sulu."

"Oh, they do me a great injustice. I used to be a thief, but I don't steal any more."

"Indinan, I read in the records of the former governors that there will be no peace and order for anybody in Sulu until after you have been killed. What have you got to say about that?"[9]

When the interpreter spoke these words the datu's bodyguard began muttering and some picked up their weapons. But Scott had the measure of his man and Indinan continued the discussion, protesting that authorities did not understand him and that he was a completely law-abiding person. As a token of his good faith, he produced the little girl he had rescued. Scott sent her down to the launch, lectured Indinan some more, and then returned to the shore. Then Scott hit upon the idea of telling Indinan that since there were no women aboard the navy ship, he could not care for the girl. Instead, Indinan should bring her to Jolo. He sent his interpreter to summon Indinan to receive his new instructions. The order was first ignored and then repeated.

The bodyguard emerged, formed a battle line, and were joined from the adjacent jungle by a second heretofore hidden group of warriors. They advanced to within ten feet of the launch and stood with barongs half drawn. Slowly Indinan descended the ladder from his home and walked toward Scott to ask what he wanted. With only some hyperbole, Scott recalled the scene: "The interpreter had turned gray by this time, and I could hear his teeth chatter. The stage was all set now . . . the keg of powder was right close in front of the fire, needing only one little spark to touch off the whole works."[10] A nervous sailor almost provided that spark when he chambered a bullet into his rifle with a retort that sounded like a cannon shot. His captain calmly reached over and took the weapon from the sailor.

That incident seemed to break the tension. After agreeing to meet again, the launch and its crew put out from shore. Scott did not then understand why events had played out the way they did. Only later did Indinan tell him that he thought that Scott intended to arrest him and that he had been prepared to resist.

Indinan brought the girl to Jolo, but Biroa still remained at large. Again reacting to Scott's pressure, the sultan ordered the island's most powerful datu, Panglima Hassan, to go and arrest the offender. Hassan retorted angrily, "You shut up! We Moro chiefs are attending to this. Biroa has only killed a slave. If a Moro chief cannot kill a slave, what can he do? Can he drink water—can he breathe air—hasn't he any rights at all?"[11]

A few weeks later, eleven of Hassan's slaves sought refuge with the

Americans in Jolo. Scott invited Hassan to a conference, but Hassan replied, "My desire to see my father, the governor, is still small."[12] Hassan's refusal was utterly characteristic of the man whom the sultan said felt so big that "he could pick the stars from the sky."[13]

Scott had patiently worked through recognized lines of Moro authority to try to apprehend Biroa. Not only had he failed, but he had antagonized a more influential Moro datu. To cap it all off, friendly Moros reported that Hassan was plotting a surprise attack against the American garrison.

BIROA'S TRANSGRESSIONS, HASSAN'S alleged surprise attack, and recent incidents of horse thievery gave Wood his excuse to land some 450 men, including a full artillery battery, on Jolo. Once there he tried hard to provoke the Moros. He summoned the island's most prominent datus and imperiously told them the United States now governed the islands and they would have to change their ways. Specifically, they would have to obey American laws, including a ban on slavery, and would have to stop all raiding, whether against each other, the Americans, or the distant British in Borneo. Most particularly, the datus had to suppress attacks by suicidal assassins called by the Spanish word *juramentado* (from the Spanish for "to swear an oath"; in Moro, *macsabil*, "to die for the faith"). The datus would be held accountable for any juramentado attack and be judged in American eyes to be as guilty as if they had made the attack themselves. Wood did not expect them to like the new rules, but he did not care. He warned them that resistance would be useless.

It was all well and good to lay down the law to a submissive group of warrior chieftains, but Wood craved action. He led a patrol inland through a teak forest, hoping to encounter resistance. His objective was a village said to shelter Moro thieves who had stolen four American cavalry horses. Wood's patrol entered the village and arrested its leading men. His interpreter spread the word that these men would be held prisoner until the horses were returned. The villagers handed over the horses within three hours. This type of peaceful police work characterized Wood's first visit to Jolo, and it was not at all what he had hoped for.

He turned his focus to Indinan, who had relocated to the island's interior. Wood led a strong patrol to surround Indinan's home, and was again disappointed to have the Moro ruler meekly surrender. Maybe the sultan himself would exhibit a more steely resolve. Wood marched deeper into the interior but failed to find the sultan. The best he could do was send Scott to fetch the sultan's brother. When the brother pled that incapacitating skin boils prevented him from traveling, Scott subjected him to a humiliating strip search that failed to reveal the purported incapacity and then compelled the sultan's brother to travel to an interview with Wood. Eventually Wood met the sultan himself, took the measure of the nominal Moro ruler, and was disappointed. He told Roosevelt that the sultan was merely "a rundown, tricky little Oriental degenerate."[14]

Wood had campaigned in the midst of the purportedly most warlike Moros and met compliance and obeisance. In disgust, he returned to Zamboanga.

AT CAMP MARAHUI, Major Robert Bullard had been practicing his new pacification approach, which combined aggressive military action with his more familiar civil work. The former had almost cost him his life. He led a patrol into a Moro village in search of illegal firearms. He drew his revolver and stooped to enter a house. An unseen figure from inside the doorway slashed his revolver from his hand and then swung at his head. The thrust chopped through Bullard's hat and only narrowly missed decapitating him. An alert corporal shot and killed his assailant before he could do more damage. Undaunted, Bullard continued to lead fighting patrols and participated in several more hand-to-hand encounters. Following these punitive expeditions, the Moros behaved more docilely, but Bullard confided in his diary that he doubted it would last. He lamented that it seemed that the Moros needed a violent lesson once a week.

He seemed to achieve more enduring results when he engaged the Moros in their favorite activity of spending long hours negotiating. On September 9, 1903, he wrote: "Past week has nearly worn out my patience. Have wrangled with Moros about stolen rifles and pistols until I am ready to kill them. However, have recovered some of the arms and taught some of the Moros that they cannot hope to contend with white men."[15]

Three days later Bullard again almost lost his life. As was so often the case in Moroland, the danger came with unbelievable rapidity. He had been leading an uneventful patrol along the shores of Lake Lanao and was sitting in the stern of a boat that was beached on the shore. A friendly appearing Moro approached and stepped aboard the boat. Bullard's first awareness of danger came when he heard a death groan and saw a Moro with kris in hand withdrawing his darkened blade from a half-severed American head. The attack scattered friendly Moros who were serving as guides and allowed the juramentado to attack a second soldier. To Bullard this Moro seemed like a mad assassin as he inexorably fought his way along the rowers' benches. The Moro was raining blows against the prostrate form of a second soldier when Bullard opened fire with his .38-caliber service revolver. Four shots at point-blank range failed to stop the Moro.

The juramentado's second victim sat on the rowing bench, his head lolling at an unnatural angle. In desperation, Bullard scrambled toward the Moro with the intent of using his last two bullets to fire into the brain or heart. Simultaneously, the Moro advanced toward Bullard hoping to kill a third infidel with his kris. "In that hundredth part of an instant he stooped to clear a bamboo bow that looped the narrow boat over the body of the fallen oarsman; I thrust my muzzle against his close-cropped head and fired."[16] The dying juramentado fell at Bullard's feet. By the time the smoke cleared, one American soldier was dead and another gravely wounded, a Moro preacher in the American service killed, another friendly Moro mortally wounded, and a third Moro slightly wounded.

A few weeks after this episode, General Wood returned to Camp Marahui. He was worried about the way American journalists depicted events at Camp Marahui. For the second time Bullard had an opportunity to speak at length with the governor of Moroland. The conversation confirmed that Wood intended to reverse his predecessor's policy and "stop coddling" the Moros. Again Bullard grasped the nature of Wood's character: "Where General Wood is no one else can expect credit for any work. The General is manifestly out for all the credit and honor and glory."[17] The next month, when Bullard learned about Wood's intention to conduct large sweeps designed to provoke Moro resistance, he wrote in his diary: "General Wood has completely reversed General Davis's policy of patient and mild treatment of Moros. We are going after

Mr. Moro now with a rough hand, we are holding him up to all the high ideals of civilization. I wonder how it will work?"[18]

SOME SEMBLANCE OF the capable, concerned administrator remained, as if an echo of the man he had been in Cuba sounded faintly off the mountains overlooking Zamboanga. American authorities had already established a public school system, begun a public health program, improved commerce, and built roads and port facilities. To help finance these activities they had imposed taxes and customs regulations. Wood issued additional orders to reform Moro education and improve the health services. He supported the notion of redistributing land to the native population. Wood also imposed changes designed to undercut the power of the datus. Wood explained to an English friend that while British colonial administrators were content to maintain in power rajahs, sultans, and the like, "we, with our plain ideas of doing things, find these gentlemen outside of our scheme of Government." Instead, the American way was "to develop individualism among these people and, little by little, teach them to stand upon their own feet independent of petty chieftains."[19]

Wood regarded most Moro laws and customs as "rubbish" and had his Provincial Council replace the Moros' religious courts with Western jurisprudence. Whereas previous American administrations had tolerated slavery because the Moros claimed that it was permitted by sacred Islamic law, Wood was certain that it should be banned. Again his Provincial Council provided the legal veneer to impose this change. That the five-man council invariably acted unanimously was hardly surprising considering Wood himself sat on the council and its secretary and engineer were always army officers. In the rare event that the council deadlocked on a motion, with the two civilians opposing the two army officers, Wood himself could vote, and his counted double.

But Wood's heart was not in the administrative side of governing Moro Province. As he had found in Cuba, hard work and good intentions would merely yield complaint and personal attack from "every shyster in the country whose toes have been trodden on."[20] With the council in place and ready to do his bidding, Wood directed it to pass antislavery legislation that made the possession, purchase, or sale of slaves a crime punishable by imprisonment and fine. That this violated the Bates Agreement, the official treaty signed by the United States and various Moro datus, he cared not. He had no doubt that enforcing this law would lead to conflict, which suited him perfectly well. However, to cover his tracks he wrote the American governor of the Philippines, William Taft, a plausible rationale: "All that is needed to bring the Moro into line, and to start him ahead is a strong policy and vigorous enforcement of the law. He must learn that for every offense against the law, he is going to be followed, taken and punished. He will welcome and appreciate protection to life and property and an honest administration of justice. He does not care under what law or procedure it comes."[21]

Recalling the lessons from the Geronimo campaign—it took Apaches to track Apaches—he created an American-officered constabulary composed of native Moros. One third of its 353 enlisted men were Moro, with the balance of the recruits drawn from among Christians and pagans. It served like an American state police force with the primary responsibility of maintaining the public peace. The ability of its disparate recruits to cooperate at work and to live in the same quarters without incident surprised many. While the Moro Constabulary wore red fezzes because of Islamic prohibitions against brimmed hats, it seemed as if the Moro recruits had successfully transferred the loyalty they had once shown their datus to their Christian officers. The Moro Constabulary worked in the tribal wards and developed an esprit de corps that made them a dependable force. The Moro Constabulary was fortunate to have James Harbord, a man possessing unusual organizational and managerial talents, as its first colonel. Harbord would serve as Pershing's chief of staff in France and later become the chairman of the board of the Radio Company of America, exhibiting a guiding genius that made RCA one of the world's great companies.

During this time Wood also worked hard to maintain his physical fitness. In addition to riding and hunting, he played tennis. Young lieutenant Benny Foulois partnered Wood in doubles and together they defeated all comers. Wood had the engaging ability to converse freely with his young officers. Foulois, he learned, shared his opinion that the Moros needed to be "spanked." In Foulois's opinion, "they are a race of children . . . and have to be treated accordingly." Foulois perhaps exceeded Wood with his belief that "gradual extermination" was the answer to the Moro problem.[22]

Foulois's attitude was pretty much the prevailing American opinion.

The American officers in Moroland understood that their difficult campaign was taking place outside of the view of the American public. This fact allowed them a freer rein, which was necessary because, as Foulois observed, it was "next to impossible to extract" intelligence from Moro prisoners.[23] Wood's aide, the urbane Frank McCoy, expressed a more cerebral evaluation. McCoy described Moro customs in a letter to a colleague back at the War Department and remarked that it was as if life in Moroland was taking place in some previous century. To another friend McCoy noted that it was difficult to understate the contrast between law-abiding American life and Moro customs: "Over here we are living in the midst of feudalism and slavery, with pirates and bloody murder."[24]

Wood and his young entourage reached some immutable convictions. The general had seen enough to conclude that Moros were semi-savage at best and that their pretensions to autonomy were ridiculous and intolerable. The solution for the entire Moro problem should be the same one applied to the American Indian. The Moros needed to be taught a lesson, or "thrashed," as Wood put it, and thrashed hard and soon. Only then would they accept American dominion, and only then could their feudal society be reordered.

EIGHT

Leonard Wood Goes to War

Corporal Lindsay's skull, hat and shoes found in the roof of
Tugassee's house. These had been used by Tugassee as trophies.

—Officer's report to General Pershing

The Execution of Panglima Hassan

THE ALARM CALL FROM MAJOR HUGH SCOTT found Wood leading a patrol through the swamps of central Mindanao. Wood had disregarded
prevailing seasonal weather patterns and begun his campaign during
the rainy season. As the Americans floundered through neck-high water or sat around sodden campsites swatting mosquitoes, the bemused
Moros watched from afar. They had no idea what the Americans were
doing and no desire to impede their progress. Wood's men also wondered about their leader. Major Bullard, who commanded two infantry
battalions that participated in Wood's expedition, observed that Wood
exhibited a "sheer lack of knowledge of the people, of the country . . . He
seemed to want to do everything himself without availing himself of
any information from others." Instead of employing Moro guides, Wood
seemed to prefer "to stagger around in the mud, marshes, and brush and
find his own way."[1] Wood eventually found a cotta that resisted his demands, ordered up a howitzer to bombard it, and then sent in an infantry

assault. One soldier was killed and five wounded. Moro losses went un-reported.

Outside of this skirmish, the terrible weather and terrain proved the most formidable opponents. Thus it was with relief that Wood received Scott's urgent report that Panglima Hassan had assembled a host of fol-lowers in Jolo's Crater Lake region in preparation for an attack against Jolo town. Hassan was a charismatic leader of humble origins who had risen to power by a combination of wits and determination. Scott knew and respected him. He also judged the threat posed by Hassan very real since his men appeared well armed. Reports that Moro pearl divers had been busy retrieving boxes of Remington ammunition that the Spanish had dumped into eighty feet of water before evacuating Jolo seemed to confirm the magnitude of the threat.

Hassan's muster at Crater Lake was the act of Moro defiance that Wood had been waiting for. It offered him a chance to revive his fortunes by testing his combat leadership. Wood promptly force-marched his men to the coast, commandeered six boats, and sailed to Zamboanga. Here he paused long enough to collect seven infantry companies, three Gatling guns, and extra ammunition, and then sailed to Jolo. Among his forces was a battalion commanded by Major Bullard.

The Americans disembarked at a port full of rumors about large, well-armed Moro forces eager to have a go at the infidels. Everyone was set at hair trigger. That night a handful of purported juramentados infiltrated the American camp and were killed. In response, soldiers showed little inclination to discriminate between civilian and warrior as they killed whatever moved around their camp.

At dawn the 1,250-man column marched toward what Wood called "Hassan's Palace." Soldiers continued to kill Moros indiscriminately along the way. Wood found Hassan's warriors entrenched on a hill out-side Hassan's cotta. Wood gave Bullard the prestigious assignment of leading the attack. Bullard's battalion of the Twenty-eighth Infantry used the superior range of their rifles to suppress the opposition. Then they charged. The Moros fired a ragged volley and fled with the Americans in hot pursuit. Wood worried that his units were becoming too scattered and might fall into a Moro ambush. He sent McCoy to rein Bullard in. Bullard believed that he had the enemy on the run and only reluctantly obeyed. McCoy correctly perceived Bullard's motive: he wanted the honor of capturing Hassan and his cotta all to himself. In the event,

Hassan and his remaining warriors abandoned the cotta and fled. Side by side, Wood and Bullard marched their men into "Hassan's Palace" and set fire to all the buildings.

Hassan had possessed the strongest cotta in the entire Sulu Archipelago and the Moros knew it. If they could not hold here, then where? After this campaign, the Sulu warriors composed a song: "The bravery of the Americans is very good: like a mad tiger."[2]

Hassan sent a message saying that he was ready to negotiate. Wood's entourage thought it a ruse, but Major Scott managed to persuade the general to give him a chance. Hassan did surrender, but during the march back to Jolo the column escorting the prisoner passed a nipa hut. Suddenly a howling band of krismen emerged to attack the Americans. In wedge formation they fought their way to Hassan and freed him. Hassan himself shot Scott's pistol from his hand. The slugs from Hassan's Remington chopped up both Scott's hands, causing the loss of two fingers from his right hand. In cold fury at this betrayal, Wood sent his men back to Hassan's cotta. They found Moros hiding in the adjacent mangrove swamps and volcanic rocks.

The next day, artillery delivered a preparatory bombardment and then Bullard led an assault. The Moros were hidden behind brush, trees, and boulders. They emerged fifteen or twenty paces from the Americans and attacked with "mad heroism."[3] Again the .38-caliber service revolver proved inadequate: It took multiple hits to stop a Moro warrior. To withstand these ferocious assaults required collective courage, but Bullard's men proved equal to the challenge. They coolly aimed their revolvers, knowing that only a shot to the heart would stop their foes.

Over the ensuing week, whenever the Americans encountered a hostile-seeming cotta, Wood summoned his artillery and followed the shelling with an infantry assault. There was widespread destruction and killing, including the deaths of many women and children.[4] Wood's scouts reported that Datu Andung, with a large number of hostile Moros, had taken refuge in a mountainside cotta. Wood personally led two cavalry troops rapidly through the jungle to Mount Suliman. As McCoy tersely wrote, "Then Mr. Andung's turn came." A meticulous body count found eighty-two dead Moros. This "pretty piece of work" came at the cost of one American killed and three wounded.[5] Wood's diary entry that night read: "It has been a very busy day's work and I think has given the Moros a very wholesome lesson."[6]

Wood had enjoyed the campaign, a welcome change from unreward-
ing administrative detail. He officially reported fifteen hundred Moros
killed, not distinguishing men from women and children. There were
never any prisoners or survivors. This total was about 2 percent of
Jolo's entire Islamic population. Seventeen Americans had died in the
fighting.

Robert Bullard was pleased as well. In a diary entry that revealed how
far he had compromised his soul, he proudly wrote, "My battalion did
most of the fighting and effective work and won a name for itself and
the regiment and me. All this occurred under the eye of the general."
Bullard enjoyed his newfound status, noting that fellow officers now
treated him with more respect because they thought he had big "pull"
as one of Wood's select lieutenants.[7]

Upon his return to Zamboanga at the end of November, Wood vaguely
appreciated that perhaps an official report of wanton murder might not
be well received by higher authority. At least he had a supporter in the
governor-general of the Philippines, William Howard Taft. Taft congratulated Wood, observing, "I have no doubt that the Moros richly deserved
the punishment you gave them and that the fact of their humiliating defeat will work great good in our relations with them."[8]

Wood, in turn, informed President Roosevelt that the Moros had pre-
cipitated the combat by attacking an American mapping expedition.
While the claim was technically accurate, Wood did not learn about that
attack until after he had completed his reprisal raids. He also told Roosevelt that he had killed only four hundred Moros. As one of Wood's bio-
graphers observed, "As time went on, the numbers continued to drift
about and the story changed with the audience."[9]

Events would prove that the expedition failed to achieve its primary
goal of eliminating Hassan or ending Moro resistance on Jolo. Hassan
again gathered his warriors and resumed defying the Americans. It fell
to Major Scott to hunt relentlessly for Hassan, assisted by Moro warriors
and informants. At last, in March 1904, Scott's men cornered Hassan in
a little grass hut in the volcanic crater of Bud Bagsak. The Americans
and their Moro allies, some four hundred men in all, climbed the steep
slope and took position along the crater rim. In the predawn darkness it
was clear that Hassan knew of their presence. A light came on in the hut
and a voice began to sing a Moro death song. At dawn three armed figures emerged from the hut. The Americans opened fire, killing two and

wounding the third. The wounded Moro crawled into a small ravine. From a protected position he fired his Krag-Jörgensen at everyone who exposed himself, wounding one cavalry trooper in the pelvis. A sergeant worked his way into the ravine. The Moro was ready. He aimed his Krag, but before he could pull the trigger a well-aimed shot hit his rifle, breaking its bolt and knocking the gun from his hand. Although already suffering from thirty-two bullet wounds, the Moro drew his barong and charged the sergeant. The sergeant, who happened to possess a .45-caliber revolver, fired and dropped the Moro. He pressed his .45 against the Moro's skull and finished him off.

Triumphant cries from Moro and American alike split the air. Scott was too saddened to inspect the body and instead sent his interpreter to verify that the last warrior killed was Hassan. During his entire tour of duty, Scott had hoped to befriend a man whom he respected. Instead, duty compelled him to supervise Hassan's execution.

The Trials of Robert Bullard

Bullard returned to Mindanao to find that conditions around Lake Lanao had deteriorated after the Jolo campaign. When Wood had abandoned his campaign and headed for Jolo, many lake Moros concluded that the Americans could do nothing against them. Thus emboldened, motivated by the desire to slaughter infidels and acquire prestige by obtaining better weapons, hostile Moros had killed four sentries at Camp Marahui. Like the Jolo Moros, they also sent divers into the waters of Lake Lanao to recover rifles and ammunition that the Americans had discarded. The future seemed to promise another cycle of Moro raids and American reprisals. Bullard found the prospect depressing. Compounding the problem was the rotation of veteran units back to the United States and their replacement by inexperienced soldiers. On the day after Christmas, 1903, Bullard resolved to work hard to get the new troops started right with the Moros. He wrote in his diary: "I cannot let them spoil my years work by letting them frighten away the only Moros with whom any civilized people have thus far been able to do anything."[10] Apparently his experience on Jolo had slaked his thirst for glory and promotion.

Back at his headquarters in Zamboanga, Wood cared little about any of this. From his perspective, the only important fact was that the Moros had resisted the Americans at all. This allowed Wood to request an abrogation of the Bates Agreement. Such policy changes had been common during the Indian Wars. Quite simply, the U.S. government seldom considered treaties with savages as binding. Rather, they were malleable articles of convenience to be unilaterally cast aside as policy changes dictated. Indeed, when Wood queried the War Department about skirting the Bates Agreement, authorities replied that Bates had signed nothing more than a "mere executive agreement."[11] The War Department asserted that since the sultan and the signatory datus had failed to discharge their duties under the agreement, they forfeited their rights as enumerated in the agreement. This mind-set informed the Roosevelt administration's response to Wood's request. On March 2, 1904, by direction of President Roosevelt, the United States unilaterally abrogated the Bates Agreement, claiming that the sultan of Sulu had failed to quell Moro resistance and that the treaty was a hindrance to effective colonial administration.

The Philippine Commission prepared a new treaty with the goal of doing away with slavery and polygamy—topics not addressed in the Bates Agreement—and introducing a better civil government. Additional new laws protected the common people from the tyranny of their traditional leaders. An organizational plan imposed a political structure on the municipalities. Dominated by non-Muslims, this municipal structure was designed to show the Moros how well-ordered and democratically governed local communities brought peace and prosperity. Thus, over time, the Muslims would enter into civilized Western-style life. Toward that same goal, a tribal Ward Court brought the Moros American concepts of justice. Selected Moro leaders, namely those who had collaborated with American forces against the "bad" Moros, received limited political authority.

The Progressive Era taught that all of these American-imposed reforms were justified because they advanced universal goods. Thus, the pureness of American motive in Moroland was self-evident and readily confirmed by seeing how the Americans continued to build schools and hospitals, improve public sanitation, and construct the infrastructure needed to promote agriculture and commerce. Like the Spanish governors before him, Wood perceived that Moroland had tremendous untapped agricultural potential. So he continued the Spanish policy of inviting immigrants, mostly Christian Filipinos but some foreign immigrants as well, to come and make the land productive. The underlying thought was that civilized people who possessed agricultural know-how would serve as examples to motivate the Moros and the pagans to become more productive farmers.

Of course, civilized people who benefited from public improvements should pay taxes. In 1903 the Legislative Council passed an act providing for the mandatory annual purchase of a *cedula*, or registration card, by residents of Moro Province. The council later levied additional taxes including a road tax. Henceforth ports charged fees to register vessels above a certain size and imposed import and export taxes on merchants engaged in foreign trade. More urbanized Moros paid property taxes. Forgotten in all of this by the American architects of change was the Revolutionary rallying cry "No taxation without representation."

The architects were also culturally ignorant and therefore unaware that to a Moro datu, the cedula smacked of tribute, and tribute was paid only by the vanquished to the victor. The datus did not consider themselves vanquished. They were also as certain as the progressive Americans about the superiority of their customs and laws because they were consistent with the precepts of the holy Koran. Consequently, American-imposed reforms could be nothing except attacks on their religion. The Moros viewed efforts to educate their children in public schools as a naked attempt to inculcate Christian teachings and values. Bypassing Muslim courts ignored the datus' traditional judicial functions while offending Muslim sensibilities. The establishment of neat political structures with their hierarchy of provincial, district, and town governors, all of whom had the power to pass decrees regulating daily life with no input from the people, took away the power and prestige of Muslim leaders. The political changes were a slight against Islam itself. Parceling out land to Christian Filipinos or other immigrants increased resentment. Perhaps the Moros had not tilled this land, but they still considered it theirs by right of long occupation. Selling licenses to Japanese or Chinese commercial fishing boats allowed outsiders to steal what once had been reserved for the Moros.

The Moro list of grievances was long. The American insistence upon outlawing what to them seemed the epitome of barbarism, the keeping of slaves, provided the flame to the dry tinder of Moro resentment.

MORO LEADERS PARTICULARLY saw the requirement to purchase a registration card, the cedula, as a demand for them to submit to the government and therefore an attack against their privileged position. To
maintain their place, they told their people that the cedula was a fundamental attack on holy Islam as part of the American effort to Christianize all Moros. This assertion resonated and formed the basis for a new
wave of Moro resistance. Datu Matabalo in the Cotabato Valley warned
that he and his krismen would kill any Moro who paid the cedula.

The ensuing phase of the Moro War mostly took place outside of the
view of the American public. Few journalists came to Moroland, while
the stories of those who did seldom traveled farther than Manila. A sporadic guerrilla war contested in a remote corner of the world simply did
not sell newspapers. The Moros fought from ambush or sent single brave
men to attack unwary sentries. Whether it was overt violence against
American soldiers or thefts and jailbreaks, Wood routinely used the
provocations as justification for large military reprisals. In the hinterland, his subordinates followed Wood's example.

Wood had persuaded Robert Bullard to remain in Moroland after his
regiment rotated home and to accept the governorship of Lanao Province. The forty-three-year-old Bullard had thought hard about the offer.
It would mean more time spent living in the wilderness, and he was
uncertain if the sacrifice was worth it: "I have neither home nor family,
neither the dear cares nor the thoughts for others that make life worthy.
I have worked hard for the Moros and the U.S. and my own name. For
the first two I feel that I've done something, for the last, but little." Bullard was caught between personal ambition and his sense of what was
right. He confided to his diary, "Any fool can fight and kill Moros but it
takes a man of some sense to manage them without killing them yet
without loss of prestige and dignity."[12] On the other hand, Wood had
powerful political connections and his favor could make Bullard's career. In the end, ambition won out. Bullard decided to remain in the
"wilderness."[13]

Because of the departure of his beloved Twenty-eighth Infantry, that
wilderness was Camp Vicars—Pershing's old post—in the heart of the
most hostile lake Moros. Bullard tried hard to persuade nearby datus to
maintain the peace. He told them that they had to control their unruly
warriors. This was the same message that American officers had tried
to convey to the Native Americans during the Indian Wars. Bullard's

message came with the same threat: If a leader did not control his people, that leader and all of his people would be subject to punishment. As was the case during the Indian Wars, sometimes a leader was cowed by the threat of retaliation. But sometimes they behaved like Geronimo and ignored the threat. Moreover, even well-intentioned datus could not necessarily control all their warriors, particularly when those warriors were impelled by the religious conviction that killing infidels was a path to paradise. In such cases, Bullard tried to use a minimum of force to achieve maximum psychological effect.

Seven miles across the lake from Camp Marahui was the Ramain River. A small party of men from the Twenty-second Infantry had left Camp Marahui to go duck hunting near the mouth of the river. Moros had ambushed them. The regiment's colonel made repeated demands that the sultan of Ramain surrender the perpetrators. Instead, over the next month they had attacked two sentries and stolen four rifles. Accordingly, Bullard organized a punitive expedition composed of four companies supported by a machine gun detachment. On the night of January 21, 1904, the column made a night march to the Ramain River. Then Bullard divided his command. Two companies under Major J. S. Parke clambered aboard vintas while the machine gunners loaded a Vickers-Maxim machine gun and a Gatling gun into a pair of rowboats. Parke's mission was to take his waterborne column up the Ramain River in order to outflank the village. Meanwhile, Bullard led the other two companies on a two-mile hike through the swamps. Moro security was

American infantry aboard a vinta.

routinely poor, and so it proved here. Bullard's column bumped into a small fortification about a mile from the sultan of Ramain's cotta. The appearance of Americans surprised the defenders of this position and all ten surrendered.

For the next sixty minutes Bullard parleyed with the sultan in an effort to convince him to surrender the men who had attacked the Americans. Generally in such situations, a Moro leader took no heed of the odds. His core convictions taught him that to yield was to lose the prestige that gave him his authority, whereas to fight was to ensure that he either retained his authority or went to paradise. The sultan refused Bullard's terms. Unbeknownst to Bullard, the Moros were using the time to mass their forces.

Parke's flotilla entered the Ramain River, where they were met by a small party of Moros, including several obviously agitated datus. Captain Robert Hamilton described the scene: "With red umbrellas raised over their heads, the tribesmen dashed excitedly about—arguing among themselves."[14] During a short parley, this group of Moros told the Americans that they lived in the southern village of Ditseen, across the river from the village of Ramain. They assured the Americans that the Ditseen Moros were friendly and that the "bad" Moros lived in Ramain. The Americans began paddling upstream led by the machine-gun-armed rowboats. The "umbrella men," as the Americans called the Ditseen Moros, paralleled their advance, pausing from time to time to shout across the river to unseen Moros on the north side.

The river quickly narrowed and the first stone walls of the twin cottas appeared. It was a perfect place for an ambush. A path ran along each riverbank just beneath the stone walls. Hamilton ordered a detachment of soldiers to land and move in single file along these twin paths while keeping pace with the boats. The villages extended for several miles along the river. As the column slowly moved upriver, the scene became more ominous: "Many heavily armed Moros could be seen running from cotta to cotta. They carried rifles and knives, and evidently were hurrying to a large fortress at the upper end of town."[15]

Bullard realized that further negotiation was futile and organized an assault. From the river, Parke's riflemen, the Vickers-Maxim machine gun, and a Gatling gun opened a covering fire designed to suppress Moro return fire. Then Bullard sent his two companies across the rice paddies toward the fortress's tall bamboo gate. At the head of the charging column were two young lieutenants vying to display the kind of front-line leadership that brought promotion. Moro riflemen opened fire, cutting down both lieutenants. Their loss briefly stunned the Americans. But the infantry rallied and during the ensuing assault overran the Moro fortress. Infuriated by the loss of their popular lieutenants, the Americans took no prisoners as they relentlessly pursued the Moros from one end of their village to the other. Before burning the cotta, the Americans counted thirty-two dead Moros.

Toward the end of the action, American flags suddenly appeared above Ditseen. Although the Americans believed that they had received fire from this purportedly friendly village, they spared it and returned to camp. When one of the brave lieutenants subsequently died from his wound, the regimental officers wore a badge of mourning for thirty days to honor his memory.

Expeditions like this took place from American bases throughout Moroland, although few officers truly shared Bullard's preference for negotiation over combat. Repeated often enough, these forays produced results. In the wake of the punitive campaigns, datus came to posts to pledge that they would adhere to American-imposed laws. Indeed, although the sultan of Ramain had not been killed in Bullard's assault, he and his lieutenants surrendered a few days later and promised that henceforth they too would respect American authority. This type of response convinced American officers that the only thing the datus respected was superior power. The fact that many "pro-American" datus told them that this was so reinforced the policy. The Americans seldom perceived that clever Moro leaders were quite happy to use the Americans to take down a rival datu.

Five weeks after Bullard's attack against Ramain, a large Moro force conducted a midnight raid against the regimental camp. Although these Moros had no connection to the Ramain Moros, in most American minds it was all one and the same: an intolerable sequence of attacks that would continue until met by the only means of persuasion the Moros understood.

NINE

"Like Rats in a Trap"

The people of this valley have been so hostile and intractable for generations that I have decided to go thoroughly over the whole valley, destroying all warlike supplies, and dispersing and destroying every hostile force, and also to destroy every cota [sic] where there is the slightest resistance. While these measures may appear harsh it is the kindest thing to do.

—Leonard Wood

From the time of his arrival in Moroland, Wood had been convinced of the folly of his predecessors' pacification strategy. In particular, he believed that Pershing's limited excursion against the Lake Lanao Moros had been counterproductive because the relative restraint Pershing demonstrated merely convinced the datus of American weakness. Now, in the spring of 1904, having "thrashed" and "thumped" the Moros in Jolo, he sought a reason to campaign against the Lake Lanao Moros. The most powerful Moro in the Cotabato Valley, Datu Ali, provided an excuse by refusing to obey the antislavery law. Moreover, Ali inflamed the Cotabato people by telling them that the American infidels were coming to force their conversion to Christianity. Accordingly, in March 1904, Wood assembled five companies and an artillery battery and started up the Rio Grande (Mindanao River) toward Ali's cotta "to nip these hostile demonstrations in the bud."[1]

110

The invading column had to traverse some of the worst ground Mindanao had to offer—waterlogged trails deep in mud, nasty floating bogs four to twenty feet deep, mosquitoes so vicious that in spite of the heat the men slept swaddled in blankets around a smoky fire. Although worried that the insects would drive his men mad, Wood again showed driving leadership and pressed ahead. On March 7, Datu Ali's Moros ambushed Wood's column. For once their shooting was rapid and accurate. It pinned down the Americans until a company shook out from the central column, flanked the Moros, and counterattacked the ambushers.

The expedition finally reached Ali's cotta at Siranaya. It was an imposing fortification with a huge central keep surrounded by fifteen-foot-high walls of packed earth, revetted front and rear with timber. More than one hundred embrasures pierced the walls to provide firing ports for the Moro artillery. Numerous outworks provided fortified rifle positions for Moro marksmen. To assault the fortress an attacker would have to cross some three hundred yards of flat, swampy ground. Interrogation indicated that several thousand Moros were inside. Clearly the attackers needed artillery, but the terrible terrain made it extremely difficult to bring up the big guns. Wood showed commendable patience and waited while gunners loaded a 3.2-inch artillery piece onto a split-rigger canoe and laboriously dragged the canoe into position. Finally the gun opened fire. The Moro gunners replied with heavy fire but their

In Moro country: Twenty-third Infantry on the Rio Grande, 1903.

hundred-year-old Spanish naval cannon, and even older brass lantakas, lacked the range to hit the modern American gun. After two days of shelling, a white flag appeared above mighty Siranaya. Wood's soldiers entered to find many blood splatters and numerous fresh graves. They estimated that the bombardment had killed one hundred Moros. More certain was the capture of twenty-one Spanish naval cannon, seventy-two lantakas, seven tons of gunpowder, and one wounded survivor.

Datu Ali was nowhere to be found. Unlike other Moro leaders who preferred to die in a ritualized last stand, Ali had surprised the Americans by escaping the night before the final assault with almost all of his followers. His skill earned the grudging respect of his pursuers. Frank McCoy called it "the most astonishing piece of work for any but a civilized people" and labeled Ali as "a soldier and a gentleman" whom he did not blame for fighting for his "ancient customs."[2]

Captain Robert Van Horn, the officer serving as district governor of Cotabato, praised Wood for his tactics. Van Horn claimed that Wood periodically ordered the 3.2-inch artillery piece to cease fire so civilians could escape from the cotta: "I thought this was a white thing to do. He [Wood] could easily have had a massacre at little cost, and it would have brought him Ali with great renown."[3]

One authority who disagreed with Van Horn was William Taft, who now served in Roosevelt's administration as secretary of war. When news of Wood's brutality reached Taft, he sent him a stern telegram ordering him to suppress slavery and other undesirable Moro customs by peaceful means rather than by force. Stung by the criticism, Wood replied that the Moros had struck first and he and his men had no choice but to defend themselves. Wood had one more major campaign in mind, and to buy enough time to complete it he promised Taft that in the future he would try to resolve conflict by peaceful means. He did not mean it.

Previously he had ordered Bullard to compile a list of Moro "crimes." The document showed that the lake Moros had engaged in intermittent sniping attacks, killed seven sentries, and stolen their rifles. In addition, there were regular attempts to steal firearms and ammunition, occasional "riots," and two jailbreaks. Wood seized upon this annoying pattern of violence to justify a major expedition. First, he needed some advance intelligence, and he cabled Bullard with a query about the presence of any newspaper correspondents. Upon learning that there were no prying eyes to tell the world—and, more important, the secretary of war—

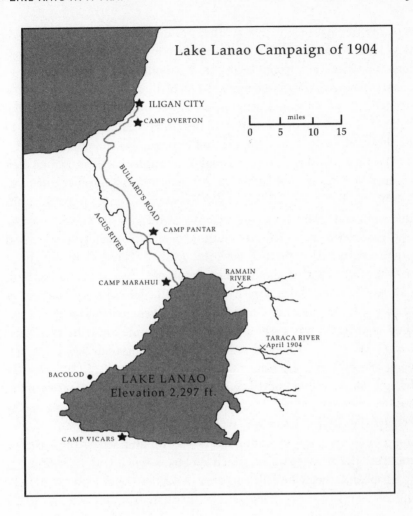

Lake Lanao Campaign of 1904

what he was about, Wood assembled his largest expedition yet: sixteen infantry companies, two troops of dismounted cavalry, and a field artillery battery. He then marched to Lake Lanao and summoned the region's datus to a peace conference at Camp Vicars.

Just as Wood intended, the most powerful datu, the sultan of Taraca, did not attend. Two thirds of all Moros living along the shores of Lake Lanao resided in the Taraca River valley, making the valley one of the most densely populated regions on Mindanao. The sultan of Taraca and his warriors had been inveterate foes of the Spanish. They boasted that the Spanish had never been able to force their way up the Taraca River and menace their riverside cottas. They considered the Americans who replaced the Spanish as just another group of white infidels. The sultan's nonattendance gave Wood the excuse to send two infantry battalions and two cavalry troops by boat to the mouth of the Taraca River. As soon as the Americans clambered out of their boats, hidden Moros opened fire, which suited Wood perfectly. He immediately marched the balance of his force overland toward the sultan's cotta. That night Moro marksmen harassed the campsite and wounded two soldiers.

The next day the column struggled through marshy terrain, often compelled to advance in single file. The column was terribly vulnerable to ambush, but it seemed that the Moros were content to remain within the confines of their fortified cotta. Meanwhile, an increasing number of Moro volunteers joined the column, apparently because they too had grievances to settle with their powerful overlord. The day's march ended with the troops within about a mile of their objective. It was Easter Sunday, so Chaplain Doherty held services. It began with the singing of "Nearer My God to Thee." Suddenly the movement around the campfires stopped. "It was a weird scene," McCoy wrote to his mother, "just beyond the chaplain I could see some men drying their socks at a fire, while the packers were eating their chow . . . a bunch of Datto Pedro's friendly Moros were huddled and squatting nearby, a trifle fearful of the strange ceremony of the dogs of infidels but interested enough to stay and see the show. It was a very dark night, and the signal man was flaring a torch message to Camp Vicars way up and across the Lake we could see the answers waved which kept us in touch with the world."[4]

Chaplain Doherty initially appeared shaken by the prospect of preaching to soldiers at war on the holiest of Christian days. But as he spoke his voice strengthened and his sermon reassured the soldiers that they were engaged in the Lord's business, part of the long, long struggle between Christians and Muslims. He preached "Holy War" with the objective of ending centuries of Moro depredations against Christians. Doherty eased the men's moral concerns, telling them that they were bringing the "Word of God" to the "land of infidels."[5] He assured them that God approved of their wholesome efforts to discipline the heathens. Of course, this was exactly what Moro firebrand preachers warned their people about when inciting them to violence and exactly what Pershing had pledged would not occur. A rousing chorus of "Onward, Christian Soldiers" ended the service. The soldiers dispersed to whatever dry ground they could find and girded themselves for what they expected would be a tough battle the next day.

Wood planned a two-prong advance. While he personally led the main force overland, Colonel Marion P. Maus embarked the Third Battalion of the Twenty-second Infantry aboard a collection of vintas and rowboats. Maus's mission was to land near the mouth of the Taraca River and hold his position until Wood's column arrived. The flotilla set out at 2:00 A.M. A four-and-a-half-hour pull across fog-cloaked Lake Lanao brought it to the vicinity of the Taraca River. As the fog lifted, small groups of Moros opened an ineffective, long-range fire. Maus's guides seemed either ignorant of the terrain or unwilling to point the way. Maus peered through his field glasses to find a landing place, but it appeared that the lake simply merged into a huge marsh with tall swamp grass everywhere. But the Moro riflemen were firing from secure footing, so Maus ordered the boats to continue along the shore. Rounding a point, the flotilla came to a small bay. A line of bamboo pilings obstructed the entrance to the bay. Fifty feet inland from the shoreline was a small cotta sited to control the bay. An agitated band of Moros occupied the cotta. The leading boat stopped fifty yards from shore. An interpreter translated Maus's explanation to the crowd onshore that the Americans merely wanted to land and set up a camp and that the Moros would not be molested if they did not resist. A Moro datu defiantly replied that he would not permit a landing.

The parley continued amid rising tension as the interpreter repeatedly warned that the Moros were preparing to open fire. "Suddenly swamp and cotta blazed with fire. Bullets and slugs whistled through the air, struck boats and splashed into the water. Lantacas [sic], service rifles, Mausers, Remingtons, and flintlocks delivered an almost perfect volley."[6] Miraculously, the Moro fire wounded only two soldiers. The American riflemen · returned the fire, but it was the two automatic weapons, the Vickers-Maxim machine gun and the Gatling gun, that dominated the exchange. Their stream of bullets swept the cotta's walls and searched the adjacent swamp grass wherever gun flashes could be seen. The infantry landed to assault the cotta, but the overwhelming American fire had disheartened the defenders and they retreated before contact. Maus had strict orders to coordinate his movements with the other column. After overrunning a few nearby cottas, he stopped the pursuit. His men policed the battlefield—a meticulous body count found sixty-five dead Moros—and then they settled in to await the arrival of the second column.

Wood personally commanded the landward column. McCoy described the scene: "As we moved out along the high bluff from Vicars we heard the boom of Moro lantakas . . . and faintly heard the pom-pom of the Vickers-Maxims. The ball opened early, and the infantry with us stepped out lively at the sights and sounds."[7] For all their boastful belligerency, the Taraca Moros could offer no effective resistance to the American combination of artillery bombardment and infantry assault. The cottas along the Taraca River were so close together that their perimeter walls abutted one another. Wood's columns methodically overran them one after another. During the ensuing days, Wood's advance along both banks of the river seemed to confuse the Moros. At night, American officers gathered around the campfire to discuss Moro strategy, or more precisely, their puzzling lack thereof. The Moros failed to maneuver in organized groups, utilize their local knowledge and superior mobility, and take advantage of the terrain to attack isolated and vulnerable American detachments. As McCoy observed, "The Moro state of mind is past our understanding. During the ten days in their neck of the woods they made every possible military mistake, leaving themselves open in every way."[8] McCoy did not understand that each cotta was separated from its neighbor by walls, and within each cotta the resident datu was his own commander in chief. The Taraca River represented an even greater political boundary, dividing loose associations of clans from one another. These facts explained the lack of a unified Moro response to the American invasion.

Before Wood came to Moroland, General Davis had pondered the question of Moro battle strategy. Davis wrote about the futility of Moro battle tactics and their impact on American strategy: "Were the Filipinos or American Indians defending the Lanao country we would have on our hands a problem of vastly greater difficulty than the one which now confronts us, for the force would be brave, desperate, resourceful, and elusive, while now we know beforehand exactly where to find the enemy and what will be his general plan of operations. The moment his cota is captured he is powerless, and the survivors either surrender or take flight to some other chieftain."[9] Davis's other key military conclusion was that the Moros had no capacity to mass their forces for offensive operations. Their offensive operations were limited to the ambushing of small parties and attacks against unwary sentinels. Wood's campaign against the Taraca Moros verified Davis's conclusions.

As the days on the Taraca River passed, Wood perfected his methods. He demanded that the datus allow him to search their cottas for weapons and gave them ten minutes to decide their fate. Their predictable refusal surprised no one but gave Wood a rationale to attack. The extremely partisan McCoy claimed, "The General's idea was not to slaughter a lot of people, but to thoroughly demoralize the chiefs" by showing them that the Americans could penetrate anywhere into Mindanao's interior and there was nothing the Moros could do to stop them.[10]

In a handful of cases, the big guns could not be brought to bear against a hostile cotta. In a letter to a friend, Wood described what happened next: "We smother their fire with rifle fire and send men over the pit and up the parapet on two or three sides simultaneously, and the finale usually is that the Moros are killed like rats in a trap."[11] Indeed, the infantry charged up to the parapet and then fired down into the trenches until nothing stirred. When describing the campaign in his diary, Wood, the former surgeon, repeatedly used a medical metaphor to describe the American action as "cleaning up" the Moro positions. Characteristic of Wood's operations, there were no prisoners or survivors. Wood explained, "The people of the valley have been so hostile and intractable for generations that I have decided to go thoroughly over the whole valley, destroying all warlike supplies, and dispersing and destroying every hostile force, and also destroy every cota where there is the slightest resistance."[12] This was a far cry from his reassurance to Taft that he would settle the conflict "by peaceful means."

From the perspective of the infantry or cavalry private, assaulting a cotta was far from a routine thing. Some of the cottas dominated the nearby terrain, appearing to rise above the adjacent rice paddies like a fortified island surrounded by a deep ditch and covered with cunning traps and obstacles. Yet time and again the soldiers willingly charged such positions, and time and again they conquered them. Then they methodically searched for Moro weapons, unearthing caches of firearms concealed beneath a nipa hut, a brass lantaka hidden in the slimy waters of a carabao wallow, or iron cannon abandoned in a nearby stream. To McCoy the soldiers now appeared as the "toughest men" he had ever seen: their campaign hats soiled and turned down over their unwashed, unshaven faces, flannel shirts open at the neck, cartridge belts sagging, torn and muddy breeches, only a lucky few still wearing leggings, shoes worn out, but still "stepping lively" as they paraded before their conquering general.[13]

During one action, the Americans noted that a prominent cotta flew the American flag. The cotta stood on tactically powerful ground. American gunboats were pounding the nearby cottas with their pom-poms and machine gun fire. Yet beneath the American flag a Moro stood calmly, observing the American infantry charging across his front. After that day's "cleaning up" was complete, soldiers interrogated this leader. He explained that he and his wife trusted American promises. Pershing had visited them the previous year and persuasively explained that the American word was golden. Pershing had said that if people lived within the law, they would be left alone. Since the Moro knew he had not done anything wrong, he had faith that he would not be harmed.

In contrast, almost all the other Taraca Valley Moros believed that the Americans would not take prisoners. The Americans, in turn, believed that the Moros were too fanatical ever to surrender. Consequently, Moro casualties were staggering. According to Wood's tabulation, during the campaign his men destroyed 130 cottas along with any Moros who chose to defend them. At one large cotta, when the Moros tried to escape in canoes, American rifle fire slaughtered them. On the shore, firing a borrowed rifle, stood Leonard Wood. There were no survivors. Through it all Wood remained firmly convinced that he was dealing with a treacherous, unreliable group of savage slaveholders and land pirates who would see anything less than the utmost firmness as American weakness. They would then exploit this weakness and set off a new carnival of crime.

McCoy explained the campaign's remorseless logic to his mother: "Each of the great Moro communities has had its lesson now, and hard ones. But they're the only sort that the savage Moro feels enough."[14]

WOOD'S TENNIS PARTNER, Benny Foulois, participated in the 1904 Lake Lanao campaign and added three notches to his pistol. His first kill came during an assault on a small blockhouse surrounded by a moat. A log laid across the moat offered the only way to enter the blockhouse. The scene was preternaturally quiet and the silence alarmed the young lieutenant. Before crossing the moat, Foulois stood to draw Moro fire. Nothing. Leading from the front, Foulois crawled across the log bridge followed by his men. He cautiously approached the entrance to the blockhouse and pushed the door open with his .38 revolver. He immediately heard a swishing sound and reflexively pulled back his arm. The descending kampilan blade missed his arm and merely grazed his fingertip. Foulois and two soldiers fired their revolvers and the dead Moro fell atop Foulois. While he disentangled himself, his men entered the blockhouse. About a dozen Moros huddled inside, demoralized by the death of their guardian. The Americans were not inclined to take prisoners and killed most of them.

Foulois's next kill came during a Moro ambush. The Moros were hidden in the towering cogon grass, where fields of vision were reduced to a few feet. Suddenly a Moro warrior carrying a kris in one hand and a knife in the other charged Foulois, who emptied his revolver into the man at point-blank range. Standing over the fallen victim, Foulois was shocked to see that it was a woman.

Foulois's fifth career kill, and the last of this campaign, came about a week later. Again the American infantry was advancing cautiously through tall cogon grass, with visibility limited to the length of their rifles. Again leading from the front, Foulois was walking point when he heard movement. It could only be the enemy. The noise increased. Foulois cocked his revolver and pointed it at the sound: "The grass parted, and I was face to face with the toughest, biggest Moro I had ever seen! There was a split second of silence, and then we both reacted. He raised his *campilan* over his head with both hands and I fired. The bullet caught him squarely in the center of his forehead, and he collapsed."[15] As was his habit, Foulois picked up his foe's weapon to add to his collection. It was a beautifully forged steel sword with an edge sharper than a fine razor.

That night one of Wood's aides saw the kampilan and said to Foulois, "That weapon is the finest I have ever seen. I think you should give it to the general for a souvenir."

Once again Foulois's ready wit served him well: "I think the general would rather go out and get his own souvenirs."[16]

FROM ACROSS THE lake, men of the Twenty-second Infantry, based at Camp Marahui, came in boats to join Wood. Back at Marahui, the wives could hear the boom of cannon and at night see some of the flashes of battle. It was an anxious time: "After dark each night, each wife kept waiting and dreading to hear the sound of the ambulances approaching the Post from the direction of the lake. They would be bringing the casualties of the day back from the battle, and each wife wondered if one of the ambulances would stop at her door with her loved one!"[17]

In the event, American losses for the entire campaign were slight: two killed and eight wounded. After a weeklong campaign, Wood led the column back to Camp Vicars. In his mind, the only blot on the campaign was the failure to capture or kill the sultan of Taraca. Friendly Moros told him that the sultan had fled across the lake to the shelter of a kinsman, the sultan of Bacolod, who had rebuilt his cotta following its destruction the prior year at the hands of Pershing's men. Wood ordered Bullard, whose rested men had served as a garrison at Camp Vicars, to go get the sultan. A grueling four-day march brought Bullard to his objective. The ensuing assault easily overran a pair of cottas at the cost of only one American wounded. Although the infantry destroyed fifteen Moro cannon and ten muskets and reclaimed some stolen army property, they failed to bag the sultan.

Bullard returned from this expedition sick and exhausted. He had been living on an unhealthy diet of raw eggs, malted milk tablets, and bread, and had lost a great deal of weight. Unofficial leave at Zamboanga only partially restored him. During the second week of June he was again in the field marching to secure another datu whom Wood wanted to punish. This time, the Americans found the offending Moro's cotta abandoned. On the return march to Camp Vicars, Bullard's morale gave out. Service as district governor had won him respect among his fellow officers on Mindanao, but at the cost of his health and a deeply troubled conscience. Disheartened and exhausted, he wrote a resignation letter to Wood. Subsequently, Wood tried to persuade him to remain, heaping heartfelt praise, telling Bullard that his combination of knowledge about the Moros and combat leadership was indispensable. Bullard refused to reconsider. He simply wanted to return to the United States, where even the boring routine of army garrison life seemed appealing in contrast to the sordid killing in Moroland. With a characteristic tinge of self-pity he summed up his service in Moroland in his personal diary: "I feel that I've added considerably to my military reputation in the last two years, but has it been worth the labor and pains and sacrifice. I doubt it."[18] Bullard's next active service would be under Pershing on the Mexican border, and then in France in 1917. He never returned to the Philippines.

General Wood had campaigned against the Taraca Valley Moros in large measure to burnish his military reputation. He was keenly aware that back in the United States the Roosevelt administration had pulled out all the stops to win him confirmation to the rank of major general. During the acrimonious Senate debate, many anti-administration senators, in a repeat of their performance when Wood was up for promotion to brigadier general, had questioned Wood's combat record. The Taraca campaign was Wood's response to his critics.

Yet Wood himself was honest enough to understand that his triumphs against a badly overmatched foe lacked luster. He wrote his friend President Roosevelt, "As a fighting proposition the Moro has been a great disappointment; in the open they are relatively helpless. If you assault them in their cottas, and have to pile into a narrow passageway or a door to get in, you will be met by fanatics armed with butcher knives two or three feet long, and of course you are going to lose a good many men. To adopt this style of fighting is to abandon all the advantages which our superior intelligence and equipment give us."[19]

Wood returned from his Taraca campaign to learn that a new man, General Henry Corbin, was coming to Manila to assume command of the Division of the Philippines. This was personally stunning news. Roosevelt had promised him the post. Zamboanga was supposed to be a prelude. Wood felt betrayed. He lost his temper and immediately sent an angry sixteen-page letter to the president. Had Wood taken the time to reflect, he would have realized that Roosevelt had invested a lot of political capital to secure Wood's promotion to major general just two months earlier. The president did not want to reopen that ugly wound. Indeed, Wood's ingratitude stunned Roosevelt. Yet the president composed himself, in a manner foreign to Wood, to write a deferential but frank reply. Roosevelt explained that his administration had acted on Wood's behalf in an unprecedented manner and that to follow up this exercise so soon by promoting Wood again would create another crisis. Instead, he had chosen to observe the seniority system.

Wood belatedly realized that he had overreached, and he accepted that he would remain as governor of Moroland for a while. After all, Wood well knew that Corbin was an elderly officer who was not likely to remain in the Philippines for too long. Wood resolved to wait for his opportunity to replace Corbin. Indeed, only twenty months passed before Wood ascended to the command of the Division of the Philippines. Because of Wood's personality, it seemed like a long time. Because of his policies, it seemed like an eternity to the Moros.

TEN

Eye of the Storm

*But as for the infidels, let them perish; and their works
shall God bring to naught.*

—The Koran, Sura 47, 9

IN AMERICAN EYES, MORO CIVIL CUSTOMS and behavior seemed to come
from feudal times. Moro chieftains practiced slavery, piracy, and polygamy while pursuing blood feuds and engaging in frequent war. These
behaviors contributed to the American notion that the Moros were uncivilized and beyond redemption. More sinister still was the Moro practice of the juramentado ritual. Early in the morning, a candidate received
absolution from an imam, shaved his body hair, wrapped himself tightly
with cloth so he would not bleed to death before accomplishing his mission, dressed in a white robe and turban, attached a charm to ward off
blows, and sallied forth to kill as many Christians as possible before
dying (or "run amok," in the language of the time). He thereby entered
a paradise of unalloyed pleasure featuring eternal youth and limitless
concubines. Regardless of a datu's control of his people as a whole, no
leader could prevent individuals from turning juramentado. The practice
of juramentado was widespread, particularly on the volcanic island of
Jolo, and it posed a perplexing challenge to that island's district governor,
Major Hugh Scott.

The essence of the problem lay in the fact that an adult male Moro customarily wore a blade when out in public view. It was easily concealed beneath his robes. A Moro's skill with edged weapons made him a deadly assassin, yet to a Western eye there was no way to distinguish a potential assassin from any other Moro male. The practice of juramentado had terrorized the Spanish and now plagued the Americans. American soldiers related stories of how "periodically a Moro would work himself into a religious frenzy and start through a barrio to cut and kill everything he met."[1] As Hugh Scott noted, any Moro man who despaired of his future prospects believed that he could enter paradise by killing Christians: "He cares no more what Christian he kills than you care which one of a bunch of railway tickets you receive, any one of which will take you to your destination and he has no more animosity against the Christian than you have against the ticket; he is simply a means to an end."[2]

Vigilant American security initially prevented many juramentado attacks. Then Moro suicide attackers adjusted to the new environment by changing their habits. Instead of engaging in ritual preparations that attracted attention and made them vulnerable to informants, they prepared in private. An assassin then watched and waited patiently before trying to smuggle a weapon inside Jolo's fortified perimeter. In a typical incident, an unwatched sewer conduit provided a portal for a juramentado to push his barong under the wall. He then entered unarmed through the gate, retrieved his barong, and attacked two American soldiers walking down the street. If a juramentado could not enter the city, he instead attacked the American sentries at the gates.

The first juramentado attack on Jolo had occurred one month after Scott became governor. A Moro laborer concealed his weapons in the tall grass just outside a gate. When the nearest American sentry turned his back, the Moro seized his spear and barong and attacked. The panicked American dropped his rifle and ran, hotly pursued by the Moro. The Moro entered the garrison's parade ground and cut down two off-duty soldiers. A bugler sounded the alarm, his call intermixing with the Moro's battle chants. When the garrison turned out, general pandemonium led to a cross fire that sent bullets into nearby buildings; one panicked shot even struck a warship in the harbor! It took four bullets to kill the juramentado. Meanwhile, a wild shot killed an American bugler. Scott pondered what he could do to stop such attacks. In Western law, the government's ultimate sanction, the death sentence, checked violent

Moros entering Jolo had to surrender their weapons.
The weapons lockup closet at one of the guard posts.

crime. But this was useless given the Moros' disregard for death. Scott reckoned that he could send his troops out to sweep the island from one end to the other but, as he ruefully noted, "it has always seemed to me a poor diplomacy that seeks to civilize a country by killing everybody in it."[3]

Because of their ability to masquerade as peaceful civilians one moment and turn into frenzied assassins the next, juramentados imparted a unique fear among American soldiers. An officer who had served in the Indian Wars remarked, "Even the veteran Indian fighters . . . had to learn that a Moro *juramentado* was more dangerous than a renegade Apache and twice as hard to kill."[4] Stories abounded about incidents such as the one in which a juramentado fought for five minutes, struggling and slashing the whole time, in spite of his fourteen bullet wounds, including three to the skull. Such incidents led to a reevaluation of the standard American handgun, the .38-caliber revolver.

A revolver's purpose was simple: to kill at close quarters. Solders understood close quarters to mean a range of twenty paces or less. At longer ranges revolvers were too inaccurate. In hand-to-hand struggle, edged weapons—the American bayonet, the Moro kris, kampilan, or barong—dominated. The whole point of the service revolver was to allow an American sentry to drop a Moro in his tracks before he came close enough to use his assortment of deadly edged weapons. By 1902, experience had already proved that the .38-caliber revolver lacked the hitting power to accomplish this. In kill-or-be-killed moments, the Americans did not have a reliable handgun.

Consequently, officers and men alike strove to obtain Colt .45-caliber revolvers because that handgun had superior stopping power. They even welcomed the old-style single-shot Colt .45s. This Colt "hand cannon" had proven itself on the Texas frontier since the 1850s, prompting a veteran of the fight against the Comanches to remark, "It is the only weapon with which we can hope ever to subdue these wild and daring tribes."[5] Officers in Moroland agreed. One departmental commander on Mindanao personally issued to his men as many Colt .45s as he could find. Robert Bullard described the Colt .45's superior performance: "A Moro who had just surrendered in our assault on a Moro fort, suddenly snatched a dagger from his clothing and sprang upon a soldier, stabbing with that invisible speed with which only a Moro can work a knife. He reached the soldier's bowels with his very first stroke, but he never made another. A single shot from the .45 of an officer nearby dashed him into eternity as if by a million volts of electricity."[6]

Coincident with the distribution of more powerful revolvers was an ethical change among many Moro religious leaders. Once they perceived that the Americans were not like the Spanish in that they did not try to covert the natives, religious and political leaders reconsidered the practice of juramentado. Since the Americans had established a secular government, the Moro leaders decided that Islam was not under assault and therefore it was not necessary for the devoted to die in defense of their religion. Imams ceased granting approval to individuals for mounting suicide attacks. This decision ended the practice of juramentado as a regular institution. Henceforth, individuals could and did continue to mount suicide attacks, but these were isolated events and not part of any pattern of violence.

The Peaceful Interlude

By the summer of 1904 Moroland seemed pacified at last. Whereas before Americans had encountered armed opposition throughout the lake region, now even small American patrols marched throughout the interior in complete safety. The Americans had practically suppressed piracy and slaving. Wood observed that while nominal security existed everywhere, it would be years before relations between Moro and American became truly friendly. "They are friendly now on the surface," Wood candidly reported, "in part because they know we are stronger than they, and, in part, because they have been honestly dealt with."[7] The peaceful interval gave Wood the opportunity to rediscover the man he had been in Cuba.

Wood's expeditions throughout Mindanao had convinced him that Moro Province had enormous economic potential. He urged the U.S. government to finance a railroad to link the interior with the coast so that the crops grown on the rich volcanic soil—coffee, cacao, hemp, rubber, bananas, coconuts—could find access to world markets that craved these goods. As Wood pondered the province's economic development he recalled his meeting with the famous British colonial administrator Lord Cromer. Cromer had said that the difficulties Wood was likely to encounter would differ in detail from those Cromer encountered in Egypt. He added, "One thing, I think, is true of all fanatical Mohammedan tribes. The only way you can get them to work with you is to interest them in trade. When you once get them interested in trade they stop going to war."[8]

Wood took Cromer's advice and established a Moro Exchange in Zamboanga. His overarching goal was to undermine the authority of the datus who had dominated the islands for so long. He wanted to create a country of yeoman farmers who could lift themselves up as individuals. Toward this end the government-supervised commodity exchange gave the people a place to sell their goods in a secure environment. In times past, farmers and fishermen bringing their harvest to town had to contend with Moro robber barons and outlaw bands. If they managed to evade their fellow Moros, they still had to deal with Chinese middlemen who squeezed the maximum profit out of them. The Chinese method was simple. A farmer brought his produce to Zamboanga. The tropic heat rendered the produce highly perishable. In addition, the farmer needed to return soon to his land to deal with pressing work. The Chinese, working in concert and in cheerful cooperation with other foreign merchants including Japanese, Dutch, and Americans, refused to buy until the farmer became desperate. The farmer, in turn, had only two choices: accept the ruinous price or carry his goods back into the mountains. The net effect of this sharp practice was that farmers either refused to come to Zamboanga to trade, thus condemning themselves and their families to a life of subsistence farming, or worked extremely hard simply to inch up the economic ladder.

Wood's stern imposition of law and order greatly reduced the control of Moro robber barons, thereby allowing farmers to bring their goods safely to Zamboanga. The Moro Exchange, in turn, offered farmers, whether Moro or pagan tribesmen from the remote hill country, a fair chance to better their lives. It published exchange rates that informed farmers before they came to town of the prices they could expect and provided storage places where they held their produce until the agreed price was indeed met. To encourage local participation, the Americans built a lodging place run by Moros where Moro traders could stay overnight and eat food uncontaminated by infidel hands. Wood promised the Moros that they could do anything they pleased at the Moro Exchange except fight. Lord Cromer's insight seemed vindicated as the Moro Exchange quickly became a thriving hub of prosperity. Moros, non-Christian tribesmen, and the Zamboanga business community all benefited. An unforeseen bonus was that Moro leaders met one another on neutral territory and resolved many of the disputes that had plagued the island since time immemorial.

As the months passed the number of exchanges increased. In addition, the American genius for engineering led to extensive public works projects including bridges, roads, schools, and government buildings. The construction of new wharves at Zamboanga attracted trading steamers from Hong Kong, thus increasing profits at the Moro Exchange and providing additional customs duties. As a result, during Wood's second year as governor, the province's revenues increased by almost 50 percent. One quarter of those revenues went to education.

But at the end of the day, Wood deeply doubted the progressive vision originally enunciated by President McKinley and practiced by Governor Taft—namely, that the riches of the Philippines could or should be exploited by the inhabitants. To Leonard Wood, Moro Province was "white man's country." In his view Mindanao was like Cuba in that inherent racial and institutional patterns inhibited development. Wood's solution was to open the land to white immigrants.

Wood took Taft's replacement, Luke Wright, on a tour that retraced the route of several of Wood's most brutal campaigns. The trip proceeded without incident. He took the governor up to Cotabato to meet prominent datus and to Jolo to meet the sultan. Wood also took his wife boating on Lake Lanao. The last time he had been here he had borrowed a rifle to participate in the slaughter of Moros trying to flee in canoes. This time all was quiet. The job seemed done. On October 25, Wood wrote that the "Moro question . . . is pretty well settled. They have had all the trouble they were looking for and perhaps a little more, and each one of the three big aggregations has been pretty well smashed as far as their power of resistance is concerned."[9]

On October 26, 1904, Wood fell ill. His brain tumor was growing, pressing on various nerve bundles and inducing pain and partial paralysis. The old surgeon remained unaware of the cause of his sickness.

THE YEAR 1905 brought renewed disturbances on Jolo. The influential Datu Usap strongly opposed the cedula and had fought against the Americans in support of Panglima Hassan's cause. He refused to come to Jolo to meet District Governor Scott and reputedly gave shelter to outlaws in defiance of American law and order. His defiance peaked when a religious preacher, Hajji Masdali, urged him to resist the Americans, persuaded him to rebuild his old cotta, and sold him charms to render his people invulnerable. Masdali was one of many Islamic preachers who had made the pilgrimage to Mecca, thereby earning high status, and subsequently engaging in the profitable business of selling *anting-antings,* or charms, that purportedly deflected American bullets. By preaching to the credulous, Masdali and his ilk often stirred up trouble.

Datu Usap buried Masdali's charms in each corner of his cotta and gathered four hundred fighters to resist the next American incursion into his territory.

Conflict came in January 1905 when an American column, purportedly on a peaceful surveying expedition, drew fire from Usap's cotta. Because Wood had told authorities in Washington that Jolo was pacified, the need to fight there again embarrassed him. Wood told Scott to use his artillery—the precision weapon of this era—to fire from long range rather then risk American lives in close assaults. Scott, in turn, knew that Usap's cotta was strongly built and thought it likely to resist his mountain guns. Accordingly, Scott borrowed a heavier naval gun and through great labor had it hauled into position to bombard Usap's cotta. The naval gun's armor-piercing shot, designed to penetrate a ship's steel plating, cracked the cotta's huge volcanic boulders, creating a breach. The ensuing assault overran the cotta, killing three to four hundred of Usap's followers. Lieutenant Jewell received a mortal wound while scaling the cotta wall. When Scott reached him he was lying calmly on the ground. Scott expressed his sorrow and Jewell stoically replied, "Don't feel that way, colonel; it's only the fortune of war."[10]

Nine Moros survived the assault and surrendered. This uncharacteristic surrender prompted Wood to ask why they had fought. Had they a grievance against the white man or against Scott himself? They replied no. They were poor chattel of Datu Usap and had been ordered to come to this cotta and fight. They knew that if they disobeyed, Usap would cut their heads off. Because Usap had died in the battle they felt able to surrender.

In contrast, another of Usap's warriors was captured while unconscious, having taken four serious shrapnel and bullet wounds. While lying on the operating table at an American hospital, this terrible warrior woke up, lashed out ineffectively, flung his betel nut box at the surgeon, and cursed him roundly. He then turned away from the surgeon and composed himself to die.

Although the American authorities captured the troublemaking Islamic preacher Hajji Masdali and deported him to Singapore, the situation on Jolo continued to deteriorate. Datu Pala, a supporter of the deceased Panglima Hassan, had fled to Borneo to escape the Americans. He returned to Jolo and called for a jihad against the Americans. Wood collected a force and steamed to Jolo to direct the first large expedition in more than a year. On May 1, their first day on Jolo, Wood's soldiers killed more then fifty Moros with the loss of one American.

Among Wood's command was a provisional company of Moro Scouts and Philippine Constabulary commanded by Lieutenant Benny Foulois. Within hours of landing, Foulois's command entered combat. The next ninety-six hours witnessed almost nonstop fighting. On May 5, elements of the Fourteenth Cavalry, Seventeenth Infantry, and Foulois's Scouts surrounded a fortified position on Mount Talepac, a huge volcanic mass rising steeply out of the jungle. A coordinated uphill assault ran into sporadic rifle fire but continued to gain ground. As Foulois's Scouts closed in, the Moros counterattacked. A scout fired point-blank at a charging Moro who held a barong high over his head. Although mortally wounded, the Moro completed his descending blow, cleaving open the scout's skull. Undaunted, the scouts overran their objective. Overall, the attackers lost four killed and six wounded while killing twenty-three Moros. Unremarked at the time was the bravery of the Moro soldiers serving in the Philippine Scouts.

The next day, Wood received a message from Major Scott. Datu Utig had attacked Scott's command and killed three soldiers before withdrawing to his cotta. Scott had pursued and now occupied a position on high ground overlooking Utig's cotta. Wood hastened to join Scott and demanded Utig's surrender. Utig replied that he would never surrender to a "dog of an infidel." Wood ordered his artillery to shell the cotta for an hour. At 7:30 A.M. the Twenty-second Infantry advanced through heavy underbrush against the objective. Company A encountered a stout bamboo fence outside the cotta. The company deployed into a firing line and began exchanging shots with the hidden enemy. Company D moved up on the firing line's right flank and took a position at right angles to the bamboo fence. This adroit maneuver brought enfilade fire against the Moros. After thirty minutes the infantry had almost silenced the Moros. The Americans charged from four directions, overran the cotta, and killed everything moving, including women and children. Frank McCoy related how the battalion "finished the business killing Utic [sic] and his whole outfit like mad dogs in their fighting and death."[11] Seven American soldiers died in the combat, an unusually heavy total that Wood attributed to friendly fire, with at least another thirteen wounded.

Three days later found Wood supervising the investment of Datu Hati's cotta. This cotta perched on the edge of a volcanic crater on Jolo's east coast. The route to the top would be difficult; a narrow, steep path swept by enemy fire the entire ascent. Booby traps with sharpened bamboo stakes dipped in poison lined the path. Scott asked Wood for time to negotiate. He sent a Moro envoy, who soon returned with the word that Datu Hati refused to budge. Scott assured Wood that this was typical behavior and sent his envoy up again. He returned a second time with the same answer. Wood was growing impatient, but Scott persuaded him to allow a third attempt. While Wood and his officers discussed how best to proceed, word came that Hati wanted to surrender. Wood and his entourage were deeply suspicious. In their experience, once a Moro resolved to die, he never would surrender. Foulois described the scene: "Slowly and cautiously, about 450 Moros—men and women—came in a single file down the trail as we covered them with every gun we had. They were dressed in their finest and brightest turbans, sashes, and heavily embroidered jackets as they always were when they made up their minds that they were going to die fighting."[12]

They laid down their arms and waited docilely as if expecting to be shot. Wood addressed them through an interpreter. He told them to cease fighting the Americans and return to their homes in peace. Wood's words prompted a great joyful shout and the incident concluded peacefully. Later the Americans learned more about this unprecedented occurrence. The night before the surrender, two U.S. Navy destroyers and a gunboat had appeared just offshore. They trained their searchlights on the volcanic crater. Apparently this display of modern technology awed the Moros. They reckoned, what chance could they have against an enemy who could turn night into day?

Wood's two-week campaign, from May 1 to May 13, 1905, squashed Moro resistance on Jolo at the cost of eleven troops killed and twenty-five wounded. Whether the excitement and strain of field duty contributed or not, Wood's seizures increased. He was prostrate for hours and complained of lack of muscle strength. Doctors examined his teeth and extracted some nerves, but their intervention did not help. His entourage noted his physical decline. Wood felt a growing numbness in his left hand and tried to compensate with daily exercise, including shaving and pistol shooting with his left hand. Proud to the point of vanity about his physical prowess, Wood grew increasingly irritable. "You remind me," his wife remarked, "of the professional beauty who sees her looks begin to go." Finally a new post surgeon at Zamboanga convinced Wood that the growing lump inside his skull was the problem. Wood replied, "Very good. Let's go to the hospital and operate on it this afternoon."[13]

It became clear that neither surgeons in Zamboanga nor those in Manila were capable of performing a complex brain operation at a time when neurosurgery was in its infancy. Wood reluctantly returned to the United States. On July 7, 1905, in a private hospital in Boston, a surgeon removed a disk of bone containing a small tumor. The surgery relieved Wood's symptoms. At the time, no one realized that the surgeon had been too timid and botched the operation. Most of the tumor remained beneath the fibrous meninges over Wood's brain.

Wood returned to Zamboanga on October 27, 1905. In his absence there had been a few insignificant skirmishes as well as one notable success: Frank McCoy had tracked down the notorious Datu Ali and killed him and three of his sons.

The Hunt for Datu Ali

In Moroland, the American military hunted Datu Ali as fervently as a later generation pursued Osama bin Laden. Ali was a formidable opponent, a clever, ruthless fighter with an enormous talent for survival. He eluded his hunters longer than any other Moro leader. Ali was royalty, proudly tracing his lineage directly back to Mohammed. He was the third son of Datu Utu, who had ruled Mindanao back in the 1880s. A small vial hung from Ali's neck, said to contain seven-hundred-year-old oil brought from Arabia by a forebear. A three-hundred-year-old sarong, blessed by an ancient man of religion and said to be bulletproof, encircled his waist. Ali, by birthright, possessed the necessary prestige to rule. His father-in-law—Datu Piang, a lowborn son of one of Datu Utu's slave women by a Chinese trader—provided the muscle and brains. Because of Datu Piang, Ali controlled the trade of the rich Cotabato Valley in the Lanao District of central Mindanao. Piang's good relations with Chinese traders allowed Ali to control the export of Cotabato's bounty of rice, beeswax, coffee, paint resins extracted from almaciga trees, and a natural latex tapped from gutta-percha trees. Then the Americans arrived.

The first American assessment of Ali underestimated his capacities: "Ali is of royal blood, one of the aristocrats of the valley, but lazy, indifferent, spoiled, with great conceit, unresponsive, and apparently dull."[14]

Datu Ali with wife and one of his sons.

The assessment did accurately note that Ali was naturally a fighting man and this activity seemed to engage him like no other.

Whereas his father-in-law, Datu Piang, became an American ally, Ali's attitude toward Americans was a mixture of contempt and curiosity. In 1904 the latter got the better of him and he resolved to visit the United States. Piang loaned him a substantial sum to finance Ali's royal tour. Ali and his entourage descended from the hills to the port of Cotabato, and there he lingered because the Americans refused to accommodate his travel desire.

The reason was politics. The 1904 election would pit the Republican Theodore Roosevelt against the New York Democrat Alton B. Parker. On the fundamental issues there was little to distinguish the rivals: both solidly supported the gold standard, championed labor and consumer rights while condemning monopoly, and favored Philippine independence at some indefinite future date. Unless something surprising transpired, the election would turn on personality, and here Roosevelt held a decided advantage over the colorless, bland Parker. Having a "little brown brother" appear in America at a time when the anti-imperialist movement continued to have political impact might just be the type of surprising event that would upset the electoral calculus. So American authorities kept delaying Ali's departure, and meanwhile the Moro potentate gambled away his travel budget. Ali soon returned to his hilltop cotta with diminished finances, reduced in prestige among his people, and bearing a grudge against the Americans.

Wood had targeted Ali's cotta as his first objective upon entering the Cotabato Valley and destroyed it along with many of Ali's followers. But Ali had escaped the American cordon around his cotta and thereafter adopted guerrilla warfare. From remote hiding places he issued orders to some twenty thousand sympathizers living in the upper Cotabato Valley. They, in turn, conducted attacks against the Americans and alerted Ali when American patrols entered the valley, thereby allowing him time to flee deep into the swamps or high into the hill country. American frustration grew as "one picked captain after another took his picked men on a hike into the bosque. They came back, one and all, saturated with mud and dew, famished, discouraged. A regiment might, probably often did, pass within a yard of the hiding Moros without seeing them."[15]

Among the units sent after Ali was Company F, Seventeenth Infantry. Because the Americans neither knew the geography nor spoke the language, they were entirely dependent upon their native guide. On May 8, 1904, the guide led them for mile after mile along a narrow trail encased in towering tigbao grass that formed an interlocking, dense mat. In places the trail became more like a low and narrow tunnel. Company F came to a ten-foot-wide mud hole blocking the trail. The first notice the unit received of a hostile presence was when gunfire erupted all around them. Several soldiers fell in the initial onslaught. Company commander Harry Woodruff and his subordinate gallantly rushed forward to rally their shocked soldiers, and both went down from Moro bullets. The surviving lieutenant managed to extract the company from the deadly ambush, but only by abandoning the fallen. Moro krises and kampilans completed the deadly work, disemboweling and beheading the wounded Americans. In one of the deadliest attacks in the entire Moro War, Ali's warriors killed two officers and thirteen enlisted men and captured two prisoners. In contrast to the usual Moro practice of killing or enslaving prisoners, Ali cared for and later returned the two wounded Americans.

The combat became known among American soldiers as the "Simpetan Massacre." The Moro desecration of the fallen enraged American soldiers. Benny Foulois personally knew the F Company men, including their commander, Harry Woodruff, having competed against them

during garrison baseball or football games. He eagerly participated in
subsequent hunts to find Ali. The pursuit was exceptionally difficult. It
seemed that Ali haunted a jungle that was two-thirds underwater. Indeed, fruitlessly marching along narrow trails deep in mud and through
fetid swamps while being broiled by the tropical sun wore out Ali's
hunters. At night swarms of mosquitoes were so dense that the troops
could not sleep. Soldier-poets recorded their experiences in a 1905 song
about campaigning, "In the Valley after Ali," sung to the tune of "I've
Been Working on the Railroad":

> *Oh, sing a song of hikers,*
> *On Datu Ali's trail*
> *On straight tips from old Piang,*
> *Who ought to be in jail*
> *Three commands of doughboys,*
> *And one of horseless horse*
> *Through mud and slime,*
> *Through filth and grime*
> *We wend our way perforce*

As time passed, soldiers developed a grudging respect for their prey.

Unable to track down the elusive Moro datu, Wood tried to negotiate
his surrender. A former member of Wood's Legislative Council and one
of Ali's old acquaintances, Dr. Najeeb Saleeby, visited Ali and remained
with him for a month. Try as he might, Saleeby could not convince Ali
to surrender. Instead, Ali wrote a defiant letter to Wood asking, "Which
is better for you, to kill me or not? . . . Until I die all the people will not
submit to the government, because I will try to kill all the people who
are friends of the Americans."[16] Wood responded the following day by
posting a $500 reward for Ali's capture, dead or alive. From time to time
thereafter, American officers met with Moros who claimed knowledge
of Ali's whereabouts. The Americans hatched various plots to poison Ali
or send a relative to assassinate him, but they came to naught.

The new year of 1905 saw Ali withdraw deeper into the rugged Cotabato Valley. Intelligence reports said that he was weakened by malaria.
From this remote lair Ali no longer threatened American posts or patrols,
but conversely, he seemed completely safe from American strikes. His
apparent immunity irritated American officers who feared that Ali's

defiance made him an example for other Moros to emulate. Instead, a Moro betrayed him.

A minor Moro leader—angered that Ali had taken his wife—bided his time until he had the opportunity to travel to an American outpost. He told the Americans that Ali had moved from his remote base and was now camped along the Malala River on the Gulf of Davao. This was the break the Americans had been waiting for, and Frank McCoy seized it with both hands.

Although best known as one of Wood's devoted aides, the debonair McCoy was beginning to stand out among his peers. He even impressed jaded, cynical war correspondents. The correspondent for *Collier's* wrote, "After you have met dozens and dozens of American officers . . . you come across McCoy. Then you catch your breath."[17] McCoy prepared carefully for snaring Ali. To date, the Americans had always entered the Cotabato Valley from the port and marched inland, using their over- whelming force to seal off all avenues of escape. Indeed, that approach was precisely the one proposed by the acting department commander, General James Buchanan. McCoy convinced Buchanan that Ali's su- perb intelligence network covered this route too well, and therefore the Americans should try something different.

So it was that Buchanan began his campaign on October 13, 1905, with an ostentatious show of force that marched out of Cotabato port and followed the standard route. Meanwhile, McCoy planned to enter the valley via a rear entrance. Although everyone knew that McCoy's ex- pedition would be dangerous, there was no shortage of volunteers. His 100 handpicked men from the Twenty-second Infantry along with 140 Filipino bearers and 10 Philippine Scouts disembarked at Digos on the Gulf of Davao. It was an elite force commanded by distinguished offi- cers, none more famous than Lieutenant Gordon Johnston. In the close- knit circle of American officers serving in the Philippines, Johnston stood out. A son of a Confederate general, Johnston was a Princeton Uni- versity graduate and had served as a private in the Rough Riders. Dur- ing the Philippine Insurrection his conspicuous valor attracted armywide admiration and later earned him the Distinguished Service Cross. Thereafter, with the personal support of Theodore Roosevelt, Johnston received an officer's commission in the regular army. Although he was assigned to the Signal Corps, Johnston's craving for action prompted him to volunteer to join McCoy's team.

McCoy judged that a rapid forced march could outpace any contact reports from Ali's intelligence net. Accordingly he marched inland at a grueling pace. Each night the men built a protective barrier of underbrush around their campsite. The barrier had only one entrance, a narrow, twisting passageway that required soldiers to crawl to get in or out. McCoy figured that this elaborate barrier would fox even the most nimble juramentado. Four days of effort traversing jungle-covered mountains exhausted his scouts, bearers, and thirteen of his regulars. McCoy left them behind and pressed ahead with seventy-seven infantry who carried their weapons, one day's cooked rations, and nothing else. A forty-eight-hour speed march brought them to the banks of the Malala River at dawn on October 22.

McCoy's men stealthily moved through thick brush and tall cogon grass to surround Ali's residence. McCoy gave stern orders forbidding anyone from shooting until he gave the signal to advance. Then they were to kill everyone encountered. McCoy gave Lieutenant Philip Remington the post of honor because he was the best pistol shot in the entire regiment. As the Americans closed in they encountered four bolo-armed Moro guards. Four Americans tackled them and pinned them to the ground. When firing commenced, the Americans shot the pinioned Moros and joined the assault. Meanwhile, Remington led his men into the clearing, where they saw Ali and two of his men standing in a doorway. Although surprised, Ali quickly disappeared inside and reappeared with a Mauser rifle. He leveled his rifle to fire a snap shot at the charging Americans. At nearly the same time Remington leveled his revolver and fired. Ali's shot killed an American private. Remington's bullet dropped Ali to his knees. Ali struggled to his feet and went inside. He tried to escape out the back door but ran into the squad detailed to guard that exit. Fifteen more shots struck Ali before the combat ended. When the Americans' fire ceased, Ali, his son, and ten followers lay dead. McCoy's picked company lost two killed and one wounded. The Americans captured some fifty of Ali's party, most of whom were women and children, some of whom were wounded. One of Ali's women showed characteristic Moro courage by refusing medical treatment. She ripped off the bandages applied by the infidels and chose to bleed to death.[18]

A week later, the merchants of Zamboanga gave a public celebration for McCoy and his officers, toasting them with warm champagne at ten in the morning. A less than sober triumphal march proceeded down

Zamboanga's main street with Johnston holding a palm leaf over Mc-
Coy's head as a token of conquest. Speeches and more drinks followed
at the Mindanao Club, hosted by Wood himself, who had just returned
from his stateside medical leave. Someone proposed a ghoulish toast to
Ali, saying he "was a royal good fellow that unfortunately got in the way
of progress, and had to have a hypodermic injection of gray matter
[lead]."[19] President Roosevelt's congratulatory telegram added to the festivities. Wood's annual report claimed that Ali's followers had numbered twenty thousand and that the late datu personally had kept the
entire Cotabato Valley in a state of rebellion. His demise promised a
brighter future.

The June 9, 1906, issue of *Collier's* featured an article entitled "The
End of Datto Ali" with the subtitle "The Last Fight of the Moro War."
The article began in thrilling style: "Shortly after dawn of October 22,
1905, a second lieutenant in the United States infantry put a revolver
bullet through the heart of Datto Ali." *Collier's* provided its readers with
needed background regarding this strange and faraway war: "The Moro
War, to be inclusive, began in 1597 and it ended the other day in 1906."
According to *Collier's*, Ali's death marked "the last phase in that war of
extermination which the American race has waged for nearly three centuries against, first the red and then the brown race."[20] Because of his
association with Wood, McCoy was already well known and liked by
both the members of Roosevelt's inner circle and the president himself.
His successful hunt for Datu Ali and the favorable report in *Collier's* allowed McCoy to emerge from Wood's shadow onto a much wider stage.

ELEVEN

Storm at Bud Dajo

Work of this kind has its disagreeable side, which is the unavoidable killing of women and children; but it must be done, and disagreeable as it is, there is no way of avoiding it.

—Leonard Wood, 1906

PHOTOGRAPHS OF AMERICAN SOLDIERS serving in the Philippines in 1905 show men who appear both familiar and distant. Their felt campaign hats, which look to the modern eye more suitable for cowboys than for soldiers, seem oddly out of place in the twentieth century. The Krag-Jörgensen rifles they carry more comfortably fit into a modern notion of appropriate firearms. For handguns, many soldiers now possessed the older-model (1871 to 1875) .45-caliber Colt pistol. Although the .45 had superior stopping power, it was an unreliable weapon with a misfire rate of about one third. The army's failure to provide an adequate handgun was a terrible thing, since a misfire often meant the difference between life and death (or—worse than death in many soldiers' minds—disfigurement and maiming).

The army had also let down its men with some of its other standard-issue equipment. The uniform was poorly made, ill-fitting, and much too heavy for duty in a tropical environment. Standard equipment included a mess kit, blanket roll, poncho, canteen, haversack, and cartridge belt. The model 1903 cartridge belt was unsatisfactory. Its pockets

Soldiers of the Twenty-third Infantry with Krags, 1904.

were too small to contain easily the standard ten-round bullet clips. In an emergency—and most fights in Moroland were emergencies—the extra time needed to extract the clip from the tight confines of the pocket could prove lethal. The cotton khaki uniforms and canvas leggings were acceptable, but the army-issue suspenders had a tendency to shrink in the tropical climate, chafing during a long march and restricting breathing when a soldier needed to run. Likewise, the staple at the back of the suspenders cramped the shoulders and irritated the skin. In jungle climates, minor skin irritations could quickly develop into oozing, debilitating sores. The suspenders also prevented free range of motion in the arm, thus impairing both accurate shooting and hand-to-hand combat. It was worse for taller men since the suspenders did not fit them.

The regular infantry served a two-year tour of duty in the Philippines. During this time, men ate an awful diet: canned meat, which they called "embalmed beef"; nausea-inducing "goldfish," their term for Alaska canned salmon; rancid bacon and hardtack, the same ration their Civil War fathers had relied upon; dehydrated vegetables; and roasted coffee. In theory, these rations could be supplemented by Mindanao's bounty, but most men preferred to hoard their pay for alcohol-fueled debauches during their infrequent furloughs. The fact that the government callously disregarded nutrition and supplied its fighting men with revolvers that misfired and other equipment ill-suited to the reality of combat in the southern Philippines was deplorable.

The treatment the veterans received upon going home was little better. A veteran wrote, "Instead of glad hands, people stared at a khaki-clad man as though he had escaped from the zoo. When forced to ask directions to a certain street, whoever you accosted shied away as though you were an Apache with the smallpox."[1] Given their government's shabby treatment and the fact that the public largely ignored the entire war, military morale could well have been shaky at best. This was not the case at all.

When the war with Spain began, patriotism was a tremendous motivating factor for the "Boys of '98" to join the army. Victory over Spain reduced the nation's war ardor. Volunteer units returned home and disbanded. Some of the men who had served in those units had discovered that they had a talent for war. Others compared their dismal civilian prospects with a military life that at least provided basic necessities, and so they opted to enlist in the regular army. Adding to their ranks were thousands of recent immigrants who had discovered that life in America for poor, uneducated workers could be brutally hard. Yet in 1907, when the average American worker earned $542 per year, a first-year private earned just $156. The lowest civilian wage, for a farm laborer, was more than twice as much as what a private earned and slightly more than what a sergeant made. Paltry as these wages were, they represented a minimal security that was unobtainable for many in the civilian world.

Most turn-of-the-century Americans thought that army life entailed boring or degrading duties and labors. Army recruiters had to overcome the perception that soldiers stood beneath ordinary citizens on the national social hierarchy. The train carrying Benny Foulois's company passed through Lake Tahoe on its way to the West Coast. Two elderly women carrying a tray of doughnuts for the troops approached Foulois and several of his buddies. The women asked what unit they belonged to, and when told that they were regulars the women "stared at us for a moment as if we had just run off with the town's bank funds, then turned and hurried away." Foulois learned "that most people thought that regular soldiers were illiterates, thieves, and half-wits who joined the Army to say out of the clutches of the sheriff."[2]

A 1904 army promotional booklet, *The Life of an Enlisted Man in the United States Army*, explicitly acknowledged this perception, noting that many citizens thought that "an enlistment in the Army . . . means that those years of a man's life have been wasted."[3] Throughout the army's history, recruiters had relied upon new immigrants, the poor, the mentally unsound, and the criminal class to meet their quotas. But the more modern army of the early twentieth century tried to change that practice. It sought physically and mentally fit men ages twenty-one to thirty-five who either were or intended to become American citizens and were literate in the English language. In 1905, the power to reject a recruit based on a physical examination passed from civilian doctors to army doctors, and this measure improved the recruit pool.

Perhaps as important as all other factors motivating recruits was something commonly shared by young men in the first decade of the twentieth century: curiosity and sense of adventure. For the vast majority of the era's young American men, particularly those living in rural areas, prospects for adventure were slim. Their lives ran along routine channels. They expected to live most of their lives in the same place and to die near where they had been born. Travel was a luxury denied them. The rail trip to the stateside training bases and particularly the voyage across the Pacific to the exotic Philippines thrust recruits into a world outside of everything they had known.

They came to Moroland with deep-rooted prejudices against their "little brown brothers."

All three battalions of the Twenty-second Infantry Regiment waded ashore on the beaches of Mindanao on December 6, 1903. There to greet them were an assembly of minor Moro leaders, all of whom professed friendship. But, as an infantry captain observed, it was friendship of "a doubtful character."[4] The captain's opinion was far more restrained than most, particularly that of the rank and file. When a new cavalry regiment rotated into Sulu, Hugh Scott worried about the potential for abuse: "Among some of the more reckless and irresponsible young men there was talk of 'killing goo-goos.'"[5] While some soldiers relished the killing, for most it was just part of the job. And it was a job they were confident they could perform.

While ambush, sniping, and particularly juramentado attacks could and did unnerve them, their veteran noncommissioned officers had told them that to date in pitched battles, the army's combination of artillery bombardment and small-arms fire had won every time. Furthermore, victory came at a minuscule price. This tradition of victory helped inspire them to conduct "bullet-eating" assaults up and over a cotta's earthen walls. If some died—in soldier slang, were sent to the "Fourth Battalion" (each regiment had only three battalions)—it was simply the cost of doing business. In sum, belief in cultural superiority and a tradition of victory earned at low cost infused the American soldier in Moroland with high morale. They expected to defeat their enemy and they did, killing Moros with untroubled conscience because that was the natural order of things.

If the American soldier found the Moro strange at best, and more commonly a savage worthy of extermination, in turn the conduct of the American soldiers perplexed the Moros. They were accustomed to Spanish habits and traditions. The Spanish seldom ventured outside the confines of their fortified perimeter and then only in large armed groups. In contrast, on Sundays, the day the Spanish attended Mass, the American garrison of Jolo went outside the walls to a riverside meadow and threw balls at one another and occasionally used a heavy stick to hit the ball long distances. The next day they put their combat boots back on and returned to the business of killing Moros. The Moros wondered what kind of people they confronted.

Yet there was no denying that Moroland was enjoying unprecedented wealth and had, in fact, become the most prosperous province in the entire Philippines. Third-quarter revenue in 1905 was twice that of the previous year. The Sulu Moros were paying taxes to Manila for the first time in history. American officials reported that the Moros were beginning to cooperate with the American-installed courts, seeking redress by legal means rather than resorting to blood feuds. The more influential Moros seemed to recognize the benefits of American rule, although, as Wood's aide-de-camp George Langhorne observed, "It will take time to convince them all that a government which taxes them without their having a voice in the matter of taxation nor use of the funds is really the best sort of government for them."[6]

Economic progress came at a price. By the beginning of 1906 the Moro people understood that the American objective was to dismantle their society's traditional hierarchy by pushing their datus aside. The Americans ignored sharia and instead new judges came from Manila.

Bud Dajo from Jolo Harbor.

Then, as a writer who interviewed many Moro elders who survived the American occupation wrote, "Moros were judged by laws we knew nothing of and were sent away to jail. They did not come back. But their message came to the people. Prison and jail were worse than death."[7] The datus clearly saw that the American innovations threatened their hereditary privileges, and they responded in predictable fashion by telling their people that it was all an underhanded American plot to Christianize the country.

SIX MILES SOUTHEAST of Jolo town stood Bud Dajo, a 2,175-foot-high extinct volcano rising out of the jungle floor to dominate the region. It was the tallest mountain on the island. Thick jungle covered the mountain's slopes. The jungle appeared impenetrable but in fact concealed numerous minor trails known only to the Moros.

Toward the end of 1905, Hugh Scott began receiving reports that some two hundred Moros had gone up Bud Dajo and did not seem inclined to come back down. The crater had abundant water. To become self-sufficient all the holdouts needed was food, so they planted crops inside the crater rim and tapped the abundant water pools to irrigate them. Their ranks included entire families who had been displaced by previous American campaigns. Many were relatives and supporters of a datu who had refused to pay for a cedula and whose cotta had been attacked and destroyed by one of Governor Wood's expeditions. In a sense, their stance on the mountain was a tax protest, but that was not how most Americans viewed it. Rather, the recalcitrants were "the rag-tag-and-bobtail remnants of two or three revolts, the black sheep of a dozen folds, rebels against the poll tax, die-hards against the American occupation, outlaws recognizing no *datto* and condemned by the stable elements among the Moros themselves."[8] Some of the menfolk on Bud Dajo reportedly sold their draft animals to buy guns and began building fortifications.

By now, Scott had acquired considerable experience negotiating with Moro datus. Keeping them alive while enforcing the law required an intellectual and ethical balance. Scott possessed this talent for compromise: "It took time and infinite patience to listen to complaints over the ownership of a buffalo long enough to arrive at a just decision. Sitting in an office crowded with natives in that moist, tropical atmosphere not far from the equator, the testimony over what in reality was a trifling matter, interpreted back and forth between two languages, droning along interminably in the heat, all day, day in and day out, year after year, seemed at times to be without purpose and without result. But the results in the end were prodigious; nothing less than the trust, confidence, and affection of the huge majority of the Moro people."[9] In addition, Scott frequently visited the Moros in their own homes, risking his own life to conduct a parley. Many had learned to trust his judgment, so he was almost always successful in persuading the Moros to surrender their arms and ammunition and accept appropriate legal punishment. The exceptions came when the Moros fired on the Americans as they approached for a parley. At such times, "something desperate seemed to wake in them that made them die . . . fighting to the bitter end."[10]

Scott was fairly certain that the situation on Bud Dajo could be resolved by talk. The alternative, a bloody assault, made no sense to him: "It was plain that many good Americans would have to die before it could be taken, and, after all, what would they be dying for? In order to collect a tax of less than a thousand dollars from savages! Obviously the thing to do was to get the rebels down off that mountain peacefully before it became necessary to make the assault."[11] So in December 1905 he sent Captain James Reeves to investigate the situation at Bud Dajo. Reeves talked with Moros living around the base of the mountain and learned that the number of troublemakers had increased significantly. People reported that 250 men and 375 women had "gone up there to die, and that they would fight, and further that they would force our hand by committing depredations."[12]

Scott listened to Reeves's report and decided that it was largely hearsay. He was willing to tolerate the Moro occupation of Bud Dajo as long as they did not promote open defiance of American authority. Meanwhile, he continued with diplomacy by trying to talk the Moros into leaving. They answered that they would leave as soon as their crops ripened enough to harvest. That time came and passed and they did not budge. But life atop an isolated mountaintop was not all that pleasant, and slowly their numbers dwindled. By early 1906, the time Scott departed for home leave, only eight men and their families remained on Bud Dajo. But those eight purportedly included hardened criminals whom every American officer except Scott thought would commence robbing and pillaging at any moment.

In Scott's absence, Captain Reeves became acting district governor. As always, promotion in the small, "peacetime" U.S. Army was agonizingly slow. The Moro encampment on Bud Dajo offered the chance for a captain to distinguish himself, and Reeves seized it with both hands. Wood had long demonstrated an intolerance for Moro provocation. Reeves followed suit by insisting that a minor crime was a significant challenge to American authority in Moroland. In fact, Moro raiders, probably based on Bud Dajo, had "attacked" a U.S. rifle range located outside of Jolo town, burning a corrugated hut housing the range's targeting material including flags, target discs, and target frames.[13] For Reeves, that vandalism was enough.

To begin, Reeves wisely chose to adhere to the letter of American law stating that civil authorities could request military intervention only if they confronted a problem beyond their capacities to solve. Given that the district governor wore two hats and was effectively the chief civil and military authority, Reeves easily performed this legal nicety. Rather than focusing solely on the "attack" against the rifle range, he found another crime to enhance the case against the Bud Dajo Moros. Reeves issued a warrant of arrest for a Moro thief who purportedly had stolen property owned by Charles Schück, who lived a few miles outside of Jolo town and also happened to be employed as chief translator and guide by the American government. Schück assured Reeves that the offending Moro had taken his loot up Bud Dajo, where the thief was protected by hordes of armed Moros. This claim provided the legal cover for Reeves, wearing his civilian hat as acting governor, to summon the army.

Accordingly, on March 1, 1906, Reeves reported to the provincial secretary, Captain George Langhorne, that the Moros were acting in open defiance of American authority, claiming that they occupied an impregnable position and that the Americans could do nothing about it. By asserting that they were "patriots and semi-liberators of the Moro people," Reeves wrote, "they had forfeited any right or claim that Colonel Scott had promised them." This dangerous situation would fester until "we finish the job and these people are whipped."[14] Reeves was preaching to the choir. By the time his letter arrived, Wood had already decided on action.[15]

Wood had returned to the Philippines in mid-January. In Manila he received the welcome news that he would ascend to the post of commander of the Department of the Philippines effective February 1, 1906. Brigadier General Tasker Bliss would replace him as governor of Moro Province. But affairs on Jolo, which Wood perceived as a rebel uprising, persuaded Wood to delay the transfer of command. On February 9, his trusted aide, Langhorne, informed Wood that the Bud Dajo Moros would probably have to be "exterminated."[16] Wood readily agreed. To him, the holdout atop Bud Dajo was "a ridiculous little affair" that a couple of infantry columns could easily "clean out."[17] Wood suggested that a strong American patrol with about one hundred soldiers could sneak up the mountain under cover of night and open fire from the crater rim at dawn to "clean the place out." Wood wanted to know when this would take place so he could be there to observe.

His ambition confronted what should have been an insurmountable obstacle. Secretary of War Taft had previously issued an order that required explicit authorization for any large-scale military expedition against the Moros. The War Department's bureaucracy fully supported Taft. It was clear to everyone including Wood that the underlying intent was to control more tightly Wood's aggression. Exhibiting more strategic ability at defeating bureaucratic shackles than he had ever displayed in the field, Wood plotted how to advance his campaign against the Jolo

Moros. In essence, he deliberately muddled the chain of command so he could freely exercise his judgment over the impending military campaign against the Bud Dajo "rebels." Then, at the end of February, he issued secret orders setting the "cleanup" operation in train.

Wood slipped out of Manila without properly informing his superiors and sailed to Zamboanga to monitor events more closely. He spent the morning of March 5 at Zamboanga doing routine paperwork and the afternoon sport shooting with Langhorne and Bliss. The next day the cable line to Jolo failed. Anxious to know what was taking place, at 9:00 that evening Wood, Bliss, Langhorne, and McCoy sailed for Jolo. They arrived early in the morning of March 7, "just in time to see through our glasses the khaki dots swarming over a cotta silhouetted against the sky."[19] In fact, they had arrived just in time to witness the beginning of a massacre.

Blood in the Mist

As part of his strategy to deceive higher authorities, Wood had carefully selected an officer he believed would be an obedient puppet to command the forces arrayed against the Bud Dajo Moros. His name was Joseph W. Duncan. The fifty-one-year-old Texan had advanced up the ranks to become a colonel. He had a reputation as a competent field commander but had never before served in Moroland. Wood ordered Duncan's Sixth Infantry to move from Leyte to Zamboanga but did not tell Duncan why. On the night of March 2, the recently arrived officers of the Sixth Infantry were attending the weekly dance at Zamboanga's Overseas Club. They were just comfortably settling in when couriers entered the dance hall bearing orders for them to return to barracks and prepare for an expedition. Duncan received a terse note from Wood ordering him to take two companies "to Jolo at once. Nothing but blanket rolls, field mess outfit, 200 rounds per man, seven days rations."[18] Subsequently, Duncan met Wood for the first time and received a briefing.

Companies G and H, Sixth Infantry, disembarked on Jolo early on the morning of March 3, 1906. The town was alive with rumors about the buildup of hostile Moros on nearby Bud Dajo. Duncan and his officers spent the afternoon studying a clay model depicting in detail Bud Dajo's terrain. It was apparent to all that Bud Dajo would be the most formidable challenge yet encountered by American troops in Moroland. The coast guard cutter *Busuanga* delivered some 220 exceedingly welcome reinforcements that evening, raising Duncan's strength to about 800 men.

At 8:30 the next morning, March 4, 1906, two troops of the Fourth Cavalry assembled outside Jolo's town gates. Escorted by the cavalry, Duncan and his principal subordinates set off to reconnoiter the Moro position on Bud Dajo. A two-mile ride brought them to the Schück homestead. The troopers enjoyed a brief but welcome rest because the day was already becoming warm and humid. Hurrying along the trail from Jolo came a surprising visitor, a French army lieutenant who wanted to accompany the expedition as an observer. The world's military customarily sent officers to study the latest developments in weapons and tactics. Given that France was involved in counterinsurgency campaigns in North Africa, it made sense to send a junior officer to observe America's ongoing guerrilla war. So Duncan obliged the lieutenant, Schück provided guides, and the column divided with the main body under Duncan's personal command heading southwest, while a second column commanded by Captain Henry Lawton rode northwest.

With a circumference of eleven miles, Bud Dajo was too big to be effectively surrounded and besieged. The only alternative was to assault the mountain by following three main trails built by the Moros. Indeed, Wood had told Duncan to utilize all three of these avenues of approach. As shown on the clay model Duncan and his officers had studied, the trails followed narrow hogback ridges separated by deep ravines and jungle. For the first three quarters of the ascent, the trails were steep but passable. However, on the south and east sides, the last five hundred feet rose at a sixty-degree slope with the final ascent to the crater requiring a near-vertical scramble. Upon reaching the crater rim, one gazed down some three hundred feet into a bowl-shaped crater about five hundred feet in diameter. From a conventional military standpoint, Bud Dajo was a superb defensive position. It was, as Wood later informed President Roosevelt, "an ugly and difficult place to take."[20] Based on his study of the terrain model and Wood's verbal instructions, Duncan's provisional plan called for establishing base camps at the foot of each of the three main trails. The impending reconnaissance would give his officers the opportunity to see if the actual ground conformed to the clay model.

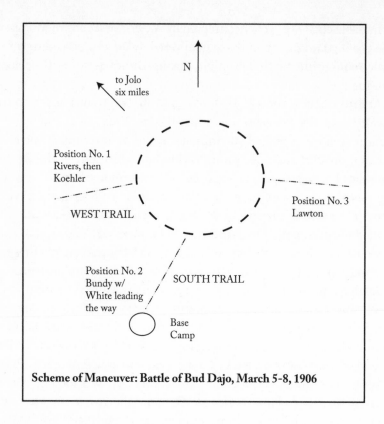

Scheme of Maneuver: Battle of Bud Dajo, March 5-8, 1906

Around 10:30 A.M., the scouting force came to the foot of the west trail, which offered the easiest climb to the summit. Duncan knew that the Moros had built their most formidable defenses to block this trail. Therefore, he did not intend to make his main effort here. Instead, he would order Captain Tyree Rivers to establish a blocking position here with two companies of the Nineteenth Infantry in order to prevent the Moros from escaping via the west trail. Rivers's projected position, which Duncan called Position No. 1, appeared favorable for this purpose. There was decent defensive terrain that controlled the trailhead, nearby ground to establish a camp, and a small stream that provided fresh water. The scout continued around the mountain for another forty minutes, reaching what Duncan called Position No. 2 at the foot of the south trail. Here Major Omar Bundy would establish a base camp to support what would become the main attack. Guides led Duncan farther around the mountain to a commanding position that had been identified weeks earlier by an artillery captain who had scouted the terrain. From this position, Duncan reckoned that his field artillery could effectively support an assault up both the south and west trails. Looking toward the summit, Duncan saw armed Moros moving in and out of their fortifications. Erasing any doubt about their intent were the red war flags flying above the largest cotta at the top of the west trail as well as the basso profundo reverberations of the Moro war drums. Duncan was well satisfied with the morning's work and turned the scouting column back to Jolo town.

There he found that Captains Lawton and Reeves had returned from their reconnaissance of the east trail. The two captains were brimming with confidence, having discovered an excellent position that commanded the east trailhead. No one paid attention to the fact that this position, which Duncan labeled Position No. 3, was about seven miles from Position No. 2. It was self-evidently difficult to coordinate converging advances from all three positions, but for now this did not perturb Duncan. That evening the colonel wrote a comprehensive field order complete with separate paragraphs describing the objective—"to capture or destroy the malcontents on or in the vicinity of Bud Dajo"—terrain, instructions for getting into position, order of battle, disposition of troops, and assignment of guides and interpreters.[21] Duncan's detailed, precise orders contrasted with the improvisational approach employed by Leonard Wood and highlighted the difference between an experienced, professional fighting man and an inexperienced officer who desperately wanted to be thought of as a skilled combat leader.

At 4:00 A.M. on March 5, 1906, Duncan's entire command, about 750 officers and men, debouched from Jolo to march to their designated positions at the foot of Bud Dajo. At the head of the column was a company of Moro Constabulary led by Captain John R. White. Born in England in 1879, this restless, redheaded adventurer had eschewed university education to join the Greek Foreign Legion seventeen years later. After recovering from a combat wound, White next headed to Canada to seek his fortune during the Klondike Gold Rush. He failed at mining and found himself penniless. The Canadian Pacific Railroad offered employment, but White was uninterested in mere manual labor. Instead, he worked as a dynamiter, setting charges for tunnel construction. Having acquired travel money, White headed back home to England. His journey took him through Seattle in the spring of 1898, where he caught that city's war fever and joined the U.S. Army as a private. Service in the Philippines earned him the rank of sergeant, but his foreign birth made him ineligible for additional promotion. Consequently, he transferred to the constabulary in 1901. Assigned to a desk job, he talked his way into a field assignment where he quickly acquired a reputation as a hard-drinking, brave, aggressive officer. His talents caught the eye of Colonel James Harbord, who picked him to be his adjutant, even though White was only twenty-three years old. In this capacity White helped build the Moro Constabulary.

White was at headquarters in Zamboanga on March 2, 1906, when his superior received a telephone call from General Wood. Wood wanted a company of Moro Constabulary to accompany Duncan's expedition to Jolo. None was immediately available, so White gathered the odds and ends—constables on recuperative leave, men in transit between posts— to create an ad hoc company composed of twenty-nine Moros, twenty Filipinos, and two white officers. White described the scene two days later as his detachment marched out the Jolo gate in the predawn hours. The officer of the guard wished White luck and lamented that he and his men were not going to take part in the battle. White's constabulary proceeded "past waiting mule trains and cursing packers, past long lines of American soldiers resting on their rifles and joking with one another somewhat nervously; up dew-wet grassy slopes between groves of bamboo and breadfruit . . . on through the heavy tropic darkness, until we reached our place near the head of the column that moved out to attack the mountain." As the sun rose the constabulary "could see along the crest, clear cut against the sky, many flags and banners waving defiance over the Moro forts. The Moros themselves lined the parapets. Their cries and taunts floated faintly toward us."[22]

Duncan's orders were purposely vague regarding the battle's conduct. He wanted his columns to occupy their three designated positions and then send scouts to develop the situation. Duncan instructed the column commanders to avoid an assault unless he specifically ordered one. Captain Rivers's column reached Position No. 1 at the foot of the west trail at 8:00 A.M. At 10:30 Rivers led a reconnaissance up the trail. Forty-five minutes later a Moro shell wounded him in the right leg. While stretcher bearers carried Rivers back to the Jolo hospital, Captain Lewis Koehler assumed command and continued to scout the Moro position until nightfall. Everything Koehler saw confirmed that the west trail would be a very tough nut to crack.

The second column, commanded by Major Bundy, arrived at Position

No. 2 at the foot of the south trail about 9:30 A.M. Bundy's column included Captain White's constabulary company. White had asked for the honor of leading the assault, and Bundy readily assented. Beginning at 1:30 P.M., the constabulary began climbing the south trail with Company M, Sixth Infantry, following in support. The constabulary scouts examined all possible routes to avoid the main trail, but the heavily wooded slopes presented no alternative. There was nothing for it but to ascend single file up the steep trail. In places the hogback ridge was only eight feet wide. A misstep put a man in the treetops or, worse, over a cliff edge. The climb proved exhausting. In many places the constabulary and regulars had to crawl on all fours along the jungle floor, all the while enveloped by stifling heat and humidity. From time to time an opening in the jungle allowed a view of the fortifications atop the summit where the Moros awaited them. By late afternoon the constabulary had climbed two thirds of the way to the summit. Here they encountered the enemy behind a bamboo and log barricade. Darkness was fast approaching.

Moro and Philippine Constabulary.

White sent a messenger to report the contact to Major Bundy. Bundy's return message ordered White to hold in place for the night.

During the previous day's reconnaissance, Colonel Duncan had not had enough time to inspect personally Position No. 3 at the foot of the east trail. In company with Captain E. F. McGlachlin and his Twenty-eighth Field Artillery, Duncan arrived at Position No. 3 around 10:30 A.M. Captain Lawton told him that his men had been in action since they arrived but so far only one man had been wounded. Duncan saw an ongoing firefight between a company of the Nineteenth Infantry and a group of Moros hidden somewhere up the slope. McGlachlin's four guns unlimbered and opened fire at a range of 750 yards. A forty-minute bombardment did little visible damage. Apparently some of the ammunition was defective, because a number of the common shells failed to explode, while the star shells seemed to have no effect.

Duncan ordered the battery to limber up and accompany his recon-naissance. He intended to move all the way around the mountain and arrive at Position No. 2. Although the most knowledgeable guides were leading the way, after ninety minutes the trail petered out in a deep, overgrown ravine. A detour would traverse five or more miles and cer-tainly wear out the battery horses and mules. There was nothing for it but to countermarch, a decision that appeared wiser in hindsight when Duncan learned that the Moros had lined the rim of the ravine with boulders and logs and were only waiting for the Americans to enter be-fore releasing a man- and horse-crushing avalanche.

By 3:30 P.M. Duncan was back in Jolo. From his personal perspective, March 5 was largely a wasted day. On the positive side, he had seen that Lawton appeared to be capably conducting operations at the base of the east trail. Duncan had also acquired a personal understanding of the terrain. These small accomplishments came at the price of absenting himself from headquarters and thus limiting his ability to coordinate all three of his columns. Throughout military history, coordinating a con-verging attack has challenged the world's best combat leaders. The next two days would severely test Duncan's ability to meet this challenge.

The regulars and constabulary spent a troubling night listening to Moro gongs, drums, and chants while enduring occasional sniper fire. Because Wood had ordered them to travel light, no one had blankets or shelter tents. The soldiers resting at the base camps fared much better than those who occupied the advanced posts along the trail. Unless those unfortunates wedged themselves against a tree or boulder, as soon as they nodded off they began tumbling down the steep slopes. In addition, they knew that, in all likelihood, sometime soon they would be called upon to conduct a difficult uphill assault. Physical discomfort and nerves made for a restless night.

ON MARCH 6, the American vise around Bud Dajo tightened. Duncan was well aware that standard artillery doctrine recommended massed battery fire. However, the previous day's ineffective bombardment had persuaded him to ignore this doctrine. He had left one gun with Lawton at the east trail before returning to Jolo. During the night, two of Mc-Glachlin's remaining three mountain guns relocated to the base of the south trail and one moved to the base of the west trail. Events would prove that Duncan made a good tactical decision by dispersing his artillery among the assault columns.

At 2:00 A.M. Duncan and his headquarters units departed Jolo to establish field headquarters at the head of the south trail. When there was sufficient light to see, Duncan ordered the two nearby 75 mm mountain guns to relocate to previously selected firing positions that partially enfiladed the west lip of the crater and the fortifications at the top of the west and south trails. At 7:15 A.M. the guns commenced a measured bombardment. The angle was so steep that the gunners had to dig the trails of the weapons into the ground in order to sight the targets at the summit. The shelling continued for five hours.

High up the south trail, White's constabulary resumed their advance shortly after daybreak. They met no resistance at the trench they had encountered the previous day and gratefully crawled into its protective depths. They were now about five hundred feet below the crater rim. Suddenly Moro riflemen opened a sputtering fire. Major Bundy had assigned four regular sharpshooters to support the constabulary. For the first time these marksmen could see a foe. They began picking off any Moro who showed himself on the skyline. It was, as White wrote, "like shooting crows out of a tree."[23]

Under cover of this fire, White and twelve of his men climbed toward a trench one hundred yards upslope. They ran into a line of abatis (sharp wood or bamboo stakes planted in the ground) that blocked further progress. Private Diukson tried to move through the barrier. A shot rang out from a heretofore unseen trench higher up the slope. The bullet hit Diukson in the head. He hung in the abatis, slowly bleeding to death. Diukson was the expedition's first fatality. Another soldier stood to try to pull apart the barricade. He fell with a serious wound. For the next two hours, the constabulary remained pinned in position by the defenders' fire. White personally searched for a route to flank the abatis, but the barrier spanned the entire width of the hogback ridge. He concluded that there was no alternative to a frontal attack. White reported his finding to Bundy. While he waited for a reply, shrapnel shells fired from the mountain guns below began bursting dangerously around his position. He and his men retired downslope to the trench.

During this time, Bundy's regulars had advanced up the south trail. The trail followed a narrow lava ridge between two deep ravines. It was so steep in places that soldiers had to use tree roots as handholds to pull themselves up the slope. The heat and humidity enervated the men, reducing the column's progress to a literal crawl. Bundy kept climbing until he found White and his constabulary occupying the first Moro trench. From this vantage point, Bundy saw the line of abatis that had resisted White's probe. Barely discernible through the foliage about 150 yards above the abatis was the main cotta guarding the summit of the south trail. The Americans did not yet perceive that two additional trenches lay between the abatis and this cotta. Bundy concluded that any attack required direct support from the artillery. He sent a courier down the mountain requesting assistance.

Back at the base of the south trail, the gunners of the Twenty-eighth Field Artillery had received Bundy's request for help. They responded in the best artillery tradition, reckoning that where a goat could go, a man could go, and where a man could go, he could take a six-hundred-pound mountain gun with him. Determination, ingenious use of block and tackle, and brute force brought one gun and its ammunition to White's position just before nightfall. Bundy closed up his entire column behind the trench so that everyone would be in position when the attack order came. Then his force hunkered down for a second night on the slopes of Bud Dajo.

At Position No. 1 on the west trail, the Americans had also been busy. Following a short bombardment from the mountain gun, Captain Koehler began a reconnaissance in force. His men overran the first barricade, where Rivers had been wounded. Koehler's column ascended another

650 yards to capture a second Moro fortification. After a climb of another 350 yards, the attackers came to the most formidable position yet: an immense banyan tree whose roots formed a natural arch over the trail. Lurking Moros hidden in the adjacent jungle were in position to deliver flanking fire against anyone who attacked straight up the trail. In spite of the position's great natural strength, Koehler's men successfully assaulted it at 12:35 P.M. They continued to a point about 250 yards below a cotta that stood on the crest. Koehler imprudently made two assaults against this cotta, but the stubborn defenders refused to yield. Rather than endure excessive losses, Koehler had his men bivouac for the night close to the crest.

From his headquarters near the base of the south trail, Duncan tried to follow the attacks' progress. Technical and human problems impeded his effort. To facilitate communications, General Wood had personally assigned one of his favorite officers—Lieutenant Gordon Johnston, a former Rough Rider—to command the expedition's small Signal Corps detachment. But the flags, mirrors, and flares used for visual signaling required clear sight lines. Consequently, Johnston was reduced to using a courier system. The steep trails and rugged mountainside terrain precluded mounted couriers. Foot couriers required two hours to deliver one of Koehler's reports to Duncan. A response took even longer since the messenger had to climb up the mountain. Johnston failed to appreciate that as the day progressed, his couriers' physical stamina steadily eroded and communication slowed even more. He and Duncan were either unaware or unconcerned that there was no uniform rate for the back-and-forth transmission of reports and orders. Duncan and his subordinates inadvertently worked at cross-purposes by responding to out-of-date information. A meticulous, detail-oriented signal officer would have detected these problems and informed Duncan. Johnston, very much a man of action, was not this type of officer.

The erratic communication between headquarters and the two nearest assault columns on the west and south trails made coordination awkward. The difficulty of communicating with Lawton on the east trail was even greater because there was no known direct path linking headquarters with the head of the east trail. Johnston resorted to using local Moros as both guides and runners, but this did not rectify the trouble. Consequently, Duncan knew very little about what was taking place with Lawton's command. He had heard Lawton's artillery open fire early in the morning and then nothing. In fact, Lawton had aggressively attacked and made surprising progress.

Using one mountain gun as a close support weapon, two companies of the Nineteenth Infantry under the command of Captain A. M. Wetherill fought their way up the east trail. The Moros continually harassed the assault column with sniper fire and by rolling giant boulders down the volcanic slope, injuring three soldiers. Undeterred, the regulars steadily advanced to within fifty yards of the cotta at the summit. Thereafter, the combination of shelling and rifle fire leveled the cotta's walls and silenced the defenders. Wetherill climbed to the crater rim to scout the Moro position. He encountered a sentinel, fired his shotgun, killed the Moro, and returned to report. His men were eager to assault. They understood that they were in more danger staying put than climbing the last fifty yards. Wetherill sent a messenger to Lawton reporting that he occupied an excellent jumping-off position for the final attack and noted that unless he received orders to assault, he saw no reason to remain in the exposed position.

Now if ever was the time for Lawton to exercise initiative. His men could occupy the cotta at the top of the trail and hold it until reinforcements arrived. However, this would expose them to a Moro counterattack. Lawton balked at the risk. After all, his orders had told him to scout the Moro position, not assault it. Now the American effort again paid the price for operating converging columns along an extended front. As Koehler had done on the west trail, Lawton followed the strict sense of his orders. He ordered Wetherill to hold his position and sent a message to Duncan informing him about his troops' position and that he was waiting for orders. Lawton appended Wetherill's note that he would not remain in his exposed position indefinitely. When timely orders failed to arrive, Wetherill retired back down the east trail.

This then was the situation on the evening of March 6 as Duncan understood it. At Position No. 3 on the east trail, he mistakenly thought that Lawton's men were in position just below the crater rim. Duncan had been receiving reports from the commander of his reserves back in Jolo that Moro bands were preparing to assault Lawton's rear. Duncan sent a forty-man company to the east trailhead to handle this threat. From Position No. 2, on the south trail, Bundy sent word he was ready to conduct the final assault at daybreak but that he hoped a mountain gun could be brought up the trail to support the assault. From Position No. 1, on the west trail, Koehler also reported that he was ready. Fifteen yards

Command decisions. Three officers confer: Major Bundy (left), Colonel Duncan (center, dark blouse facing camera), Captain McGlachlin (right, back to camera).

above Koehler's bivouac was a blockhouse apparently defended by only four Moros. Koehler informed Duncan that after capturing the block-house "we have a clear shoot for the crest a little over two hundred yards to our front."[24] The only distressing aspect of Koehler's situation was that his assault troops numbered only 130 men and six officers. Duncan still had no firm idea about the strength of the Moro force defending the Bud Dajo crater.

For three days Duncan had orchestrated a patient advance that had kept his losses to a minimum. With all three columns in position he decided to order a dawn assault. The major problem he envisaged was the danger of friendly fire when the attackers gained the summit, par-ticularly since Lawton on the east trail and Koehler on the west would potentially confront each other across the crater rim at a range of under two hundred yards, well within American lethal rifle range.

Either Lawton or Koehler would have to stay off the rim. Duncan chose the numerically weakest command and ordered Koehler merely to maintain a blocking position. His orders to Lawton and Bundy re-quired them to unleash simultaneously the final assault at daybreak. To assist Bundy, Duncan ordered the crew of a Colt automatic gun, a fore-runner of the gas-operated modern machine gun, to bring the gun from its reserve position in Jolo.

So, for the second night in a row, companies of American regulars and a handful of constabulary endured a disturbed night on the chilly slopes of Bud Dajo as the Moros again serenaded them with beating gongs and drums, taunts, song, and lantaka discharges.

DUNCAN'S COMMAND AWOKE on March 7 before sunrise, stiff, hungry, and anxious. A mist hung over the crater. Reporters would describe the ensuing engagement as the "Battle of the Clouds." From its firing location near Position No. 2, a mountain gun fired five times in the direction of the cotta atop the south trail, the prearranged signal to begin the assault. The mountain gun near the top of the south trail blasted the Moro fortifications and then the infantry went forward. Again Captain White asked permission to lead the way with his constabulary. It was an odd request given that spearheading an infantry assault had never been part of the Constabulary Field Manual, but Major Bundy obliged, happy to use native troops as cannon fodder.

The constabulary crawled up to the line of abatis where they had halted the evening before. A deluge of fire swept the trail. White had to physically force his men to advance through the narrow gap in the bamboo abatis: "It seemed like they were killed or wounded almost as fast as I could push them through. For, once around the corner, we came under the direct fire of the large fort which crowned the summit. Between us and the loopholes which spouted fire, there was nothing that would shelter a rabbit."[25] Moro fire killed two and wounded another thirteen of the thirty-eight constabulary who made the attack.

So steep was the climb that Captain Bayard Schindel ordered a halt on the fire-swept ground so that the panting soldiers could lie still for a few moments to collect their breath before making a final dash. For once, American firepower had been unable to suppress the Moro fire. Consequently, the defenders' inferior shoulder arms and antiquated artillery wrought a fearful toll at point-blank ranges of under one hundred feet. Paradoxically, safety lay directly beneath the cotta's walls if the attackers had the courage and luck to reach that position. The constabulary struggled ahead to the base of the wall. Here, on closer inspection, they saw that the Moros had loopholed the cotta at intervals of two to three feet by inserting bamboo tubes through the walls. The tubes created six-inch-wide firing portals designed to sweep the ground below the fort. When

the attackers pressed against the wall itself, they were between the defenders' fields of fire and relatively safe.

In places the cotta's wall was only head high. By standing straight up,
men on opposite sides of the wall could fight one another. A desperate
hand-to-hand combat ensued. White stood up and felt the brush of a
spear thrust parting his hair as nearly simultaneously he fired his shotgun at the spearman. The discharge caught the Moro full in his belly.
All along the wall, small-arms fire proved more effective than sword and
spear as the attackers slowly began to dominate the fight. An American
sergeant raised his hat on his rifle, thus luring Moros to expose themselves as they tried to thrust. White stepped back to secure a good field
of fire and killed them as they rose to the lure.

The frontal assault by the constabulary occupied most of the defenders' attention. Hard on the heels of the constabulary came Schindel
with Company M, Sixth Infantry, followed by Company K, a twenty-man
detachment of Company E, and then thirty troopers belonging to Troop
I, Fourth Cavalry. The regulars began working around the sides of the
cotta. Who was hit and who was not was largely a matter of luck. Company M and the constabulary were directly in the line of fire from the
cotta and suffered 40 percent losses, while the adjacent units suffered
far less. White sensed a turn in momentum and climbed up the wall to
urge his men over the top. He saw a gaudily dressed datu gather himself
to swing his long, two-handed kampilan. White dodged but lost his
footing, falling back beneath the wall in front of one of the bamboo firing tubes. A Moro fired a Krag-Jörgensen, undoubtedly stolen from the
Americans, and the heavy shot pierced White's knee, sending him into
shock. Two constabulary carried White downhill, where they encountered Lieutenant Gordon Johnston striding up the slope.

Although formally serving as the expedition's signal officer, the restless Johnston, just as he had done when joining Frank McCoy's hunt for
Datu Ali, could not resist participating in the fighting. He had appeared
at dawn at the trailhead and volunteered to accompany Bundy's column.
Just getting close to the action was not enough for Johnston. While Bundy
was deploying his infantry, he asked permission to join the attack. So it
was that he encountered White's devoted constabulary carrying the
bleeding captain to safety. Johnston paused to take White's shotgun and
ammunition belt, then resumed his climb. Moro riflemen from a firing
pit outside the cotta targeted Johnston as he clambered up to the base of

the wall. Johnston disregarded the bullets slapping at the dirt around his feet and climbed atop the parapet to encourage the attackers. A warrior assaulted him, inflicting an incapacitating shoulder wound. Someone killed the warrior before she dispatched Johnston—for indeed, the fierce assailant turned out to be a woman.

The regulars carried the Moro position on the crater rim with a bayonet assault. Some two hundred kris- and spear-bearing Moros launched a ferocious counterattack, a tactic the Americans called a "bolo rush." American rifle fire killed most of them, but a handful closed the range and again a terrible hand-to-hand struggle took place. After killing this audacious handful, the regulars spread out along the crater rim and opened fire at the Moros fleeing across the crater floor. Now the Americans could clearly see their enemy, and now they began inflicting horrific casualties. However, because he expected Lawton's column soon to appear on his right and was unwilling to risk exposing his men to Lawton's fire, Bundy stopped his men at the crater rim at about 7:30 A.M. It soon became apparent that Lawton had not attacked. From the heights, a signalman waved his flags to inform headquarters. The morning hours passed atop the south trail with no sign of Lawton. Something was clearly amiss.

In the early afternoon, a machine gun detachment arrived with the army's Colt automatic. The crew opened fire at Moro positions on the west rim. At 1:30, toiling artillerymen joined them, having employed block and tackle to haul their mountain gun to the summit. It opened fire at point-blank range against targets of opportunity, particularly the cotta at the top of the west trail that was blocking Koehler's column. The two weapons inflicted additional losses but did not change the tactical situation. The momentum of Bundy's attack was gone, the troops exhausted and no reinforcements available.

LEONARD WOOD AND his entourage passed through Captain Koehler's camp at the base of the west trail in midmorning. There was little apparent activity, which annoyed Wood, who did not realize that Duncan's plan did not involve an assault from this direction. Wood continued around the base of Bud Dajo until he arrived at the camp at the foot of the south trail. Here too what he saw did not please him. There were many Moros freely circulating and very few soldiers present. Wood did not know that almost every able-bodied soldier was needed for the assault. To Wood's eye, the presence of a potentially hostile crowd of Moros amid the unprotected camps indicated a lack of military professionalism. Adding to his anxiety was the sight of one of his favorite officers, Gordon Johnston, being carried through the camp on his way to the hospital in Jolo. Then two lieutenants rode into camp trying to find Colonel Duncan. They came from Lawton's camp and brought a disturbing message.

In the absence of any contact with headquarters the previous evening, Lawton had withdrawn his column from its close embrace of the summit to a more secure camp. The next morning, around 10:00, an officer arrived in Lawton's camp and told him that Duncan had expected a dawn assault up the east trail. Lawton was astonished. He had never received the necessary orders. He did not know that the fault lay with Johnston, who in his capacity as signal officer had so mishandled the flow of information that he had to rely upon a Moro courier to carry the critical assault order to Lawton. Then Johnston had omitted the standard staff practice of having Lawton sign that he had received the order. The Moro messenger either got lost or decided to betray the Americans. Consequently, Lawton had not received the order, and Duncan did not know this fact.

When finally informed about his expected role, Lawton displayed a stunning lack of initiative. Instead of acting, he sent a request to Duncan: "Please send me orders; have received none since I sent those messages to you yesterday. Have just heard that you sent message to me to assault at daylight. No such message was received by me. I withdrew those companies after they had been up there all day. Shall I go up now, and what about my artillery fire?"[26]

When Wood read Lawton's message, it confirmed his notion that the assault was being botched. Wood sent Lawton's officers, along with his aide, Langhorne, back to Lawton to order him to assault immediately. They also carried the strict injunction not to allow artillery to fire over the crater rim, since such shelling might hit friendly troops. Thus, Lawton's delayed assault would have no artillery support.

At this point a display of military professionalism partially relieved Wood's anxieties when a naval detachment from the gunboat *Pampanga* made a surprising appearance. Under the command of Ensign H. C. Cooke, the nine sailors and their Moro *cargadores*, or bearers, and a mule pack train had carried two of the gunboat's Colt automatics all the

way from Jolo town in hopes of participating in the battle. Wood sent
Cooke's detachment on to Lawton. Sometime during this stressful morning, Wood suffered one of his seizures and collapsed to the ground.
Thereafter, although he recovered and rode on to join Colonel Duncan,
this man who so desperately wanted to showcase his military skills exercised little command presence at the most famous battle that took place
during his time in Moro Province.[27]

Langhorne delivered Wood's orders to Lawton at 12:30 P.M. The two
officers agreed that the assault column would follow the east trail as far
as possible and then, in order to avoid casualties, try to flank the main
cotta at the summit by advancing through the underbrush.[28] Although
Langhorne emphasized that time was of the essence since Bundy's column was having to bear the brunt of the fighting alone, because of the
terrain it still took over an hour to organize the assault column. Around
1:30 P.M. the ascent began. In places the regulars had to crawl using
bushes and vines as handholds. Lieutenant Josephus Cecil commanded
the vanguard composed of Company D, Nineteenth Infantry. Captain
Wetherill followed with Company B. The two companies numbered a
total of about one hundred men. Two more similarly numbered companies of the Sixth Infantry followed. As the column neared the cotta
crowning the summit, the advance stalled in the face of heavy defensive
fire. Soldiers now paid the price for Lawton's caution the previous day.
Lieutenant Cecil "had to push men by force up the steep hillside and
into the destructive rain of bullets and other missiles."[29] Not content with
merely stopping the Americans, individual Moro warriors and sometimes small bands clambered over the crater rim and counterattacked
downslope toward the American line only to die in a fusillade of rifle fire.
While the men directly beneath the cotta huddled in the dirt, to their
left soldiers moved off the trail and began hacking through the underbrush with machetes in an effort to outflank the cotta.

Following in the wake of Lawton's infantry came the naval machine
gun detachment. The exhausted mules gave out about halfway up the
slope. Thereafter, the sailors, with a helpful assist from some infantry,
hefted the guns and 4,500 rounds of ammunition the remaining distance until they joined the front line assault troops. From a position fifty
yards below the rim, Gunner's Mate Ernest Fleming opened fire at the
Moro trenches. The return fire was intense but Fleming ignored it and
resolutely continued firing until he silenced the enemy and cleared the

crest. The effective machine gun fire reenergized the infantry, who began loudly cheering. Lawton ordered a bugler to sound the charge.

It was a charge in name only. The slope was so steep that only a handful of men could run at the enemy. The others had to crawl forward on all fours or pull themselves up by grasping the underbrush. The terrain to the left of the trail was less steep and here the infantry managed to move from tree to tree and gain ground while avoiding the Moro hail of rocks, javelins, and rifle fire. The Moros had dug a trench along the crater rim adjacent to the cotta at the top of the trail. Logs laid along the front of the trench provided extra protection and almost entirely concealed the defenders. One Moro waited until the first soldier neared his position before throwing his knife. His target was not quick enough to dodge but was lucky enough to lose only part of his ear as the knife flew past his face. Having come so far, the implacable American advance could not be denied. At the cost of three killed and a handful of wounded, the infantry successfully captured the trench at the top of the east trail. Only then did they see several more trenches crammed full with defenders dug into the reverse side of the crater rim. The hardest fighting was yet to come.

The sailors carried a machine gun to the summit and sited it in a firing position that enfiladed the Moro trenches along the crater rim. Captain Lawton described the ensuing ten-minute combat, during which the Moros offered "a desperate resistance with rifles, spears and bolos, killing and wounding many of our men, but being shot down in their tracks with terrible slaughter so that their cotta and lip of the crater were soon piled up with dead."[30] The Americans lost five more killed and fifteen wounded during this stage of the battle. The Moros had no answer to the lethally effective machine gun and rifle fire. After the battle the Americans found trenches filled with bodies stacked five deep. The sailors then trained their Colt against the Moros in the crater. A veteran related what took place: "They turned that machine gun on them and they'd stand there, the Moros would, and just look like dominoes falling."[31]

Lawton's column gained the crater rim around 4:00 P.M. He sent a company along the rim to make contact with Bundy's command, but this effort failed when Bundy's artillerists mistook them for Moros and drove the company back with shell fire. Meanwhile, Lawton gazed down into the crater to see numerous shacks built by the Moros during their long occupation of Bud Dajo. He sent Captain Langhorne into the crater to burn the shacks and kill anyone he encountered. Langhorne's detachment met surprising opposition. The Americans did not know that they were assaulting the building used as a mosque. Moros hurled homemade grenades—fabricated by filling large seashells with gunpowder—at the attackers. Frank McCoy later recalled, "It was most remarkable the fierce dying of the Moros. At every cotta efforts were made to get them to surrender or to send out their women but for an answer a rush of shrieking men and women would come cutting the air and dash amongst the soldiers like dogs."[32] Toward the last it appeared that the Moros deliberately exposed themselves to American fire, as if committing suicide.

By nightfall on March 7, Lawton and Duncan had placed their commands in a continuous half arc running from Lawton's position at the summit of the east trail around the crater to the southwest. The only visible fortifications still defended by the Moros were those guarding the west trail. Officers established outposts partway down the interior slope while the soldiers manning positions along the rim settled in for their third night on Bud Dajo. Just before dusk, a photographer clambered up the east trail. His camera produced what would become the iconic photo of the Battle of Bud Dajo—Wetherill and his soldiers gazing across a large trench filled with mutilated Moro bodies (see page 168).

Stretcher bearers carried the wounded down to camp. There were so few medical personnel that Lawton personally returned to his base camp to care for the wounded. Finally he found someone who understood how to administer morphine shots, and this helped relieve the suffering. Casualties among the assault columns had been higher than anyone expected. To alleviate the strain, that night the steamer *Sabah* returned to Zamboanga to pick up medical supplies, doctors, and nurses.

At the summit, Bundy, in his capacity as the senior officer at the crater, made plans to complete the "cleanup" of Bud Dajo. He understandably believed that his own command had done enough. So he ordered Lawton to carry the attack against all remaining Moro positions. Lawton's command was particularly well placed to assault the defenses confronting Captain Koehler since it could approach them from the rear.

At daybreak on March 8, Lawton commenced a patient advance, with the naval detachment again providing supporting fire. After all the visible enemy had been killed, Lieutenant H. H. Bissell led two squads against the cotta at the top of the west trail. Suddenly there was a fusillade of fire accompanied by a bolo rush. A bullet passed through Bissell's hat. A

Moro lunged at the soldier next to the lieutenant. Bissell shot the Moro in the head. After Bissell withdrew from this violent attack, Lawton pondered what to do next. He could not see into the cotta and called for a volunteer to climb a nearby tree to obtain a better view. Nineteen-year-old Ordinary Seaman Joseph Fitz immediately stepped forward.

Born in Austria, Fitz had immigrated to Iowa and then joined the U.S. Navy. This roundabout journey seemed likely to end on the crater rim of Bud Dajo when a Moro marksman spotted Fitz in his exposed perch and fired. Although seriously wounded, Fitz calmly tied himself to the tree, drew his revolver, and opened fire at those still alive in the cotta. Having silenced the visible enemy, he resumed spotting for the machine guns. With Fitz's direction, the machine guns delivered a deadly fire. By the time the action ended Fitz was too weak from blood loss to climb down from the tree. His comrades had to climb up and free him. Fitz later received the Congressional Medal of Honor for "bravery and extraordinary heroism" exhibited on this day.

Leonard Wood (seated, turning to face camera) at Bud Dajo crater rim, March 1906.

The victors posed over the bodies of the defeated; the iconic photo of Bud Dajo.

Informed by Fitz that very few live Moros remained in the cotta, Law-ton gradually advanced his line and then launched a spirited bayonet charge. This time there was no opposition. Sixty-seven Moros lay dead inside the cotta. No more defended fortifications remained. The Battle of the Clouds was over.

TWELVE

The End of the Storm

> O Dewey at Manila
>   That fateful first of May
> When you sank the Spanish squadron
>   In almost bloodless fray,
> And gave your name to deathless fame;
>   O, glorious Dewey, say,
> Why didn't you weigh anchor
>   And softly sail away?
>
>   —Boston Transcript, ca. 1900

ABOUT THE TIME LAWTON'S MEN WERE capturing the last Moro position, Leonard Wood and Tasker Bliss climbed the south trail all the way
to the summit. As they looked around they saw hundreds of dead Moros.
Wood estimated the number at six hundred, while other observers more
reliably guessed that the number was closer to eight hundred or nine
hundred. Because Moro warriors habitually gathered their women and
children with them to defend a stronghold, many of the slain were noncombatants. The carnage did not seem to bother Wood. Several of his
officers wanted to search for survivors and count the fallen. Instead,
Wood ordered everyone except a small constabulary burial detail and a
dozen Moro laborers to retire from the crater, descend the trail, and return to Jolo. That evening he dined at the officers' club with Jolo's acting
governor, Captain Reeves, the officer who had aggressively manufactured

evidence to provide a rationale for the campaign. Then Wood embarked on the *Sabah*, along with some fifteen wounded, to return to Zamboanga to write his reports.

The casualty total for the regulars and Moro Constabulary numbered twenty-one dead and seventy wounded. Three sailors received wounds. These were by far the heaviest losses suffered in any post–Philippine War engagement. Around four hundred regulars and constabulary had entered the close fire zone. About one man in four was killed or wounded. Regarding Moro losses, Wood reported, "All the defenders were killed."[1]

The American soldiers and sailors had displayed splendid battle courage. Their uphill charge, in which soldiers literally crawled in order to close with the enemy, was remarkable. Had it occurred at a different time and place and been well publicized, their conduct would have entered the pantheon of famous American battlefield performances. Instead, Wood worked hard to censor the news of Bud Dajo, an effort that had a variety of lasting consequences, one of which was to deny the American servicemen their due.

The detachment of Moro Constabulary had also fought courageously. Even General Wood noted its "excellent work."[2] Given that their purpose was to serve as the Philippine government's armed police force, charged with the task of maintaining order, detecting and preventing crime, and enforcing the law, their performance on the fire-swept slopes of Bud Dajo should have earned them enormous acclaim. But few Americans were interested in praising their "little brown brothers," while Filipino authorities positively feared public praise of Moros fighting on the government's behalf. Filipino political leaders in Manila, all of whom were Christian, were firmly focused on acquiring control of the natural resources of Moro Province however and whenever the U.S-Moro conflict ended. To praise the brave Moro Constabulary might encourage Moro separatism. The only constabulary member to emerge from the battle with enhanced prestige was Captain John White. White deservedly became the constabulary's youngest officer ever to earn the Medal of Valor, the highest medal available to the police force and an award equivalent to the military's Medal of Honor.

MOST AMERICAN MILITARY men considered Bud Dajo an unqualified success. An officer stationed on Luzon praised Frank McCoy for doing "fine work in Jolo cleaning out that nest of vipers. Wish I had been there."[3] News of the battle reached Robert Bullard at Fort Snelling, Minnesota, where he was basking in the glow of favorable publicity generated by his recent article in *Atlantic Monthly*. That national publication had previously accepted his first article about the Moros right around the time of the Battle of Bayan. Bullard ruefully wrote in his diary, "This makes the second time, by a strange coincidence, that the appearance of an article by me upon the Moros has been promptly followed by a slaughter of the bad ones by U.S. troops."[4] Whereas Bullard accepted the necessity of the battle, John Pershing held a different view. He wrote his wife, "I would not have [that] on my conscience for the fame of Napoleon."[5]

President Theodore Roosevelt held no such qualms. He sent Wood a congratulatory telegram praising "the brilliant feat of arms wherein you and they so well upheld the honor of the American flag."[6] Thereafter, in spite of Wood's efforts at censorship, Manila reporters obtained information about the battle and it spread outside of military circles like a tsunami, reaching Manila as a powerful wave and flooding Washington with alarm. On March 9, 1906, the *New York Times* headline read: WOMEN AND CHILDREN KILLED IN MORO BATTLE . . . PRESIDENT WIRES CONGRATULATIONS TO THE TROOPS.

The report reenergized the moribund Boston-based Anti-Imperialist League, established in 1898. At its organizational height in 1900, its members included many of the nation's most renowned politicians, educators, social reformers, and business and labor leaders. Among its members were such luminaries as Mark Twain, William James, Charles Francis Adams, and Andrew Carnegie. The Anti-Imperialist League strongly backed Democratic presidential candidate William Jennings Bryan in 1900 because of his opposition to the annexation of the Philippines. McKinley supporters had hit back hard, with Secretary of War Elihu Root publicly questioning the patriotism of the anti-imperialists. The pro-McKinley *New York Tribune* charged that Bryan was more of an insurgent leader than any Filipino and that "every American soldier that is killed during these months can be laid directly to his door."[7] The election ultimately turned on economic issues. Bryan had no answer to the Republican platform, based on "Four more years of the Full Dinner Pail," and McKinley won easy reelection.

Bryan's loss disheartened the Anti-Imperialist League. However, during the Moro campaigns the League continued to publish graphic stories of American brutality. Wood's bloody victory at Bud Dajo gave it an easy target. With sarcasm dripping from his pen, Twain wrote: "With six hundred engaged on each side, we lost fifteen men killed outright, and we had thirty-two wounded—counting that nose and that elbow. The enemy numbered six hundred—including women and children— and we abolished them utterly, leaving not even a baby alive to cry for its dead mother. This is incomparably the greatest victory that was ever achieved by the Christian soldiers of the United States."[8] However, Twain decided that his comments were too controversial to publish and withheld them for his autobiography, which was not to be published until after his death.

Meanwhile, the anti-imperialist press and Roosevelt's congressional foes worked hard to keep the issue at the forefront of public debate. A drawing in the *New York World* entitled "Peace in Jolo" showed General Wood standing atop the crater surrounded by bodies with blood dripping from his sword. An editorial in the *Nation* on March 15, 1906, demanded a congressional inquiry. It asked if "there is any definite policy being pursued in regard to the Moros . . . There seems to be merely an aimless drifting along, with occasional bloody successes and now and then the report of a victory of peace. But the fighting keeps up steadily and no one can discover that we are making any progress." In the halls of Congress, Mississippi senator John Sharp Williams recited his newest poetry, borrowed from Lord Tennyson's "Charge of the Light Brigade":[9]

Chased them from everywhere,
Chased them all onward,
Into the crater of death,
Drove them—six hundred!
"Forward the Wood Brigade!
Spare not a one," he said.
"Shoot all six hundred!"

The growing criticism alarmed the Roosevelt administration, and it began asking its own questions. Secretary of War Taft telegraphed Wood: "It is charged there was wanton slaughter Moros, men, women, and children, in the fight Mount Dajo; wish you would send me at once all the particulars with respect to this matter, stating exact facts."[10]

Taft's cable angered Wood, particularly the word *wanton*. Wood acknowledged the deaths of women and children but pled extenuating circumstances: "Moro women wore trousers and were dressed, armed much like men, and charged with them. The children were in many cases used by the men as shields while charging troops . . . Action was most desperate, and was impossible for men fighting literally for their lives in close quarters to distinguish who would be injured by fire." The Moros "apparently desired that none be saved."[11] Nonetheless, Wood accepted entire responsibility for his troops' actions, a decision that had profound consequences for his career, since it ended the rancor held by many army officers toward the onetime contract physician. Henceforth, in the face of outside political pressure, they closed ranks and treated Wood as one of their own.

Wood's explanation satisfied Taft and Roosevelt. Roosevelt sent a special message to Congress transmitting Wood's report. It also contained Taft's assessment, which said, in part, that the unfortunate loss of life occurred because of the Moros' deliberate sacrifice of their women and children. Furthermore, the "treacherous" efforts of the Moro wounded to resist American medical assistance was entirely characteristic of "the uncivilized Mohammedan."[12] From his headquarters in Manila, Governor Henry Ide assured his friend and former boss, William Taft, that indeed nothing untoward had occurred at Bud Dajo.[13]

Wood reacted to the political firestorm in Washington with a mix of contempt, bemusement, and indifference. He wrote in his diary on March 16, 1906: "Press dispatches from the United States indicate that the Administration is being vigorously attacked on sensational charges incident to fight at Mount Dajo. Can find no evidence of any telegrams bearing out statements made by press." With untroubled conscience, the next day Wood competed at target shooting with Bliss at the La Loma Gun Club and achieved a very fine score of 18, though Bliss bested him with the "remarkable score of 22."[14]

But Wood being Wood, he had to gild the lily. He persuaded Governor Ide to file an official report stating that press claims about the battle were "extremely sensational and in all essential details false." Ide's report contradicted every eyewitness by asserting that "some women and children were killed or wounded by preliminary shelling at a distance" but there had been no "wanton slaughter."[15]

The hostile Mississippi senator John Sharp Williams immediately seized on the discrepancy between Wood's and Ide's reports: "First they tell us that Moro children were used as shields, now they say the children were killed in a bombardment. What is the truth? Doesn't this cast doubt on the credibility of the government's entire explanation of the battle of Mount Dajo?"[16]

Amid accusations of cover-up and lying, the Roosevelt administration agreed to provide Congress with all relevant telegrams associated with the battle. To buttress its case, the administration even summoned Major Hugh Scott to the War Department. Since leaving Jolo, Scott had been enjoying his leave in New York City until he heard the news of Bud Dajo. Fully aware that the press would hunt him down if he remained in public, Scott lay low until summoned to Washington. He closeted himself in the War Department, and, with administration officials close at hand, wrote a memorandum on the "Moros of Jolo Island." Of course it exonerated his commanding officer, General Wood, of all blame.

As part of the administration's publicity campaign, officials also gave interviews to reporters. A former commander of the Department of the Philippines, Lieutenant General Henry C. Corbin, explained to the popular magazine the *Outlook* that Wood had confronted a different kind of enemy at Bud Dajo: "The Moros are religious fanatics, and are not amenable to the influence of other peoples." The *Outlook*'s writer ignored the issue of dead women and children and observed, "The disparity in the losses of the two forces is a significant illustration of the inequality between an army with antiquated arms and insufficient training in an almost perfectly defended position and an army with arms of precision and military science."[17] Such protestations may have convinced a wavering few, but many still challenged the veracity of the administration's claims.

Wood recognized his career was in peril. He had assumed command of the Department of the Philippines on February 1, 1906. At that time he made the unusual choice to hold on to the position as civil governor of Moro Province until after Bud Dajo was "cleaned up." Undoubtedly he thought that he would acquire more glory by retaining this position and then supervising a victory on Jolo. Instead, surprised by the outpouring of criticism—after all, what he had done was merely a repeat of what he had been doing for years—he decided to distance himself administratively by resigning his position as civil governor of Moro

Province and belatedly passing that title to Tasker Bliss effective April 15, 1906. At the time few noticed that this transfer came six weeks beyond the date originally specified by the War Department.

He then proceeded to cover up his personal responsibility for Bud Dajo. He asserted that he had ordered his men to offer every assistance to wounded Moros. He did not mention the fact that this did not take place because almost all the Moros were dead. He said he had deliberately left Moro bodies where they had fallen so they could be properly buried by their neighbors according to Islamic tradition. In fact, he had ordered the troops to retreat from the crater to escape the overwhelming stench. Bodies remained unburied for another six months until an American tourist complained. Likewise, he lied about the facts preceding the attack. He falsely claimed that Scott had told him that negotiation was futile and the mountain would have to be stormed. He asserted that he had issued attack orders only after personally assessing the situation. As previously noted, he actually resolved to attack only three days after returning from his stateside sick leave and well before he knew all the facts. Only in his conclusion did Wood express his opinion candidly: "This action was unavoidable unless the government decided to give up all attempt to control in the Island of Jolo."[18]

Wood also provided proof of his good judgment by inviting cowed datus aboard his personal yacht for a discussion about Bud Dajo. He asked leading questions that yielded the desired answers, namely, that Wood's decision had rid Jolo of only the "bad" Moros and thus benefited the majority. One datu, when asked if he agreed that all his bad people had been "managed," replied with sarcastic candor that went over Wood's head: "Yes. You killed them." Wood finished the interviews with a lecture explaining that all the Moros who had resisted American control were now dead, and if any resisted in the future they also would be killed. Then he brightly pointed the way forward for the newly pacified Moroland: "What you need now is to have large families to make up for those killed on Dajo. That is the thing, let the children come and take the place of those who are gone. You want now big crops of babies, hemp, rice, and coconuts, not more fighting."[19]

The sensational story of Bud Dajo continued to dominate newspapers until April 18, 1906, when a terrible earthquake and fire destroyed San Francisco and took precedence in the news for months. The U.S. Army units charged with imposing martial law, the Fourteenth Cavalry and

Twenty-second Infantry, were Moroland veterans, having just rotated home the previous year. Thereafter, memories of Bud Dajo haunted only a handful of minds. In January 1907, the Anti-Imperialist League reprinted and distributed three thousand copies of the horrific photograph taken after the assault (see page 168). The clear image of a dead Moro woman with a very young child lying on her lap lying among the slain was a powerful commentary on the bloodshed at Bud Dajo. Among those who saw the photo was W. E. B. Du Bois, who wrote to the president of the Anti-Imperialist League that it was "the most illuminating thing I have ever seen. I want especially to have it framed and put upon the walls of my recitation room to impress upon the students what wars and especially Wars of Conquest really mean."[20]

In spite of such powerful propaganda, the influence of the Anti-Imperialist League waned, leaving the history of Bud Dajo to be framed by the victors. In his annual report for 1906 Wood observed, "The general condition of public order has improved much during the year. There have been few military operations of importance in the department, with the exception of the operations resulting in the death of Datu Ali, in October, and the destruction of his following, and the operations in Jolo incident to the capture of Mount Dajo, a volcanic crater 2,100 feet high, occupied by from six to seven hundred Moro fanatics who had banded themselves together, and by their lawless acts made themselves a menace to the peace of the community."[21] The new governor of Moro Province, Tasker Bliss, endorsed this view in his own official report. He "regretted" that a number of women and children were among the killed but asserted that it was unavoidable because of the Moros' "religious fanaticism."[22]

With those words the storm of Bud Dajo came to an end. Neither the War Department nor the White House wanted to probe deeper into what had transpired on the volcanic slopes, and the press also was content to move on to new topics. Thereafter, official accounts referred to the slaughter as "a necessity that existed for destroying a band of outlaws" and focused on the gallantry of the Americans and the peace that came afterward.[23]

In June 1906, Hugh Scott returned to Moroland and toured Jolo's countryside. He saw cultivated fields with bumper crops of hemp planted in areas that had been controlled by the most hostile datus. Instead of continuing a life of brigandage, datus were returning stolen cattle and property. A Moro Exchange had opened in Jolo town and was well attended. The island's inhabitants were anticipating the benefits of roads and schools. Scott informed Wood, "It is amazing to see the fruits of our three years of work ripen so fast. Never were the people so pliable and plastic."[24] The fact that a cowed and beaten people were complying with American wishes was heartening progress. But Scott knew the Jolo Moro better than any other American did. He wondered if peace could last.

The Philippine Commission also reported marked improvement in conditions in Moro Province after Wood's reign of terror. Further progress would be "a work of time, tact, and constant watchfulness to change the feelings of the Moros toward us from suspicion and distrust to friendship and confidence. Still more than a beginning has been made."[25]

Leonard Wood departed Zamboanga to assume command of the Division of the Philippines, leaving behind a record of violence. The decision to impose direct American rule, made before Wood arrived, had played perfectly into his keen desire to display his military craft. During his thirty-two months as governor of Moroland, there were more than one hundred reported clashes between Moros and Americans. In his last battle, Wood had weathered the storm that arose from the massacre at Bud Dajo and remained poised to ascend to the top of the U.S. Army.

THIRTEEN

Tasker Bliss and the Return to Benign Assimilation

*Force is not a desirable agent for peace and benevolence. Some
fighting might have been necessary at times, but it certainly is
unnecessary all the time . . . Can a tiger be struck with a stick and
be expected to hold his patience and peace? And knowing the nature
of the beast as we do, do we try to tame him with a stick or
with a piece of meat?*

—Najeeb M. Saleeby

AFTER THREE YEARS OF SERVICE ON JOLO, it was time for Hugh Scott to
go home for good. During this time, from 1903 to 1906, Scott had listened patiently to Moro complaints and concerns and thereby created a
deep reservoir of cooperation. What he had found on Jolo in the after-
math of Bud Dajo dismayed him: "Some of my successors ruined all
that cooperation by failing to continue the reciprocity. They did not want
to be bothered with the 'dirty natives' and would not listen to their little
complaints, with the result that in the day of their need of help [intelli-
gence] it was not forthcoming, and their administrations were a failure
on Jolo."[1]

The War Department had offered Scott the opportunity to become
superintendent at West Point. His superiors in the Philippines tried to
persuade him to stay, saying that he had already accomplished more

than anyone thought possible but that much remained to be done. Scott believed that work at Jolo could never be completed in his lifetime and decided to accept the prestigious West Point assignment. In his memoirs Scott asked, "What had been the result of the expenditure of so much blood and effort? What had come out of those three years of toil and danger?"

He answered, "It is given to no man to civilize a wild people overnight, as so many of our good citizens seem to expect. Neither may it be done in a generation, and often many generations are required."[2]

Scott was among the most sensitive and sensible officers ever to serve in Moroland. When he departed Jolo, many Moro leaders expressed deep and sincere sorrow. Yet for all Scott's talents he lacked fundamental insight about Islam: "For some reason the attempt to collect the tax [cedula] was regarded by the Moros as an attack upon Islam."[3] Had he matched his knowledge about Moro personality with knowledge about Islam, he could not have failed to understand the Moro viewpoint. The Moros' uncharacteristic docility and willingness to cooperate with American rule stemmed from the fact that the majority had concluded that they were powerless to resist. There were a few scattered pockets of resistance, but even the Jolo Moros seemed exhausted. However, while there was an absence of open rebellion, seething resentment remained just below the surface. An American misstep easily could lead to renewed conflict.

This was the situation confronting the second governor of Moro Province, Tasker Howard Bliss. The contrast between Bliss and Wood hardly could be starker. Whereas Wood delighted in physical pursuits, Bliss was a scholar with a particular passion for ancient history. Wood had combat experience; Bliss's closest approach to battle had come when he accompanied Wood to the top of Bud Dajo. Wood had used the platform of the governor's office to conduct remorseless military campaigns and thereby vault up the ranks to achieve the post of commanding general of the Division of the Philippines with headquarters in Manila. When Bliss assumed command in Zamboanga, he had the opportunity to do the same.

In contrast to Wood's boyhood experiences and subsequent celebration of physical culture, Bliss had grown up in an intellectual environment. Born in 1853, this son of a deeply religious college professor led an inward-looking, insular life. Until his late teens he never ventured farther from his birthplace in Lewisburg, Pennsylvania, than he could walk. Bliss seemed poised to follow in his father's footsteps. He had

Tasker Bliss (behind cat) and staff.

completed his first year at his father's place of employment, Lewisburg University (subsequently Bucknell), when the family's financial situation deteriorated. Government-financed education offered the only alternative. His first choice was the Naval Academy at Annapolis, but there were no appointments available. The alternative was West Point. He had befriended a decorated Civil War combat veteran and asked this man, "What kind of soldier do you think I would make?" The veteran prophetically replied, "You'd make a good professor at West Point."[4]

Indeed, upon graduating from West Point in 1875, he spent the next thirteen years teaching, first at West Point and then at the Naval War College. Promoted to lieutenant colonel on the eve of the Spanish-American War, he served exclusively in staff positions. Bliss's assignment for the two years preceding his arrival in the Philippines was as president of the Army War College, an institution he helped found. In his career to date, Bliss had exhibited a love of learning coupled with a high intellect. Other men with his brains would have become discouraged by the military's torpid pace of promotion and lack of challenging assignments and availed themselves of the abundant opportunities open to talented civilians. But Bliss had been brought up in a household where modesty was taught as a virtue, and he never conceived that he had any exceptional capacity. He had also been taught to respect life's obligations. The nation had given him an education, and it was a debt he had to repay. So this humble intellectual officer assumed the position as military governor of Moro Province on January 9, 1906, and then, after Bud Dajo, inherited the civilian role as well.

He wrote to his wife describing what was at stake: "The authorities forget that the most critical time is after slaughter has stopped. Then is when we need here men of influence and power to get the people started in the right way, to get them to cultivate their fields, and make them understand that peace is better for them than war."[5] Bliss understood that the Moros had suffered terribly. He completely altered the American approach that had inflicted this pain. Instead of seizing upon every incident as an opportunity to chastise the Moros, Bliss ended large punitive expeditions. He treated the Moros' incessant raiding, murders, and tribal feuds as criminal actions instead of direct challenges to American sovereignty. He accepted that isolated crimes and disturbances would occur, that unwary sentinels would occasionally be killed for their arms, and that juramentados would sometimes fulfill their lethal wishes. But Bliss believed that in the larger picture all of this was tolerable. He did not hold a starry-eyed view of Moro history or habits. When sending a constabulary detachment against an outlaw band, he reported that practically all the Moros in the district were "murderers and slave stealers."[6]

Bliss saw the only possible route for Moro advancement as economic development brought by whites. He thought the notion of Moro self-government preposterous. He asserted that even the advanced Moro did not understand the concept. Experience had proven that placing a local headman in any position of authority led to his taking advantage by exploiting his people for personal gain. Bliss predicted that for years to come "to confer on any one native element the power of government would, stripped of all misleading verbiage, amount to the naked fact that the United States would have to hold the larger part of the people by the throat while the smaller part governs it." Bliss was too intelligent to ignore the obvious hypocrisy: "It is true that we constitute a still smaller part and are forcefully holding the people while we govern them."[7] But at least, he thought, American governorship provided the people with some benefits, whereas native leadership meant a reversion to pillage and murder.

Bliss's theory of governorship soon received stern tests. It was one thing to tolerate ongoing Moro attacks against American and Filipino civilians, but something else when the attackers targeted American soldiers. The Moro goal was to secure modern firearms. On the night of June 27, 1906, five Moros killed Private James W. McDonald as he stood guard at Parang. American investigators learned the names and general whereabouts of the assailants. Military officers followed the Bliss approach and treated it like a civil case of murder by seeking their arrest through civil authorities. This effort failed. Bliss faced a choice: he could mount a military expedition to arrest the Moros, or he could accept that the Moros had gotten away with murder. If the former, he had to overcome civil government law and, more important, risk provoking a renewed war. Bliss judged the risk not worth the capture of five criminals. But he knew that this decision frustrated his soldiers and bred their resentment against the civil government.

It also annoyed his superior, General Wood. When Wood received Bliss's report about the "murder" of an American soldier, he replied that if Moro acts of violence were not met with a timely response, then the violence would only worsen. The proper response was to give the Moros an ultimatum with a hard deadline and then follow through if the Moros failed "to do the square thing." Wood asserted that three years of experience had taught him that this approach "was the whole secret in handling the Moro situation."[8] As time passed, Bliss's tolerant policy continued to upset Wood, who thought that the new governor was too passive and too willing to accept insult to the American flag.

The Return of the Pirates

In 1907 the navy withdrew the shallow-draft gunboats that had been patrolling the Sulu Seas on the grounds that they were no longer needed. Bliss complained that this decision was premature, observing that it was inconceivable that a few years of peace were enough to change Moro culture. Unlike naval authorities, Bliss understood the fundamental nature of Moro piracy: "The Moro does not regard acts of piracy as resistance to the government. It is a legitimate source of income to be worked if it can be done without detection. Where the danger of detection is great he does not attempt it."[9] The presence of American gunboats, with their ability to pursue native sailing craft everywhere in the Sulu Seas, had practically eliminated Moro piracy. Their absence brought a return of the pirates, including the era's most notorious Sulu buccaneer.

His name was Jikiri. Born on a small island five miles south of Jolo to a Samal fisherman and Moro woman, his life's path seemed destined from birth. One of his eyes was much larger than the other and this defect became the source of cruel taunts throughout his childhood. He grew to become a broad-shouldered, tall youth and served as the Sultan Jamal-ul Kiram II's betel nut bearer. But the taunts continued, particularly from the krismen who served as the sultan's bodyguard. Jikiri turned to a life of crime, boasting to one of his lieutenants that the strength of his kris arm would one day comfort the women who had scorned him.

The relative peace that Bliss's reign had brought to the Sulu Seas had encouraged intercoastal trade. The burgeoning pearl shell trade between Zamboanga and Jolo made a tempting target for pirates, and here Jikiri began operations as the leader of a seven-man crew in the middle of 1907. Thereafter he conducted a series of raids all over the Sulu Archipelago, and his targets were not limited to the pearl traders. On the night of November 1, 1907, a Chinese trader named Tao Tila put to sea in his vinta, a small coastal trading vessel. A swiftly sailing vinta overhauled him, and one of his two Moro crewmen heard a voice call out, "Kill them." This Moro dove overboard and escaped while Jikiri's pirates seized the vinta and killed both Tao Tila and the remaining crew. The surviving Moro swam to shore to tell the tale of a brutal seaborne scourge who displayed mercy to neither Moros nor infidels.

As time passed, Basilan Island became Jikiri's special target because here he received assistance from a local strongman known as the Salip Aguil. On Christmas Eve 1907, Jikiri attacked the American-managed Kopuga logging camp on Basilan. Around two in the afternoon, two vintas carrying seven Moros hauled up on the shore near Kopuga. A pair of Moros appeared in the camp to barter, but the American overseer, a man named Case, said he had nothing to trade and sent them away.

Jikiri's scouts returned to the vintas to describe the camp's layout. Three hours later the pirates struck. It began when one of Jikiri's men summoned Mrs. Case to the company store, saying he wanted to buy cigarettes. As she turned to reach the shelves she heard a scream. Looking out the window, she saw an American logger named Verment go down beneath the blows of two Moros. The Moro in the store began

Gunboats ensured the uninterrupted flow of supplies along the coast, on Lake Lanao, and along the Rio Grande.

clambering over the high counter to get at Mrs. Case. She managed to escape out the window and ran through the jungle to a nearby village to summon help. When a constabulary patrol reached the scene they found that Mr. Case had been beheaded while Mrs. Verment was lying in the dirt with a ghastly slash from shoulder to hip that proved to be a mortal wound. The store and camp had been looted, but Jikiri's band was nowhere to be found.

Following this raid, Jikiri became a minor celebrity when he returned to Sibago, his base island. The locals celebrated his feats. Jikiri, in turn, used some of his proceeds from the raid to buy a Remington rifle. The constabulary received reports that Jikiri was on Sibago, but when patrols arrived they found that he had wisely dispersed his band to wait out the pursuit. For three months an American-led force of two hundred men searched for the pirate but could not find him. During this time Jikiri hid out in a swamp on Jolo. Upon resuming activities he used his Remington to wound a trooper of the Sixth Cavalry and killed with his kris Albert Burleigh, an American private detailed as a schoolteacher on Jolo.

A typical raid came on March 22, 1908, when Jikiri and his ten-man band of pirates landed on Jolo and attacked a store. They killed three Chinese, wounded several others, looted, and then burned down every store in town. In response, authorities put a price on Jikiri's head.

A typical Sulu Seas sailing vessel with outriggers.

When that did not work, they raised it. Jikiri purportedly replied that he would run juramentado in the streets of Jolo, but not before he had cut down the hundred men he had sworn to slay. The *Mindanao Herald* noted that Jikiri's exploits were earning great respect from the island's Moros. He was coming perilously close to emerging as the unifying war leader that the Moros had always lacked.

In response, Sultan Jamal-ul Kiram II sent his personal bodyguard, including men who had once taunted the deformed betel nut bearer, to capture or kill Jikiri. They too failed. His ability to elude the authorities amazed many. The *Mindanao Herald* marveled at his unpunished depredations, including multiple murders, and his ability to evade justice. The newspaper observed that in one year he had won more glory than most Moros looked for in a lifetime.

On August 22, 1908, Jikiri attacked a pearl schooner, killed four of the crew, and seized its valuable cargo of black-lipped pearl shell. Success brought more recruits. His pirate band grew to some one hundred men. Along with a handful of other pirates, Jikiri laid siege to the intercoastal trading routes with a series of attacks unmatched since the sixteenth century. In January 1909, Jikiri led four pirate vessels against a small pearl fleet. Two pearlers fled to Zamboanga. The remaining two, the *Ida* and the *Nancy*, stoutly defended themselves. A three-hour duel ensued, featuring an exchange of long-range riflery interspersed with blasts from swivel guns and lantakas fired by the pirates. The pearlers were holding their own until the *Ida* ran out of ammunition. The crew jumped overboard and swam for safety, leaving the pirates to loot their schooner. The pirate fleet massed against the *Nancy*. Jikiri himself, by now recognizable because he always concealed his face with a white head scarf, ordered his command to close. Disregarding losses caused by the *Nancy*'s marksmen, the pirate craft drew near. Close-range pirate rifle fire drove the *Nancy*'s surviving crew to shelter behind the bulwarks, allowing the pirates to board. In the ensuing hand-to-hand melee, the pirates slaughtered the crew and captured the vessel. Thereafter, because of Jikiri, the pearl fleet remained in port, too frightened to risk another pirate attack.

The Americans created a special military detail to capture Jikiri, led by Captain Frank DeWitt, who spoke the local dialect fluently. DeWitt's tactics called for continuous operations with small mobile forces in hopes that eventually he would catch Jikiri off guard. DeWitt's persistence finally paid off. Benefiting from excellent intelligence, DeWitt cornered Jikiri's band on Jolo. The outlaws answered the call for surrender with a volley of rifle fire. Four pirates died during the ensuing shoot-out, but to DeWitt's frustration, Jikiri was not among them. He either escaped or had already left for a raid on British-controlled Borneo. Jikiri's destructive raids on Borneo prompted British authorities to organize an all-Moro party to seek and capture Jikiri. This party sailed to Jolo, encountered the pirate himself, and returned to Borneo in defeat, minus their ears and fingers. They carried a warning from Jikiri himself that the British could never capture him.

Nonetheless, steady pressure gradually depleted Jikiri's band. The return of the U.S. Navy gunboats limited his seafaring activities and eventually pinned him to the land. Finally, on July 2, 1909, an overwhelming American force ran Jikiri to ground on the small island of Patian, ten miles from Jolo. Purportedly Jikiri could have escaped, as he had so many times in the past, but Moro tradition asserts that he had grown weary of running and decided on one last suicidal defense. His refuge was a cave in a high volcanic crater. The Americans methodically surrounded the crater, brought up heavy weapons, and bombarded the cave over the course of three days. After a pair of navy Colt automatics blasted the cave opening at point-blank range, the besiegers concluded that nothing inside could remain alive. On the morning of July 4, a mixed force of U.S. cavalry troopers and navy sailors cautiously advanced toward the mouth of the cave. Suddenly seven kris-wielding warriors emerged, led by Jikiri himself. The surprised Americans delivered an ineffective fire. Jikiri advanced through the fire, grabbed Lieutenant Arthur Wilson by the hair, and was about to decapitate him when Lieutenant Joe Baer rushed up, jammed his 12-gauge Winchester pump shotgun against Jikiri's head, and blew off the top of his skull.

An eye-gouging, kris- and bayonet-stabbing melee ensued during which Baer killed three more Moros with his sawed-off shotgun while a sailor skewered a fourth with his bayonet. The cavalry troopers shot down the remaining two Moros. The melee had lasted some ten seconds. When it was over, Jikiri and his outlaws were dead alongside three slain Americans. Nineteen Americans were wounded during Jikiri's last stand.[10] So died the last of the Sulu Seas buccaneers.

FOURTEEN

The Problems of Pacification

This case is one of vital interest to the Army. The principles involved are far-reaching, and must necessarily have a profound effect upon the performance of duty by officers and soldiers of the United States Army.

—Leonard Wood

The Reforms of Leonard Wood

THE AMERICAN MILITARY EXPERIENCE in the Philippines changed over time. During the years of conventional and unconventional warfare against Filipino insurrectos, the dangers of combat had combined with disease and exposure to make military service dangerous. Benny Foulois had two tours of duty in the Philippines and later risked his life repeatedly as a pioneer military pilot. Asked how he survived his early flying days, Foulois replied, "Anyone who lived through the fighting in the Philippines could live through anything."[1] After the war against Aguinaldo's guerrillas ended, a large American garrison remained in the Philippines to accomplish two strategic objectives: control the populace and defend the islands from foreign invasion.

Having just solved, or so he thought, the problem of controlling the Moros by virtue of the bloodbath at Bud Dajo, the new head of the Division of the Philippines, Major General Leonard Wood, was not particularly interested in the ongoing struggle to pacify the rest of the Philippines. This effort involved dealing with the flotsam and jetsam of the Filipino insurgency as well as a variety of outlaw bands. Wood understood that pacifying these diverse groups required patient persistence; a misstep could bring criticism and blame, and success would confer little glory. He wanted to distance himself from the career risks associated with pacification.

Wood knew that U.S. policy called for a gradual transition from American military to Filipino civil rule. He was confident that this would not take place during his time in the Philippines. Thus, for the time being, he urged that "a strong garrison should be maintained here [the Philippines] until conditions pertaining to the civil government are well established, and the animosities and disappointments incident to the building up of local government under new and perhaps strained conditions have passed away."[2] In the meantime, to maintain law and order, Wood relied heavily upon the Philippine Scouts. For Wood's career, this solution had two advantages: the Scouts could probably get the job done; regardless, they mostly operated outside the gaze of the American press.

Philippine Scouts, 1904.

Recent history informed the American decision to arm native Filipino troops. American officers serving in China during the international campaign against the Boxers had seen British-trained Indian troops perform superbly. But even as late as 1907 the memory of the Great Mutiny and the Sepoy Rebellion loomed like an unexpected typhoon over the Raj. Most American officers with any experience in the Philippines agreed with the statement, published in a leading American military journal in 1902, that the typical Filipino was "a consummate actor, a most deceptive schemer, and that his regard for veracity is absolutely nil."[3] This assessment of Filipino character gave pause to American planners who pondered the formation of armed Filipino units.

However, when the army overcame its prejudices and did organize a trial unit of Scouts, the results were overwhelmingly positive. Thereafter, American regular officers on temporary assignment commanded the Scout units. Since the Scouts typically operated in small detachments, the quality of the junior leadership was critical. Consequently, all the lieutenants were either serving or former American officers and noncommissioned officers. The rank and file came from the native population, and therein lay a problem. When companies comprised men from different Filipino tribes, the men frequently fought with one another. Wood made the pragmatic recommendation to recruit battalions on a tribal basis and then assign them to their native regions. This was both good for the Scouts, who could see how their efforts helped their own people, and good for American intelligence efforts, because it unlocked the language barrier posed by local dialects.

Henceforth, the Philippine Scouts conducted a long struggle to pacify the islands, a series of arduous and often deadly little encounters that took place outside of American public consciousness. All successful counterinsurgencies require long-term contributions from loyal native troops. While the Philippine Scouts repeatedly proved their devotion to the United States, none surpassed Private José Nisperos. On September 24, 1911, Nisperos's unit, the Thirty-fourth Company of Philippine Scouts, was patrolling on the island of Basilan, just off the Mindanao coast. Suddenly a spear-wielding band of Moros attacked. Although badly wounded in the torso from Moro spear thrusts and unable to stand, and also suffering from a broken arm, Nisperos lay on the ground and continued to fire his rifle one-handed. He thereby saved his unit from being overrun. For his splendid conduct on this day, Nisperos won the Congressional Medal of Honor. He was the first Asian ever to receive this award.

THE ABILITY OF the Philippine Scouts to control the people allowed Wood to concentrate on his second major responsibility: defending the islands against foreign invasion. Following Japan's dramatic victory over Russia in 1904–5, American strategists realized that Japan's power was ascendant. To defend against a Japanese thrust, the garrison of the Philippines in mid-1906 comprised 20,043 officers and men divided into eleven infantry and four cavalry regiments along with support troops. Impressive as this total appeared—it represented about one fifth of the entire U.S. Army—Wood believed it badly deficient in terms of its officer corps. Undoubtedly, Wood's prejudice against the army's traditional seniority system colored his opinion. But in this case the facts supported Wood's desire to reform that system.

Many officers had entered the army as a result of the war with Spain, some motivated by patriotism, some pushed into military service by the ambitions of parents, and others, like Wood, because they lacked an alternative. As a group, they found the professional aspects of postwar garrison life in the Philippines uninteresting. Officers still had the daily work associated with caring for and training their troops, but there was no excitement of combat to enliven their routines. Many were growing old and lacked the physical and mental energy to do their duty. One lieutenant colonel fondly recalled his time at Fort William McKinley, south of Manila, in 1910: "This post is like a big country club. A little work in the morning. Golf, polo, tennis, riding in the hills in the afternoon. The Club at sunset. Dinner in the evening. A lazy man's paradise."[4]

Reflecting his high regard for physical culture, Wood wrote, "Troops are energetic and efficient in accordance with the energy and efficiency of the officer who commands them, and his energy and efficiency depend very much upon his physical fitness."[5] Yet an inspector general reported in 1907 that only two of nine colonels he observed were fully fit for their duties. Overall, a very high percentage of the field-grade officers—majors, lieutenant colonels, and colonels—were in too poor a physical condition to enter the field should war erupt.

The prevailing methods to remove such officers—court-martial or judgment by an officers' board that a candidate was physically or mentally

unfit—were seldom invoked. The army viewed such methods as a hu-
miliation for aging veterans who had once been acceptable or even valor-
ous combat leaders. This problem of what to do with aging officers had
first emerged in a big way following the Civil War. It still had not been
addressed forty years later. As long as an officer managed to pass the standard examinations, the presumption was that he was fit to make colonel.
But history showed that passing these exams did not necessarily equate
with being an efficient soldier. One officer bitterly complained that too
many officers were "just a larva hatched from the effort of the Civil War,
feeding upon the routine of petty administration and its paper work."[6]

Wood accepted the notion that promoting an elderly colonel as a reward for past service was sometimes acceptable. But filling the entire upper echelon of command with antiquated officers whose major objective
was to live until retirement did not serve the army or the nation well. Not
only were such men unequal to the demands of their duty, but by clog-
ging the higher ranks they blocked the possibility of advancement for
younger officers, particularly given the fact that the postwar army was
being reduced in size. Wood urged the creation of some system based on
comparative merit, because "some searching system of elimination is necessary to get rid of those who are indifferent or worthless, either through
lack of aptitude, physical or mental infirmity or weakness."[7]

The statistics were daunting. A typical officer would serve for almost
twenty-nine years at the company grade: six and a half years before being promoted from second lieutenant to first lieutenant, nine years as
first lieutenant before becoming a captain, and thirteen and a half years
at the captain's rank. Indicative of the problem was the fact that, in
Wood's time, thirteen Civil War veterans remained on active duty, including five field-grade officers and one captain. In the absence of significant reform, the army would enter its next war led by too many
antiquated, inefficient officers. Persuaded by Wood's arguments, in
1907 President Roosevelt ordered field-grade officers to take physical
fitness tests. A War Department general order followed that required
them to take annual physicals and to pass a fitness test involving thirty-
mile horseback rides on three consecutive days. While this measure did
not address the cerebral side of efficient leadership, it was a welcome
beginning.

While dealing with the reform of the officer corps, Wood also had to
cope with a criminal issue that, in his mind and that of many other

serving officers, fundamentally threatened the ability of the United States Army to conduct a counterinsurgency.

The Trials of Homer Grafton

The soldiers of Company G, Twelfth Infantry, shared the duty of guarding the Buena Vista landing on the island of Panay. The landing served as a boat dock for quartermaster supplies for the American garrison at nearby Camp Jossman. On the lazy Sunday afternoon of July 24, 1904, Private Homer E. Grafton left camp with the first relief group and arrived at the dock to perform sentry duty. The twenty-two-year-old Grafton, a native of Springfield, Missouri, was new to the Philippines. Yet already his officers judged him a good, conscientious soldier with a record devoid of the infractions that often plagued bored peacetime soldiers serving in foreign garrisons.

Private Grafton relieved the sentry and began walking his circuit. Between 2:00 and 3:00 P.M., he was halfway between the quartermaster storehouse and a coal pile when he saw two suspicious-looking Filipino men approach. Their behavior raised the hair on Grafton's neck. Recently he and his comrades had viewed the bodies of American soldiers hacked to death by Filipino civilians. Then and thereafter, tales of unwary American soldiers killed by bolo-wielding Filipinos who had "run amok" circulated through Company G's barracks. Grafton did not intend to become another victim. The two Filipinos clambered over a stone wall and advanced up the road toward him. Grafton later testified: "One of the natives reached in his bosom and pulled out a knife and immediately he changed the handle and concealed the knife under his arm from my view."[8]

Grafton said that the men approached closer. Suddenly the knife-armed man brandished his weapon with the tip of the blade pointing toward him and charged. The second Filipino was close on his heels. When the charging Filipino was within four paces, Grafton raised his rifle to his shoulder, chambered a round, and fired. Grafton's assailant dropped. He saw the second Filipino pause. Grafton perceived that this man was unarmed. He aimed carefully. The second man ran toward him for a step or two and then turned away. Grafton squeezed the trigger and then called for help.

The commander of the security detachment, Lieutenant Harrel, came running, accompanied by several soldiers. Harrel looked around and saw that whatever had happened was over. For the next forty-five minutes the lieutenant examined the scene and then recorded what he found. Harrel saw the bodies where they fell: one in the middle of the road with a ten-inch knife lying next to him some ten feet from where Grafton had stood, and the second against a wall thirty feet away.

This evidence emerged when, according to army procedure, Grafton was tried before a general court-martial under the Articles of War on the charge of "unlawfully, wilfully, and feloniously" killing two civilians.[9] It turned out that the deceased, Florentino Castro and Felix Villanueva, were employed by the army's quartermaster service. Grafton pled self-defense. His attorney pointed out that Grafton's service record was excellent. The military court exonerated the private.

The Philippine court system—part of the American-run civil government—saw the case differently. On November 28, 1904, it charged Grafton with murder. The commander of the Division of the Philippines, General Adna Chaffee, refused to hand Grafton over to civil authorities on the grounds that he had already been tried and found innocent and that the civil authorities had no jurisdiction in this case. The civil government overrode Chaffee's refusal and began a new trial.

The essence of the government's charge was that while Grafton might have been justified in killing Castro, Villanueva was shot while running away, and this amounted to murder. The court asked, was the shooting justified?

Upon cross-examination Grafton added details about shooting at Villanueva: "He was not coming toward me when I fired; he jumped back toward the quartermaster building before I fired; he had no weapon that I saw; he was crouching."[10] Grafton asserted that he fired two shots. Yet evidence provided by Lieutenant Harrel demonstrated that the two victims lay thirty feet apart and that there were two bullet holes in the wall above Villanueva's body. This supported the claim of Filipino bystanders that there were more than two shots fired. Indeed, on several points government witnesses disputed Grafton's testimony. Two Filipino eyewitnesses swore that the knife was carried by Villanueva, not by Castro; that he was trimming his nails with it; that he left the road only after the soldier pointed his rifle at him; and that three shots were fired, two of them at Villanueva, who dropped first.

Yet this purported eyewitness testimony failed to square with the position of the knife, which lay between the sentry and Castro, and with the many military witnesses who said that they heard only two shots in spite of the singular fact that the two bullet holes in the storehouse wall were both immediately above Villanueva's body

One more piece of evidence emerged: immediately after the shooting, a Filipino civil justice who was seeking to take Castro's dying statement was forcibly warned by Harrel "to keep out of it."[11]

The civil court noted these inconsistencies. It concluded that Grafton's depiction of events was in error and that it was exceedingly unlikely that Castro was trying to attack Grafton. However, it also said: "A soldier guarding the property of the Government and the lives of his comrades can not be held to a too rigid accountability if he acts in the honest exercise of his judgment and with reasonable regard to human life." Thus the court absolved Grafton of blame for shooting Castro. However, it viewed the second shooting differently:

> In our judgment the observation by the defendant that the native, instead of advancing upon him was fleeing from him and was protecting himself in a crouching attitude against the wall, was sufficient to apprise him that there was no danger and to deprive him of any justification for the shooting. The sacredness of Government property or of the life of the soldier is not greater than that of the life of a citizen, and a sentry with a loaded rifle in his hand in the full possession of his senses, is bound to use reasonable judgment, and is accountable for human life taken by him without the justification of immediate defense of himself or of his charge. The great trust conferred upon him is the measure of his high responsibility and he may not act without forethought in the heat of strife. This soldier, observing that Felix [Villanueva] had fled from him and had reached a point where flight was no longer possible, should have been conscious that he was in no bodily danger and he should not have fired the second shot.[12]

Grafton's lawyer claimed that this charge represented double jeopardy. Furthermore, he asserted that the Philippine courts had no legal jurisdiction to bring this case because the incident took place on a U.S. military reservation. The judges rejected both claims and convicted Grafton of homicide—a lesser offense than murder—and sentenced him to a term of imprisonment of twelve years and one day.

Grafton's lawyers appealed. On April 3, 1906, the Philippine Supreme Court heard the case. The divided court, by a vote of four to three, rejected Grafton's defense of double jeopardy and affirmed the sentence. The opinion of the majority, all of whom were Filipino, cited specific United States case law as the basis for their decision. The dissenting judges, all of whom were American, wrote that they believed Villanueva participated in wrongful aggression. Therefore, they had to consider three things spelled out in the statutes: whether there was unlawful aggression, an absence of previous provocation, and reasonable necessity for the means employed to repel the aggression. The first two answers were obviously yes. So to the dissenting American judges everything hinged on whether Grafton acted appropriately.

The American judges agreed that with hindsight, the killing of Villanueva was not necessary and that Grafton committed an error of judgment in firing at him. But, they stressed, hindsight was irrelevant because the case had to be judged as it presented itself to Grafton, upon whom an unlawful aggression was being made by two men acting together. The courts relieved him from responsibility for the first killing. To hold him responsible for the second, which occurred about five seconds later, required him to exercise serene judgment at a time of tremendous stress. The American judges argued that this was both beyond realistic expectation and outside of established case law. Their dissent did not alter the majority opinion.

AMERICAN SERVICEMEN IN the Philippines, particularly those in Moroland, closely followed the trial. After all, better than anyone they understood that but for the grace of God they could have been on duty that day on the Buena Vista docks. The news from Manila infuriated them. They perceived a terrible miscarriage of justice made worse by the fact that Grafton had not even had a jury trial. An angry General Wood wrote that the case "is one of vital interest to the Army" since its principles would have a "profound effect upon the performance of duty by officers and soldiers of the United States Army acting in conjunction with the civil authorities."[13]

A colonel serving in the Philippines expanded on this topic, articulating a position that would speak to American counterinsurgencies more than one hundred years in the future: "Officers feel that their official reputations are in jeopardy as his [Grafton's] investigations are entirely one-sided and as is well known manufactured evidence can be obtained from native sources."[14] Soldiers began contributing to a subscription that eventually raised almost $15,000 to pay lawyers so Grafton's case could proceed to the United States Supreme Court. Thereafter, the law lecturer at the Army War College was made chairman of a committee representing the whole army for the purpose of obtaining top-notch legal defense for Grafton. In turn, the committee hired a prominent Kansas City lawyer, John Harrison Atwood, to argue the case.

Grafton's actions became the basis for one of the most celebrated cases in the history of military law. The U.S. Supreme Court considered two propositions: Did the Philippine court have legal jurisdiction to bring the case against an American soldier, and did the trial place Grafton in double jeopardy? The Court dealt with the first question by citing precedent regarding the dual sovereignty doctrine that limited this doctrine to cases where "the two entities that seek successively to prosecute a defendant for the same course of conduct can be termed separate sovereigns."[15] To be considered as such, the two entities had to draw their authority to punish the offender from distinct sources of power. However, both the military court and the Philippine civil court derived their authority from the United States. Because the incident took place on a military reservation, the judgments of a general court-martial were appropriate and a civil tribunal could not disregard them. The Court's second decision logically flowed from its first, namely, that Private Grafton's constitutional rights had been violated since he had been put twice in jeopardy for the same offense. (Long after the incident, the Grafton case continued to influence justice, as on June 28, 1993, when the U.S. Supreme Court again considered the issue of double jeopardy and cited the Grafton case as precedent.)[16]

On May 24, 1918, General John Pershing published the latest casualties for the U.S. Army in France. The list included four killed in action, nine mortal wounds, four accidental deaths, sixteen severely wounded, one slightly wounded, and ten dead from disease. Among those in the last category was Private Homer E. Grafton. He had returned to his old regiment in the fall of 1915. Perhaps he was among the Americans outraged by the recent sinking of the *Lusitania* and reports of German atrocities in Belgium, or perhaps he was simply down on his luck. At any event, his previous military experience did not impress the army, which inducted him as a thirty-three-year-old private in a machine gun company. Two and a half years later he was dead from pneumonia.

FIFTEEN

"Sponge Cake, Coffee, Cigars"

*Asleep in the jungle camps at night, the Americans' first warning
would be the gurgle of an expiring sentry and then the cat-footed
Moros would be upon them with flashing kris.*

—Victor Hurley

Garrison Life in Moroland

THE THREE-DAY AGRICULTURAL FAIR held in Zamboanga in February
1907 was a great success. A Monday night ball at the Army and Navy Club
inaugurated the fair. When the fairgrounds themselves opened, Tasker
Bliss was the main speaker. According to the *Mindanao Herald*, the
Americans and Europeans in his audience greeted his speech enthusiastically. Bliss's mention of Leonard Wood received "tumultuous applause."[1]
An estimated 20,000 Moros attended the fair. Around the fairgrounds,
Moro datus vied with one another to present the best exhibit. Foreign
merchants inspected their wares and dreamed of future profits. A grand
ball of nations closed the fair. The singing of "Home Sweet Home" ended
the ball.

Bliss was enjoying his assignment. He studied Moro folklore and
learned to speak conversational Malay. He hosted regular dinner parties

attended by a stimulating mix of American and foreign dignitaries, explorers, scientists, businessmen, missionaries, and fellow officers. He described to his wife a typical dinner menu: "cocktail; tomato soup, toast, peanuts; chicken and mushroom timbales, white wine; roast chicken, gravy, potatoes, peas; asparagus salad, chocolate ice cream, sponge cake, coffee, cigars." His only complaint was that the chicken meat was all white, which he attributed to the rice diet of the poultry.[2]

When his family was with him, Bliss and his wife particularly liked walking along pristine beaches collecting seashells. Indeed, most military families stationed in Zamboanga perceived that they lived in a tropical paradise. Here the threat of juramentados had so receded that families enjoyed lives free of fear. Their young children swam off the beach, sailed native craft on the canal, rode horses through nearby plantations, and roller-skated on the sidewalks. Zamboanga so enchanted a young army bride, Carolyn Richards Whipple, that more than six decades later she recalled, "It is the only place I ever was homesick for."[3]

Life was very different in the hinterland, as everyone discovered as soon as they left the security of the coastal garrisons. Army engineers labored to build corduroy roads to link the remote posts. The Pickering family rode a springless army ambulance to Major Abner Pickering's duty station at Camp Marahui on Lake Lanao. For Mrs. Pickering and her young girls the exotic journey was one of intense excitement. They

Zamboanga square with bandstand built for July 4 festivities.

thought that they were among the first white women to enter this country. The mule-drawn ambulance made slow progress on the primitive,
uneven road. The passengers experienced "a continuous bumping of
heads against the top stays of the roof . . . When we finally reached the
end of that awful corduroy section, we thought the soft mud of the next
section of road would be like heaven."[4] Instead, the ambulance wheels
bogged deep into the mud and the mules sank to their bellies. The
sixteen-mile trip to the first way station took fifteen hours.

The next day the journey resumed, this time following a trail cut out
of the side of a heavily forested mountain. The road wound through
towering mahogany and mango trees covered with brightly colored orchids. Monkeys chattered from the treetops. The ambulance's passage
disturbed brilliantly plumed tropical birds. A thick undergrowth of
brush, tall jungle grass, and bamboo filled the spaces beneath the jungle canopy, reducing visibility to only a few feet and providing perfect
concealment for an ambush.

Family quarters at Camp Marahui consisted of a palm-leaf-roofed hut
on stilts into which crowded two families. The families were fortunate if
the adults had their own bedroom. Everyone shared the communal living room, dining room, and kitchen. The climate, at 2,200 feet above
sea level, was cool. The wind easily penetrated the hut's grass sides. To
warm themselves in the morning and evening, families burned char-
coal in large brass urns purchased from the Moros.

Soldiers had cleared the trees and underbrush from around the camp's
barbed-wire perimeter to create unobstructed fields of fire. No one ventured into the jungle unless he was carrying a weapon or, in the case of
an officer's wife, accompanied by an armed escort. Each night at least
one hundred men mounted guard. It was dangerous duty and the men
of the Twenty-second Infantry loathed it: "Those Moros were just like
snakes in the grass; they would crawl up the side of the mountain and
lay in wait for the sentry, and as he passed they would jump up and take
one slash with their long sharp bolos, slashing at the arm which held
the rifle, off would come the arm dropping the gun, and the Moro
would grab the gun and be gone down the side of the mountain and out
of sight before the sentry had a chance to shoot."[5]

One night one of the young Pickering girls awoke to a suspicious
sound beneath her hut. She alerted her father, who quietly grabbed his
revolver, went out the back door, saw a Moro lurking beneath the hut,

and fired. He missed and the Moro escaped. Each night every family placed a lantern and a box of matches near the front door. Whenever the trumpet sounded the call to arms, which typically happened about twice a month, a family member would rush to light the lantern while the officer dressed. Then the officer seized the lantern and headed for his duty station. No one stepped outside without a lantern because the sentries had orders to call out halt once and then shoot to kill. Given how experience made them jumpy, their warning shout and the discharge of their rifles were often nearly simultaneous.

To help defend remote camps, Bliss ordered that each regular company have at least four repeating shotguns. Bliss explained that soldiers had found them invaluable in high grass and underbrush because "they stop men in their tracks."[6] But neither exceptional vigilance, extensive fortifications, nor weaponry stopped all Moro infiltration. Consequently, part of the evening's routine for married couples living inside the wire was to move the beds away from their nipa hut's exterior wall to avoid a possible thrust from a juramentado's bolo.

The port of Malabang, the regimental headquarters for the Twenty-third Infantry, was nominally safer. Here too the perimeter fence was heavily guarded. After Moros wounded a sentry one night, an officer and his wife took to sleeping with pistols next to their beds. The wife found this so distressing that she compelled her husband to resign from the army after he completed his tour of duty. At another base, young Rita Hines experienced a moment of sheer terror one morning when she awoke to the sounds of voices on the veranda. She ran outside to see her small daughter happily showing her dolls to half a dozen Moros who mysteriously had appeared. Before Hines could react, the Moros cheerfully chorused, "Good-bye Babee" and left.[7] From the time of its birth, the U.S. Army had allowed officers' wives to live on base with them. In Moroland, wives quartered in Mindanao's interior were among the last in army history to endure life on a wild frontier.

The presence of American women constrained officers, whether wed or not, from chasing after local Filipino women. American women made it clear that to do so risked certain ostracism and social annihilation. For officers assigned to coastal garrisons, a break in the routine came twice a month when the supply steamer arrived from Manila. It carried American girls who worked in the American administration and were eager to see the exotic Sulu islands. The officers arranged dances at their club where besotted young men, "to whom a pretty American girl looked like an angel from heaven," plied them with presents—brass trays, copper bowls, and carved betel nut boxes—in hopes of winning their attention.[8] But the numbers were not in the officers' favor, and time was short, since the girls always booked a round-trip voyage. When the steamer's whistle sounded, they were gone. The inland garrisons enjoyed far fewer comforts. Twice-monthly supply convoys guarded by a troop of cavalry traveled to each post. They provided the only break in the isolation. As one colonel ruefully acknowledged, Camp Marahui was "long on climate and scenery, but damn short on fresh meat and newspapers!"[9]

In the American army, rank-and-file soldiers had few of the luxuries or social comforts experienced by their officers. The monotony of garrison life in the tropics set in. There were many empty hours, so soldiers looked outside the wire for diversions. Noncommissioned officers and enlisted men were not constrained by the prejudices of American women, and a handful found the casual Moro acceptance of polygamy perfectly agreeable. But most knew better than to risk a husband's rage by trying to consort with Moro women. If the soldiers looked hard enough, occasionally a white planter would offer a Moro woman whom he had purchased—an illicit slave trade continued outside the gaze of American authorities—for a carnal transaction. For most of the men, a tour of duty in Moroland meant long periods of celibacy. To relieve pent-up energies, men played baseball during the day and organized minstrel shows at night. During Wood's tenure of command, every post was required to hold a sports field day once a month. Because Bliss had no interest in sports, this practice waned. In addition to sports, soldiers turned to their other traditional means for coping with the absence of women and the lack of entertainment: alcohol.

Army-issue alcohol consisted of weak, warm beer. When Pershing returned to Mindanao in 1911 he would recommend that post exchanges establish enlisted men's clubs and serve beer and wine. Although Pershing had a sincere interest in enlisted men's welfare, his real motivation was to keep them from frequenting grog shops and brothels. Improvements in the living standards for enlisted would come in the future. In 1907, soldiers tried other means to obtain strong drink, and those means sometimes proved deadly. At one camp, a sergeant and his command claimed that they killed several Moros in self-defense. The commanding officer who investigated the incident concluded that the sergeant had been buying alcohol from the Moros, disagreed about the price, killed the Moros, and then claimed self-defense. This type of incident was not uncommon on any country's military base on foreign soil, where bored soldiers committed crimes against the local population. It was another cost paid when an occupying power tried to impose its control. The monotony of unoccupied hours led to tragedy at Camp Keithley when soldiers tried to distill alcohol and the resultant brew of methyl alcohol killed eleven men.

And the Moros killed a few more. In the garrison town of Parang, shortly before dawn one day the occupants of a squad tent were awakened when a private shouted, "I am stabbed." His disbelieving comrades told him to be quiet, he was having a nightmare. Suddenly another private groaned loudly as a Moro spear inflicted a mortal wound. The remaining men inside the tent rose from their beds and began fighting back. A guard at the front of the tent fired his revolver and alerted the entire camp. In the ensuing confusion the three assailants escaped.

The Bliss Way

Bliss was perfectly aware of the violence, having been shot at while inspecting the garrisons around Lake Lanao. However, to give his own strategy time to succeed, he needed to keep his superiors, particularly Leonard Wood, from meddling. Bliss understood that in official channels the best possible news he could report was that he was keeping the Moros quiet. So his reports emphasized economic and social progress while minimizing the violence even to the point of claiming that government officials could travel throughout most of Moroland with only a small constabulary escort.

By skillfully managing the army bureaucracy, Bliss was able to hold true to his convictions about how to manage the Moro problem. He learned, as had Scott, Bullard, and Pershing, that dealing with the Moros required enormous patience. Now that he occupied Wood's former residence, all Bliss had to do to remind himself of this fact was walk into the back garden and gaze over the water at the distant island of Basilan.

For four years following the death of an iron-willed ruler, a succession fight had raged on Basilan. The American-appointed headman was a weak leader, and the island's twenty thousand Moros grew restive. Into the void stepped an Islamic religious leader known as the Salip Aguil. At one time the Salip, an honorific term referring to Aguil's position within Basilan's religious hierarchy, had allied himself with the pirate chieftain Jikiri. Then and thereafter, Aguil's activities were more akin to those of a gangster than those of a guerrilla leader. American troops hunted in vain for him, managing only to burn down his hilltop home. In early May 1908, Bliss sent word that he wanted to meet, and offered the Salip a safe-conduct pass. While Aguil deliberated, the Americans ceased patrolling. Six days later a courier presented a letter from Aguil saying that he was too frightened to attend a meeting with Bliss. Two days later, Aguil reversed course and said he would come in two days. At a meeting on May 19, Aguil agreed to bring his family and followers to a 2:00 P.M. meeting the next day. True to his word, more or less—the Moro measure of time was how long it took to boil a pot of rice—at 4:00 P.M. on the designated day the Salip Aguil and two hundred armed followers arrived.

His arrival was Bliss's reward for three weeks of patient negotiation. One major hurdle remained, however: The Salip agreed to meet Bliss at the local market but demanded that he appear unarmed and without an escort. Bliss, perhaps consciously emulating Pershing, accepted the risk. The meeting took place peacefully. Bliss optimistically reported to the captain who had been chasing Aguil that the Salip had agreed to surrender his firearms. The captain skeptically replied that if that were so, it would not take him more than a day to collect all the arms.

On June 1, Aguil returned to town and acted as if his meeting with Bliss had never occurred. Instead, he spoke to the captain about his intentions to rebuild his home. The captain ignored this gambit and told him to surrender his guns within two days or Bliss would assume that he did not intend to act in good faith. The newest deadline came and went. On June 5, the Americans resumed active patrolling with orders to kill or capture Aguil and his followers. Verbal orders to the American soldiers included the stipulation to destroy food supplies and burn buildings where Aguil had been operating. On June 6, an American patrol assembled for this purpose. The patrol's commander deceived his Moro guide by telling him that he was on a friendly visit to the Salip. The guide dutifully led the patrol to Aguil's home, where his wives said that he was absent buying food. The American officer replied that he would wait for Aguil because he had an important message to deliver. Early the next morning, Aguil appeared and the patrol compelled him to surrender his barong, a Moro's badge of manhood. The Americans then burned his home and took him and his family back to their base. During the next two days, American patrols continued burning buildings throughout the district where Aguil had been operating. On June 11, Bliss arrived on Basilan and saw that the prisoners, including Aguil, had been put to work sawing wood to build barracks.

To complete the job of pacifying Basilan, the Americans commissioned a Moro leader as a deputy sheriff and gave him orders to arrest or kill Aguil's remaining followers. On June 23, the American district governor had a long interview with Aguil and persuaded him to serve as guide to the outlaw camp under risk of death. The next day Aguil led the patrol into an ambush. In response, the soldiers received orders "to fire on all natives and identify afterwards."[10] Having inflicted an unknown number of casualties while establishing a new, more brutal approach to pacification, the patrol took Aguil back to their base, where he remained a prisoner. Eventually, relentless pressure from three regular companies and a sizable detachment of Philippine Scouts killed or dispersed Aguil's followers. Then the Philippine Scouts established six outposts across the island. Their presence slowly brought peace and order back to Basilan.

The manner in which Bliss handled trouble spots such as Basilan had its critics. Eddy Schück, a translator and guide who worked for the Americans, wrote to Hugh Scott, now serving as superintendent at West Point, that the Moros on Jolo continued to recall Scott's tour of duty with wistfulness. His successors just did not have his knack: "Some lose their temper whilst talking with the Moros, a thing you never did. Some threaten and do not follow it out, a thing you always did. These two points will make or ruin any native country. When you were here and sent word to a chief to come, he would be there at the appointed hour, but now 5 letters would not bring him in, not because they want to fight but just because they know that they can do it without being punished."[11]

More important to Bliss was the fact that his immediate superior, General Wood, continued to disagree about how Bliss dealt with Moro "criminal" activity. In Bliss's view, the best way to end intermittent Moro violence was to disperse the American garrisons into much smaller outposts spread throughout the hinterland. This was the opposite of the Wood strategy. One consequence of Wood's policy to concentrate American garrisons was that those Moros outside of direct contact with the bases seldom saw any Americans. Individual datus easily persuaded their credulous subjects that the Americans either were all dead or had left the islands. In the absence of a visible American presence, the people reverted to crime. The disregard for unseen authority inevitably led to violence against American troops and, under Wood's reign, necessitated a large-scale American military intervention.

Even though he knew that it went squarely against Wood's strategy, Bliss bravely posited an alternative approach: "Our present garrisons, were they broken up into smaller detachments, could be so widely distributed throughout the Moro country as to enforce continued respect for the law, with the probability that there would never be occasion for military operations at all. Armies have before been used in this way, resulting in a civilizing and peace-producing effect, and it could be so done here."[12] Bliss was alluding to recent American history to support his assertion. During the conventional phase of the Philippine Insurrection, American soldiers operated from fifty-three dispersed bases. In response to the outbreak of guerrilla warfare, the War Department sent substantial reinforcements, dispersed across guerrilla territory to occupy 413 bases.

However well reasoned his arguments, Bliss was never going to win an important strategic debate with Wood. He could and did keep American regulars out of large-scale combat during the entire time he served as governor of Moro Province. Still, the Bliss way also ultimately relied upon sanctions imposed by armed authority. Consequently, American-led forces continued routinely to kill Moros while pursuing the elusive goal of pacifying Moroland.

SIXTEEN

Jungle Patrols

*Do not come in the night, pigs. If you do I will crush you. Come in
the daytime so the Moros can see the dead Americans. All of you
that come I will give as Sungud [marriage portion] to the Virgin.
Durum pacal [the kris that cuts fast] is ready.*

—The Lion of God to the district governor

The Moro Constabulary

DURING HIS TIME AS GOVERNOR OF Moro Province, Bliss treated most
Moro violence as crimes to be dealt with by the police force. The U.S.
Army remained in the background, available if needed, but ideally kept
in reserve. This avoided casualties while giving time for green, new units
to obtain seasoning. The regiments with experience in Moroland had
rotated back to stateside garrisons and been replaced with inexperienced
units. Bliss was reluctant to expose them before they became acclimated
to the nature of campaigning in Moroland. He complained about newly
arrived, overly aggressive American officers who seemed predisposed to
kill any Moro on sight. In response, a regular army colonel queried Bliss:
"If I understand the policy from above alright, it is to refrain from bringing on hostilities unless some vital principle is at stake or some of these
headmen act in defiance of United States authority."[1] The rub came when

Moros continued to behave defiantly. To maintain law and order, Bliss relied upon the Philippine Constabulary.

The successful pacification of die-hard insurgents and outlaws in the northern Philippines allowed the constabulary to switch its focus to Moroland beginning in 1906. For the next bloody decade they were the frontline troops in the fight against the Moros. Constabulary patrols penetrated Mindanao's uncharted interior, sometimes entering places where no white man had ever been. Supported by the Philippine Scouts, the constabulary fought a smaller-scale version of Wood's punitive campaign.

Back on September 1, 1903, Moroland had raised its first Philippine Constabulary Corps under the command of thirty-seven-year-old Colonel James Harbord. Harbord's father had served with an Illinois cavalry regiment in the Civil War. Like so many young men of his generation who grew up in a household with a military background, Harbord badly wanted to join the military. He was the highest-ranking student officer of Kansas State Agricultural College's Cadet Corps and later tied for first place in a competitive examination for the U.S. Military Academy at West Point. When the other contestant received the only available appointment, Harbord promptly enlisted as a private in the regular army. When he achieved an assignment to the constabulary, Harbord had a forum to display his outstanding organizational qualities and personnel management skills. He accomplished a task that skeptics considered impossible: organizing an effective constabulary on Mindanao.

During the fight against the Filipino insurgents, the Americans had weighed the potential value of employing native troops against the dangers of disloyalty and lack of control. A handful of farsighted officers had exploited ethnic divisions and elevated minority groups to positions of power. The result were famous native units such as the Macabebe Scouts, who rendered invaluable service suppressing the insurgents. These native soldiers shared the same religion as their American officers. Moros, of course, did not. To control Moros, whose every instinct, or so the Americans believed, was dominated by the Sulu proverb "Big fish eat little fish," seemed like an infinitely more difficult challenge.

Regardless, for Harbord the advantages were obvious. Compared to Americans, the natives knew the local geography, with its maze of narrow jungle tracks and footpaths through the swamps, like an open book. They spoke the language and, more important, understood the mind of the Moro. A Moro employed in the Philippine Constabulary would receive a wage that, while small by American standards, was attractive by local standards. Over time, Harbord hoped that service in the constabulary would be a source of personal pride and bind loyalties to the central government in Manila. For certain it would keep otherwise "idle hands" out of mischief, since recruiting the most ambitious Moros would deplete the ranks of potential insurgents.

Bliss's strategic preference for dispersing his forces in small outposts so they would live in close contact with the people also applied to the constabulary. In once restive Cotabato, a typical constabulary post numbered only one sergeant and four privates. Yet such outposts proved sufficient to investigate routine criminal activity. In November 1907, a constabulary sergeant led a patrol to investigate water buffalo thefts by a robber named Baguisan. The constables captured Baguisan, who revealed the names of his band. The next day the constables returned to arrest the rest of the outlaws, exchanged fire with the bandits, and returned to their post unharmed. It was a sign of the times that such a small patrol could demonstrate so much initiative and survive. It was also notable that American officials followed Bliss's policy and refused to escalate such small affairs into major confrontations. The Bliss way soon paid dividends: In 1908 only five assassinations and three homicides occurred in all the Cotabato region.

The Exploits of Leonard Furlong

Every war produces a number of legendary heroes, men whose exploits astonish both their peers and the public. In Cotabato District a ninety-five-man constabulary detachment occupied four stations. Joining the constabulary were two young, promising second lieutenants: Henry Gilsheuser, a big-boned, tall, blond German with prior service in the Prussian army, and Leonard Furlong. According to one of his officers, Gilsheuser combined German thoroughness and method tempered by American experience and tolerance. Known to his friends as "Nardo," Furlong was "a slim, dark, American boy, very carefully groomed and sporting a tiny mustache."[2] At age fifteen he had joined the U.S. Navy. By age twenty-one he was fighting the Sioux in Minnesota. The next year he accompanied the first American troops to land on Mindanao, and thereafter served with the constabulary, first during Wood's time of command and then during the Bliss era.

July 1904 found Furlong stationed at Camp Kudarangan, the operating base for three regular infantry companies and two Philippine Scout companies. At this time Datu Ali was still at large. Wood ordered patrols to explore the region and determine Moro strength. Kudarangan was a particularly tough nut to crack. The region featured a vast swamp covered with tigbao grass that grew ten to twenty feet high. The natives moved through the swamp on a network of narrow trails known only to them. Kudarangan was a place where a small party of warriors could use their local knowledge to ambush or evade a much larger force. Only two months earlier, Datu Ali's men had ambushed Company F of the Seventeenth Infantry, an action known to the Americans as the Simpetan Massacre. Among those assigned for the next probe into the Kudarangan was Second Lieutenant Furlong.

Furlong had to make an intuitive decision about how many men to take on patrol. Too many and the Moros would not be tempted into a fight; too few and the Moros could overwhelm the patrol. Furlong lacked the experience to inform his decision and took just fourteen of the constabulary. They were all new recruits with less than two months of experience and included several Moros who were more familiar with krises than carbines. A seven-mile probe into the heart of the Kudarangan swamps took the patrol to an area dominated by one of Datu Ali's most renowned subordinates. An unknown number of Moros ambushed the patrol, beginning a running fight that lasted all the way back to camp. The regular American infantry greeted the returning patrol—who carried the bodies of two of their own along with several captured firearms—with the respect due to fellow soldiers who had bravely endured a harrowing ambush. Furlong's first independent patrol was the first of a six-year pattern of leading his men where no one else was willing to go.

Furlong's absolute fearlessness both attracted and terrified the Moros who served under him in the constabulary. As a warrior culture, they admired and respected his courage. As men whose lives were in Furlong's hands, they wondered about his reckless disregard for his own well-being. They suspected he had supernatural powers, including an anting-anting to ward off bullets and kris thrusts. His foes agreed, calling him a devil-warrior. His fellow officers knew him as an indefatigable hiker with a deep reserve of stamina belied by his slight appearance, a peerless mapmaker, and an expert pistol shot—all prized talents in the trackless swamp and jungle, where the first sign of an enemy usually came at point-blank range. But they too wondered about Furlong's judgment. What kind of man would lead a small patrol into a place where a regular company would hesitate to go?

Furlong's subsequent conduct reinforced these questions. He routinely led from the front—a quality shared by many officers—but as his patrol entered a combat zone he seemed to become like a Viking berserker. As his constables advanced toward a hostile cotta, he would run ahead and sail his broad-brimmed hat over the wall. He told his constabulary that if any of them found his hat it was theirs. They responded by vying with one another to secure this trophy. Meanwhile, Furlong began climbing the cotta's parapet. His startling composure in the resulting swirling melees amazed both his men and his enemies. He always regained his hat before any of his men, killing enemies along the way. Word spread among his enemies that the appearance of Furlong's hat within their cotta's walls was a harbinger of certain death.

Furlong was the only constabulary officer to be recommended on four separate occasions for the organization's highest award, the Medal of Valor. He earned one of those on the morning of July 9, 1906. At the head of an eleven-man patrol, only six of whom carried firearms, he appeared on the outskirts of Bugasan at daybreak. His mission was to capture or kill the men who had murdered a private in the Nineteenth Infantry. The patrol approached a house pinpointed by an informant and summoned the

"Nardo" Furlong and Moro Constabulary, 1905.

occupants to surrender. A band of some one hundred armed men emerged from various buildings, surrounded the patrol, and attacked. Furlong had his men form a tight wedge and put himself at the apex. He personally slew six Moros as he led the wedge through a wall of krismen and broke through the Moro encirclement. Having faced seemingly certain annihilation, the patrol escaped with no losses.

Later that same month Furlong led a patrol to meet with a notorious Moro leader, the sultan of Buldung. The sultan invited the patrol into his cotta for a conference. It was a trap. Scores of krismen attacked Furlong's men. Outnumbered twenty to one or more, Furlong backed his men into a corner against the cotta's interior wall and held his position with revolver and rifle fire during a terrible hour of carnage.

From April 28 through July 5, 1907, Furlong conducted an extended campaign in the notorious Taraca Valley. One day Furlong's constabulary received fire from the fifteen-foot-high walls of a nearby cotta nestled against the Rumayas River. A deep moat protected the cotta's three landward faces. Sharpened bamboo stakes guarded the moat. The Moros greeted the ritual American summons to surrender with their usual taunts and renewed rifle fire. Furlong chose the main gate as the point to assault. He and five of his men hefted a large log, braved the Moro fire, and tried to break down the door. The defenders' fire killed one constable and wounded two more. Repulsed at the gate, Furlong did what he should have done in the first place and ordered a thorough reconnaissance. One of his men crawled through the underbrush and found a gap in the bam-

Officers on break, Taraca campaign, April 1904.

boo stakes near the river. Furlong led an assault through this gap and up and over the cotta wall. As was usual, he was first inside the cotta, where he killed the majority of the seventeen Moros who died defending it.

Furlong's conduct along the Rumayas River was no different from his behavior in countless prior combats, but this time he earned the Medal of Valor. A regular army captain told newspaper reporters that Furlong "deserves several medals for valor instead of one. He is deserving: he is efficient: he is loyal: he is gallant: he is energetic, and all of these in a more than ordinary degree."[3] Although no one realized it at the time, Furlong's career had reached its apex.

He continued to lead his Moro Constabulary as he completed a six-year span of combat duty without a furlough. The strain of repeated jungle patrols wore on him even as other young constabulary officers emerged to vie with Furlong as premier warriors. Worse, to this prideful, thin-skinned man, his superiors questioned his conduct in the Taraca Valley. A humiliating court of inquiry followed in 1910, and although Furlong was cleared of all "these damn rotten charges," the unwelcome publicity associated with his trial seemed to change him.[4] After another tour of duty on Mindanao, his increasingly unstable behavior caused his superiors to send him to Manila for enforced rest. On the evening of July 8, 1911, he dined as usual at the officers' mess. Nothing seemed amiss. The next night he committed suicide. He was thirty-four years old.

When American writers interviewed elderly Moros in the 1930s, the faces of old warriors grew keen as they related stories of battle and conflict when the kris had been the law of the land and the measure of a man's courage. They told stories of Nardo Furlong, bestowing on him the highest praise they could give: He was the most desperate fighting man of all.

As TIME PASSED, other lieutenants serving with the constabulary emerged as highly effective fighters. Some even matched Furlong's reckless dash. At least one surpassed Furlong as a stone-cold killer. Oscar Preuss was a mercenary, drawn to his trade not for pay but for the joy of legalized killing. He had served in the Prussian Lancers during the Boxer Rebellion and as an infantry lieutenant in East Africa, and he had participated in various revolutions in Central and South America. Joining the constabulary in 1907, Preuss achieved a legendary reputation as a ruthless fighter. His reputation finally caught up with him and he too was ordered to appear in Manila before an official inquiry. Purportedly, a colonel at the inquiry said, "Captain Preuss, it is said that you, personally, have killed 250 Moros. What is your statement, sir, to that report."

Preuss drew himself to attention and replied in a calm but angry voice, "The report is in error, colonel; my count places the total at 265."[5]

The ability of Moro men to serve effectively in the Philippine Constabulary encouraged authorities to expand the use of Moro auxiliaries. At the end of 1908, Congress authorized the formation of a Philippine Scout Company with the rank and file recruited exclusively among Moros. To prevent one tribe from dominating the Scout Company, American officers traveled widely in their efforts to attract recruits. Authorities sent Lieutenant Allan Fletcher to Buldung to recruit in March 1909. Fletcher found the countryside in virtual revolt. While his small recruiting party was eating a meal, thirteen juramentados rushed out of the jungle and attacked with kris, kampilan, spear, and dagger. Fletcher's men killed all thirteen at the cost of one dead and six wounded. As Fletcher recalled, "Then and there the idea of getting recruits from Buldung was abandoned."[6]

Enough Moro recruits were found elsewhere to form the Scout Company. They took the usual enlistment oath, and in addition a pandita conducted an oath-taking ceremony during which the recruit swore on the holy Koran. Still, arming native troops on Mindanao was a calculated risk. Young Moro men who wanted to marry had to obtain a considerable dowry to win a wife. Sale of a modern firearm easily covered this cost. Over time, the Moro Scout Company proved immensely effective. Most men held to their oaths. The company had eighteen men desert, and lost thirteen rifles and 1,050 cartridges. To recover the deserters and their equipment, the Americans offered sizable rewards. The practice of putting a price on the heads of the deserters proved successful when civilians appeared toting sacks with the heads of the disloyal scouts. In this fashion all the rifles were recovered and all the deserters either killed or captured.

Effective administrative responses to issues such as desertion, coupled with good leadership at the patrol level, made the decision to arm native troops a successful component of American counterinsurgency strategy in Moro Province.

THE OFFICIAL DISPATCHES from the army officers in charge of the Philippines painted a pleasing picture of peace and progress. Leonard Wood reported: "On the whole, the conditions throughout this department are very favorable, although, in view of the fact that there is a large Mohammedan element, unexpected disturbances may occur as the result of the action of religious fanatics recently returned from Mecca, or others striving to gain popularity through preaching resistance to the government. The Moro people are a brave and hardy people, and it is believed that every day makes them more difficult to move against the government, now that they are convinced that it will deal fairly with them. Each of the great Moro centers has attempted concerted resistance to the government and each has met with exceedingly severe reverses, which, it is believed, will prevent any further organized resistance on a large scale."[7] In turn, Tasker Bliss reported progress in collecting the cedula, "not withstanding considerable opposition on the part of the Moros to the payment of any tax which to them indicated their subordination to other authorities than those to whom they were accustomed to pay tribute."[8]

Wood and Bliss were right about the progress. Increasing numbers of prominent Moro leaders willingly cooperated with the Americans. They had benefited from American-provided security and enhanced trading opportunities. Datu Piang had exhibited particular skill at dealing with the Americans. The death of his son-in-law Datu Ali changed nothing. He continued to use his connections among Chinese merchants to increase his wealth and power. But whereas most Moros saw American-imposed change as threats, Piang sensed opportunity. The Americans, in turn, learned that not all Moros were cut from the same cloth.

When American authorities demanded that datus send their sons to American schools in Manila, most sent slaves instead. Piang sent his son, Gumbay. There were others of like mind. Datu Ali's youngest sons attended American schools, while his eldest son worked closely with the American officer serving as district governor. To encourage further such initiatives, Bliss promoted commercial development. He understood that such activities would not confer glory on him or the army, but was deeply persuaded that such reforms were vital. Bliss also maintained that only the presence of American troops prevented a return to lawlessness. Therefore, he argued passionately against reducing the size of the American garrison in Moroland. He continued to support the constabulary even when it became politically difficult, as increasing numbers of American planters on the island argued that the constables were not coming down hard enough on the Moros.[9] He backed Moro land claims against white planters, telling Wood that the U.S. government should not support the planters because to do so would "keep the natives in a state of peonage" for as far as the eye could see.[10] Long before many people had any notion of conservation and environmental degradation, Bliss warned that if unchecked, foreign companies would take Mindanao's natural resources and leave a wasteland behind.

During Bliss's three-year term as governor of Moro Province there were intermittent thefts and murders, assassinations of government informers, and occasional attacks against American troops. Throughout his time, Bliss was aware how one accidental or ill-advised killing of a native could undo so much patient progress and dissolve the precarious bonds of trust. He perceived that the "Moros are in a state of savagery where they know a man but know or care nothing about a government."[11] Throughout his tenure he was distinctly squeamish about some of the violence necessary to impose American rule. When he asked one datu about his progress arresting some murder suspects, one of the datu's cronies proudly opened a bag from which three bloody human heads rolled onto the floor. The datu did not understand Bliss's agitated response: "For God's sake, take them away!"[12]

To Bliss's credit, there were no major acts of Moro resistance during his governorship. By the time he left, he judged that the Moros had been successfully pacified.

On December 14, 1908, Bliss was promoted to commander of the Division of the Philippines, replacing Wood, who returned to the United States to continue his ascent to the top. Like Pershing, Bullard, and Wood, Bliss understood that battle and bloodshed won public headlines and combat performance put one on the path to promotion. Unlike those officers, he did not compromise his core beliefs to achieve promotion. Had Bliss shared Wood's consuming ambitions, had he lusted for military glory, he easily could have provoked the Moros and begun full-scale military operations. Had he won a combat reputation in Moroland, he probably would have received a high-level front-line command in France in 1917. He chose otherwise. His forty-two months as governor of Moro Province became known among Moros as the era of peace.

SEVENTEEN

The Return of John Pershing

In the Moro Province, especially in Davao, various abuses have been committed . . . against the civilized Filipinos, and countless abuses against the Moros and non-Christians on the part of the American colonizers, with the knowledge and consent of the government and the province.

There each American is judge and executioner at the same time. There the American is king, tyrant, lord and master of the lives and properties of the Moros and non-Christians.

—El Ideal, December 2, 1910

The Prodigal Son

THE JACK PERSHING WHO RETURNED to Mindanao after a six-year absence was a more experienced and more powerfully connected officer than the captain who had left in 1903. He had served on the General Staff, attended the Army War College, traveled to Manchuria to observe the Russo-Japanese War, served as a military attaché in Japan, traveled across Asia, and observed the vaunted German war machine. While Pershing was on the General Staff, President Roosevelt had invited him to a White House luncheon. Roosevelt asked if they had previously met. Pershing answered that they had met just once, in Cuba. Roosevelt could not recall the occasion and asked Pershing what he had said. Pershing replied, "Since there are ladies here, I can't repeat just what you

217

said, Mr. President."[1] It turned out that Pershing had found Roosevelt cursing like a trooper at a mired mule team and had then helped him extract the animals and the ammunition wagon. Amid general laughter the two veterans fell to reminiscing, and it was clear to all that they got along well. Pershing subsequently so impressed the president that Roosevelt petitioned the army to promote him to colonel, but the army brass refused to violate its traditional seniority-based hierarchy.

While in Washington, Pershing met a young Wellesley graduate named Helen Frances Warren at a dinner party. A night of dancing followed. Returning to his quarters around 2:00 A.M., Pershing awakened a friend and announced, "Charlie, I've met the girl I'm going to marry." His friend was well aware of Pershing's reputation as a womanizer but patiently listened while Pershing described the girl's sterling attributes. Finally he interrupted, "Jack, if you're in love, I'm not. I want to get some sleep. If you're still in love tomorrow, come around and tell me about it."[2]

In the autumn of 1905, Roosevelt tried a new ploy, utilizing his presidential prerogative to nominate Pershing for brigadier general. As had been the case with Leonard Wood, Congress had to approve. It hurt not at all that Pershing was now married to Frances Warren, whose father was Wyoming senator Francis E. Warren, chairman of the Military Appropriations Committee. In a move that outraged many serving officers, Pershing skipped three ranks, jumped over 909 more senior officers, and attained a general's rank.[3] As one officer bitterly observed, if none of the army's colonels merited the promotion, then they all should have been dismissed, others promoted to colonel, and one of them selected as general instead of this extraordinary display of favoritism.

Pershing's run of good fortune continued with the election of William Howard Taft. Taft had enjoyed a long association with Pershing, beginning in 1901 when both men were serving in the Philippines. Taft's support had helped Pershing achieve fame on Mindanao. At the end of 1908, President-elect Taft influenced the decision to make Pershing commander of the Department of Mindanao and third governor of Moro Province. The assignment, which Leonard Wood called "the second best command in the Army," was a high honor.[4] It was a coveted army posting because it combined command of 5,500 men, mostly American regulars, and nearly total autonomy. If the ambitious Pershing again performed well, his future would look very bright.

His arrival in Zamboanga in November 1909 was like a homecoming.

While his wife dealt with the family home that once had been the domi-
cile for Wood and Bliss—she pronounced its cavernous interior barnlike
and began planning extensive renovations—Pershing toured his new do-
main. "My return after the six years' absence was something like that of
the Prodigal son; large crowds from all parts of the lake attended the meetings and hailed me like a far-traveled brother."[5] One of his orderlies noted
how the general "was always careful to observe the little courtesies that
the Mohammedans thought essential to their dignity."[6] Pershing listened
carefully to Moro tales of woe at the hands of the American military and
reached two conclusions: although the army had done much good work, it
had sometimes used force unnecessarily to enforce laws that ran counter
to age-old Moro custom, but "as a general rule it was the depredations
committed by the different tribes and peoples themselves that were basi-
cally responsible" for the army's punitive response.[7]

Pershing's first inspection tour also convinced him that Moro Province had slipped backward due to lax enforcement of law and order. He
partially attributed this slippage to the rule of the acting governors who
had been in control during the yearlong interval between Bliss's departure and Pershing's arrival. He set about rectifying this problem through
administrative and leadership changes. In Pershing's mind, the future
of Moro Province depended on its economy. He devoted his attention to
reforming local and provincial government to encourage economic
growth. To achieve agricultural and industrial development, Pershing,
like his predecessors, promoted internal improvements. Better roads and
wharves would allow products to reach expanding markets. A growing
economy would attract investments, creating a self-reinforcing cycle that
would raise living standards throughout the province.

As a former schoolteacher, Pershing was keenly interested in Moro
education. He inherited from Bliss the policy of aiding select pandita
schools, although his heart was not behind this policy. He vigorously resisted proposals that Islam be taught in public schools by Muslim teachers. Pershing was certain that Western schools were superior to traditional
Islamic-based education. In his view, the pandita schools propagated oc-
cult inspiration that was detrimental to good government. Indeed, Pershing was certain that much violence had been caused by proselytizing
Muslim preachers. Thus he was delighted to find that as time passed, the
Moros themselves showed a preference for sending their children to
Western-style public schools. Yet in his public utterances to assembled

Moro notables, Pershing always reminded them that ever since their first encounters the Americans had exhibited religious tolerance. He saw no contradiction in his personal views, asserting, "I believe that the Moros should live according to the teachings of the Koran, because I think that the Koran is the best book that they can follow."[8]

Pershing periodically sailed to Manila to confer with his superior. In the summer of 1910, he met with Major General William Duvall, the head of the Division of the Philippines, and this officer suggested that he eventually try for the Philippines command. Such an achievement required careful handling of army politics, but the fact that Duvall, a venerable general who knew this part of the game inside out, had suggested it more than hinted that it was possible. Duvall asserted that none of the three brigadier generals senior to Pershing, including Tasker Bliss, was a better candidate. It was also likely that this assignment would go hand in hand with a promotion. This intriguing possibility remained in the back of Pershing's mind for the duration of his service on Mindanao.

One of Pershing's trips to Manila attracted a cloud of newspapermen. They were curious to learn about the general's policy toward the Moros and knew that he had just sent an urgent telegram to Mindanao. They asked Pershing about its contents, and he characteristically refused to say anything. One enterprising newspaperman hoped to scoop his competitors by cornering Frank Lanckton, a soldier who worked in headquarters, and offering him a large bribe to obtain a copy of the telegram. Lanckton responded indignantly. When the reporter persisted, Lanckton punched him and a fight broke out. As Lanckton was pummeling the overmatched reporter the noise attracted the headquarters staff. After the reporter had been escorted from the building, Pershing summoned the soldier into an office.

Pershing asked, "Lanckton, did you hit that reporter hard?"

"Yes sir. I hope I did not cause any trouble."

"That's all right Lanckton. Always watch the reporters."

And then Pershing asked if Lanckton would like to serve as one of his orderlies.[9] It was a fateful invitation, whereby Pershing acquired an often-drunk orderly who compensated for his bad behavior with a lifetime of total devotion to Pershing and his family.

Every day, regardless of weather, Pershing took a brisk gallop for his morning exercise. He was a skilled, fearless rider. To the alarm of his orderlies, Pershing's fearlessness applied to other arenas, as he continued frequently to go unarmed to meet with Moro datus. Lanckton recalled how the general ordered him to leave his revolver behind before boarding a steamer on Lake Lanao to visit a troublemaking datu. Lanckton habitually ignored this order by hiding a pocket pistol in his waistband. This time Pershing noticed the suspicious bulge. "Throw it away," he commanded. "A soldier's word counts more than his gun."[10] A few months after Pershing assumed command, W. Cameron Forbes, the civilian governor-general of the Philippines, accompanied Pershing on an inspection tour. Forbes wrote the secretary of war that the change in Moro Province "is most startling and enheartening . . . [Pershing's] work there is something magical."[11]

Pershing earnestly argued that his regulars, scouts, and constabulary should be dispersed in small garrisons throughout the province. Like Bliss, he asserted that close contact between the natives and the occupying forces demonstrated to all the people in Moro Province that there was a government looking after them. Duvall might have agreed with him. But General J. Franklin Bell had replaced him. Like most conventional military thinkers, Bell disliked the dispersion of forces. He believed it was bad for discipline and training as well as being costly. He also did not much care for Pershing. Pershing tried to persuade Bell that his policy was both necessary and wise. Its military benefit was that it allowed American forces to reach quickly all parts of Moro Province, thus quelling violence before it took root. But the dispersed garrisons also had a more subtle effect. Peaceably inclined Moros and other wild tribes congregated around the outposts, taking advantage of the security to grow crops. Other farmers joined them, creating prosperous enclaves within the protective radius of the foot patrols. Pershing assured Bell, "I can conceive no better use to which scouts can be put in the Philippine Islands."[12] Every day spent otherwise—and in Pershing's mind ten years' worth of days had been thus spent—was a day wasted.

The Meaning of Government

Pershing worked hard to make real his vision of future prosperity in Moroland, but he had to contend against a perception that violent crime and murder were entrenched Moro habits. White planters had a vested interest in promoting this perception. They prospered when a repressive

American presence clamped down on violence, thereby allowing them to exploit docile, cheap labor. Pershing viewed this group with distaste, agreeing with a captain who observed, "The American has lowered the standard of the white man in the Orient."[13] Indeed, Pershing's confidential files on American planters described most of them as exceptionally low-life characters, including a former boxer with brain damage and an unredeemed slaveholder. However, the planters had some political power, particularly in Manila and to a lesser extent in Washington. They apparently used this power to persuade a former strong Pershing supporter, Martin Egan, the editor of the *Manila Times*, to write an editorial claiming that conditions in Moro Province were far worse than authorities acknowledged. Published on July 8, 1911, the editorial painted a bleak picture of murder and mayhem, a land where white men huddled behind fortified barriers and even there were not safe. In a stinging rebuttal of Pershing's policy, Egan wrote that conciliation would never succeed with the savage Moros and that the price for this failed policy was being paid with white lives. Egan posited only one possible solution: disarmament.

Egan's attack struck a nerve. Not only did Egan's claims threaten Pershing's future prospects for promotion to the Division of the Philippines, but Pershing recognized that there were kernels of unpleasant truth in what Egan wrote.

But it was the lurid story of the murder of Lieutenant Walter Rodney that captured public attention. On a tranquil Sunday afternoon in April, Rodney had taken his four-year-old daughter for a walk along the Jolo-Asturias road. On their return trek the pair passed an innocent-appearing Moro. As soon as they passed, the Moro drew his barong and slashed Rodney across the face. As Rodney fell, the Moro delivered a death stroke, almost cutting Rodney in two. After administering a few more gratuitous blows, the Moro turned to attack a nearby carriage filled with unarmed Americans. Before he could kill any more, a sentry from the Jolo garrison shot the Moro to death. The *Manila Times* reported that the little girl, spattered with her father's blood, stood over his body calling for him to get up.

Three days later, two Moros approached a guard station on the same road. Sergeant James Ferguson greeted them with his fluent knowledge of the local dialect. A private warned Ferguson to watch out because the pair seemed to be fingering something concealed in their clothes. The sergeant rebuked the private for speaking nonsense. The Moros walked up to the sergeant, a brief conversation took place, and then the Moros drew concealed blades and mortally wounded Ferguson. Guards killed one Moro and mortally wounded the other. The dying Moro confessed that both men had chosen to become juramentados with the goal of killing as many Americans as possible before ascending to paradise.

Beyond anecdotes, there were statistics. When Egan wrote his denouncement of Pershing's restrained policy, the general was working on his annual report with its list of military expeditions. On one hand, American casualties had been remarkably few: in 1909 four regulars and one scout had died in combat, in 1910 four regulars and no scouts. However, over the past two years Pershing's forces had rounded up ten different outlaw bands, killing 126 individuals, capturing 79, and accepting the surrender of another 10. These figures disheartened Pershing. If it seemed to him that crime and murder were "in the Moro blood" and "a part of Moro nature" as well as partially "in their religion," then this opinion was even more strongly held by General Bell.[14] That officer, who had been aptly called by one of his subordinates "the real terror of the Philippines" for his brutal suppression of Filipino insurgents, was growing impatient with the continuing violence in Moro Province.[15]

For the immediate future, Pershing ordered officers to carry their sidearms at all times and for soldiers to travel in groups no smaller than three. For a long-term solution Pershing chose disarmament. He was well aware of previous discussions about disarming the Moros and knew that it had been rejected because it "is next to impossible to do so without a war."[16] Furthermore, as Tasker Bliss had noted, there were legitimate reasons for the Moros to possess firearms, including hunting and self-defense against lawless Moros. Bliss also understood that efforts to disarm the Moros conflicted with their traditions and perceptions of selfhood. Pershing knew this equally well. Just six months earlier he had supervised a spectacular provincial fair designed to build civic pride. Beneath his viewing stand passed a remarkable parade showcasing the province's ethnic and tribal diversity. Whether they were part of an American district officer's bodyguard, the sultan of Sulu's entourage, or Datu Piang's followers, the Moro menfolk had proudly brandished their krises and kampilans as they saluted Pershing. A group of nearly a thousand Lake Lanao Moros brought up the rear. When they spotted Pershing they cheered loudly while flashing their weapons. Now Pershing proposed to take their badges of manhood away.

Bliss had become persuaded that disarmament would eventually be necessary, but expected that when it took place the Jolo Moros would resist. Pershing likewise thought that disarmament might produce a general uprising or even a holy war. He also knew the policy would be controversial, especially since many Americans with considerable experience in the province opposed it. He explained his motivation to his father-in-law, Senator Warren: "There have been several opportunities more favorable than the present, particularly after the Battle of Dajo (first) 1906. The Moros expected it then. The powers that were concluded best not to attempt it. The general result of the failure to disarm these people has been to encourage them to lawlessness." Subsequently, most efforts to arrest Moro criminals required large military forces and often led to a battle. Pershing would "no longer stand for that sort of thing."[17]

Having concluded that "the time had arrived to teach the Moros the meaning of government," on September 8, 1911, Pershing issued an executive order making it illegal for them to carry either a firearm or an edged weapon, except for working tools having blades of less than fifteen inches in length.[18] The government would pay for all arms turned in before December 1, 1911. Pershing proposed to change centuries of culture in a mere three months.

Pershing again traveled around Mindanao to meet with Moro leaders. Patiently he repeated the rationale for his decision: There would never be peace in Moroland until the Moros disarmed. Some promptly complied. Others headed for the hills. In the event, Pershing proceeded incrementally, first going after all firearms and later confiscating edged weapons. He issued licenses to friendly datus allowing them to retain edged weapons for themselves and a select number of their followers as long as they collected all weapons from everyone else living in their district. Then, once the deadline passed, secret service men began identifying who had illegal arms and the constabulary went to arrest them.

THE TROUBLE CAME, as everyone had expected, on the island of Jolo. Pershing sailed to the island to supervise a military response. As the Jolo Field Force, composed of American regulars from all three branches of the service as well as Philippine Scout and Constabulary units, fanned out across the island, the Moros living in the Taglibi District reacted. On the night of November 28, as soon as the moon set, the sounds of drumming and war cries split the air. A detachment of the Third Infantry manned their positions behind a belt of barbed wire that overlooked two hundred yards of cleared ground. Groups of fifty to two hundred Moros came charging out of the jungle only to confront the barbed-wire entanglements. American rifle and machine gun fire tore great swaths from the attackers' ranks. The Moros fell back, regrouped, and attacked again. Their gallant charges were absolutely futile. When they finally broke off the action, scores of Moros lay dead, while no infantryman had suffered so much as a scratch.

An uneasy peace hung over Jolo for the next weeks, allowing Pershing to return to his headquarters at Zamboanga. During this interlude, some Moro datus surrendered their weapons, while more talked about doing so. Then, on December 14, 1911, Pershing received word that about eight hundred Moros had fled to Bud Dajo. Everyone knew what had happened there before and no one wanted a repeat, particularly Republican politicians in Washington, for 1912 was a presidential election year and Taft's standing among the electorate was already shaky. Another massacre might extinguish the incumbent's dwindling hopes. Pershing's instincts matched the administration's wishes. He thought that patient negotiation could talk the Moros down from Bud Dajo without bloodshed. He wrote to Bell, "It is not my purpose to make any grandstand play here and get a lot of soldiers killed and massacre a lot of Moros, including women and children."[19] Pershing ordered a Second Cavalry squadron to reconnoiter Bud Dajo on December 16. The cavalry reported that the Moros held Bud Dajo in strength but that they were not yet fully provisioned. This intelligence gave Pershing an idea. He again sailed to Jolo to take personal command.

His Jolo Field Force included two infantry battalions and a machine gun platoon, six troops of the Second Cavalry, a field artillery battery, five companies of Philippine Scouts, and one company of Moro Constabulary, a force numbering about 1,256 officers and men.[20] On December 18, Pershing arranged blocking forces at the bases of the three trails leading to the summit. Instead of following Wood's method, he ordered his soldiers to fan out around the mountain and starve out the Moros. Pershing was certain that if he attacked, the Moros would again choose to die fighting. So he issued strict orders for outposts to be established no nearer than three hundred yards from the summit. Although there was some sporadic shooting, the Jolo Field Force obeyed its orders to defend itself if attacked but to avoid contact if possible. Meanwhile, co-operative Moro leaders convinced most of the people to leave the crater and surrender their weapons. On December 26, the Fifty-second Company of Philippine Scouts formed a line with its right flank touching the crater rim and completed a sweep all the way around the crater. The Scouts killed six Moros, raising the total killed to twelve, and bringing the campaign to an end. Total casualties for Pershing's command amounted to only three wounded.

From start to end, Pershing's conduct on Bud Dajo stood in striking contrast to how Leonard Wood had behaved. In Washington, Wood, who was locked in a bureaucratic power struggle, tried to downplay Pershing's accomplishment. Finally he grudgingly acknowledged, "That matter of Pershing's came out all right. It was a risky thing to do, but he won out, and it's a good thing."[21]

PERSHING PERIODICALLY LAMENTED that the Moros never seemed to learn from experience. Renewed fighting on Jolo in 1913 supported this view. In January, the Jolo Moros and American forces fought two sharp engagements. The first action took place just outside of Jolo town when eighty Philippine Scouts and fifty Philippine constables assaulted a jungle cotta. Even though the attackers benefited from artillery support, their first assault failed. Not since Baldwin's first assault at Bayan had the Moros repulsed a large, set-piece infantry assault. A second attack drove the Moros from the cotta at a cost of one American officer killed and three wounded, and twenty-nine scouts and constables killed or wounded.

Three days later, Moro juramentados attacked Camp Severs. Experience had taught the Americans how to build a fortified camp.

> The camp itself was a large rectangle, completely enclosed with wire. The line of company tents were about ten feet inside the wire on each side. Inside the line of tents were the saddle racks and the picket lines of horses. The fence was about seven feet high, with ten wires, making the strands about eight inches apart. Every twenty feet along the top of the fence, was a Dietz lantern with reflector to light up the high grass outside for several yards. The firing trench just inside was banked up and ready for business. In a few seconds after an alarm by the sentries, the men could be out of their tent ready to meet an attack. We felt secure.[22]

Before turning in for the night, Captain Jesse Tiffany of the constabulary verified that each of the camp's four sentinels was alert and at his station. Tiffany sensed trouble but could find no reason for his unease. Two shots and the shout "Moros! Moros!" woke him from his sleep. Tiffany snatched his .45 revolver from beneath his pillow, tore aside the mosquito net, and emerged from his tent. He saw dark figures running up the fence line and heard firing from all around the camp. Tiffany realized that he was wearing only his white underdrawers and might be mistaken for a Moro. He went back to his tent for his khaki shirt, and this delay saved his life, because during his ten-second absence six juramentados charged down the company street just in front of Tiffany's tent.

During his second sortie, Tiffany could not distinguish friend from foe. A dim figure advanced along the company street just in front of him, and he figured it was a soldier on his way to the firing trench. Suddenly a big cavalryman emerged from an adjacent tent, shoved his shotgun against the figure, and blasted the man to the ground. Tiffany felt his heart sink, mistakenly thinking that the trooper had just killed one of his own. He was about to tell the soldier to cease fire when he came to full alert: "Powder smoke filled my nostrils and I was looking down the barrel of that same riot gun. The big soldier was about to let go again. Some kind of a squealing voice came out of me: 'Hey . . . it's me . . . it's me.'"[23]

Tiffany ran on to join his "boys," who were firing rapidly. Then he heard the familiar clang of steel blade against a gun barrel and saw a constable parrying a Moro barong. Only then did he realize that the Moros were through the wire. A terrific hand-to-hand fight ensued in which the Moros hacked a constable to death. Five troopers were wounded in the combat, and one subsequently died. Seven Moros had penetrated the barbed wire, ignoring the gashes they endured while crawling through the strand. All seven died inside the camp. A cavalryman finished off an eighth Moro outside the wire. Careful examination of the dead revealed that they all had shaven heads and eyebrows, the sure sign of the juramentado.

Tiffany pondered his night of terror: "As I reflected that there might be months and months of this—with every night a possibility of night attack from juramentados, it cracked my nerves more than I cared to admit. It was jittery business, fighting Moros."[24]

EIGHTEEN

Bud Bagsak: The Last Battle

*They assembled on top of Bagsak in January and February to the
number of about from five to eight thousand and clamored for a
fight. We finally persuaded them to come down and they made all
sorts of promises and agreed to turn in their arms. They failed to
keep these promises however, so after segregating the noncombatants
from the combatant hostiles, they were given a thrashing which
I think they will not soon forget.*

—John Pershing, 1913

THE MOROS LIVING IN LATI WARD, a tribal ward near the center of Jolo,
had always been the fiercest opponents of foreign rule. Whenever government forces entered the ward, or even made military preparations
that suggested an impending expedition, Datu Amil and his lieutenants
collected the ward's entire population, an estimated six thousand to ten
thousand people, and fled to Bud Bagsak. Some claimed that since Bud
Bagsak had never been taken, it must be impregnable. Agitators said
that regardless it was better to give battle now because in a few months
all their guns would be gone. Then the Americans would come for their
barongs. Such logic appealed. However, combat veterans had few illusions about the outcome of any fight with the Americans. A Moro warrior who fought at Bud Bagsak remembered, "We could not fight your
soldiers. Their guns would kill as far as you see a man. Their cannon

Datu Amil.

could blast down a mountain. What could we do with *barongs*, and a few *sinapans* [guns] that we had smuggled in from Borneo? There was no hope in our arms. There was no hope, save Allah."[1]

During the first months of 1913, Pershing tried the same patient approach with Datu Amil's followers that he had employed at Bud Dajo. In March 1913 Amil brought fifteen hundred warriors to confer with pro-American Moros including the sultan of Sulu. They reached an agreement whereby government troops pulled back to Jolo town and Amil pledged to yield his arms at some future time. Two months passed and Amil reneged, declaring he would never surrender his weapons. He sent a message to the Americans: "Tell the soldiers to come on and fight."[2]

Manila newspapers criticized "peacemaker" Pershing's reluctance to act. Back in the States, Robert Bullard also doubted Pershing's martial skills and wondered if he had become a pacifist. In Washington, Colonel James Harbord told Army Chief of Staff Leonard Wood that Jolo town had become so dangerous that army wives and children needed to be evacuated. Cameron Forbes, the governor-general of the Philippines, cabled Pershing with strong advice to act and recommended reinforcements so Pershing could employ overwhelming force. Pershing replied, "The nature of the Joloano Moro is such that he is not at all overawed or impressed by an overwhelming force. If he takes a notion to fight, he will fight regardless of the number of men he thinks are to be brought against him. You cannot bluff him."[3] Mounting impatience at army headquarters in both Manila and Washington and hectoring from the halls of Congress pressured Pershing to act. He also knew that failure to act would scotch his hopes for promotion.

Pershing studied the behavior pattern of the Lati Ward Moros. They fled to Bud Bagsak at the slightest provocation. When government forces—typically native troops in the Scouts or constabulary—returned to the garrison, the women and children came down from the mountain to work the fields. When Pershing visited Jolo, they rejoined their warriors atop Bud Bagsak, suggesting that the Moros were watching his movements closely. The general decided to take advantage of this behavior by devising a campaign plan in secret with the object of isolating the diehards on the mountain from the innocents. On June 5, 1913, he ordered the commander on Jolo to cease patrolling and bring all his men into garrison so that the Moro women and children would return to their fields. Next, Pershing made a public announcement that he was going to Camp Keithley, where his wife and three children were spending the summer. Toward that end, on the evening of June 9 he and his aide, James Lawton Collins, boarded the transport steamer *Wright* and left Zamboanga.[4]

When the *Wright* was no longer visible from land, it altered course and raced to the island of Basilan to embark the Fifty-first Company of Moro Scouts. The *Wright* steamed south to Siasi, arriving at noon on June 10 to pick up the Fifty-second Company of Moro Scouts and its renowned commander, Captain Taylor Nichols. Then came a speed run back north. With its lights turned off and smokestack muffled, the *Wright* slipped into Jolo around 8:00 P.M. Inside the harbor Pershing found what he expected—practically all of the southern islands' launches, sampans, and barges, enough vessels to carry the one thousand men he intended to form his seaborne column. Equally important, the *Wright*'s appearance surprised everyone. The garrison officers were in their dress whites at a formal dinner when Collins entered the room with an order to assemble the troops. Most of their soldiers were at a local movie hall when they received the call to arms. While the soldiers assembled, their officers read Pershing's orders: "The objective of this movement is to disarm, with as little loss of life as is possible, those hostile Moros who have refused to give up their arms."[5]

Having surprised his own men, Pershing was fairly certain that the Moros had no idea what was afoot. To capitalize on this opportunity,

Pershing ordered a multipronged convergence on Bud Bagsak. Two companies of Philippine Scouts departed Jolo town to march nine miles and establish a blocking position south of Bud Bagsak. Fifty troopers from the Eighth Cavalry escorted the pack train on a seventeen-mile march to the coastal village of Bun Bun, three and a half miles from the objective. Meanwhile, the vessels in Jolo harbor loaded for an amphibious landing at Bun Bun. Pershing's intention was to have units in position around the mountain by daybreak in order to prevent the noncombatants from rejoining the warriors. He thus hoped to avoid killing women and children. However, his efforts at secrecy had one unforeseen consequence: Besides Captain Nichols, only one other officer was familiar with the trails leading to Bud Bagsak. Unaware of the impending maneuver, that officer had celebrated the end of the day by getting drunk. Carried aboard the *Wright*, subjected to repeated immersions in a bath full of cold water while the transport steamed toward Bun Bun, this officer began a painful return to sobriety.

Pershing anticipated meeting opposition on the beaches. In the event, his meticulous planning paid dividends when, around 3:30 A.M., the troops splashed ashore unopposed. Better still, the pack train was already there, thus allowing the gunners to shift the mountain howitzers and ammunition from the landing barges to the mules for the march to Bud Bagsak. Luck also played a part, as the drunken officer-guide revived in time to help lead the column inland.

The Bud Bagsak position was a horseshoe-shaped volcanic crater some eight hundred yards wide and a thousand yards deep. Dense jungle covered the mountain's steep sides. In most places, the last one hundred feet to the crater rim were almost perpendicular. The Moros had built five main cottas and numerous trenches along the crater rim. Long ago, flowing lava had partially collapsed the crater's northwest rim, thus forming the open end of the horseshoe and allowing access to the heights. To block this opening the Moros built Puhagan, the lowest cotta at 1,440 feet, situated in the middle of the horseshoe's open end. The other four cottas were on peaks rising from the crater rim. Flanking Puhagan to the northeast was Puyacabao, at a height of 1,500 feet. Flanking Puhagan to the southwest was Bunga, at a height of 1,900 feet. The main cotta, Bagsak, stood at the closed end, or toe, of the horseshoe. North of Bagsak, about midway to Puyacabao, was the fifth cotta, Matunkup, at a height of 1,800 feet.

Pershing knew the approximate outlines of the Bud Bagsak position and was therefore able to issue his assault orders well before daybreak.[6] He perceived that the key to Bud Bagsak was a bald knoll, Languasan, that sat squarely athwart Bud Bagsak's open end. Located only two hundred yards from Puhagan, Languasan was at about the same height as that cotta and only sixty feet lower than Puyacabao. Consequently, it provided an excellent artillery platform and also blocked the main escape route for the Moros occupying the heights. Accordingly, Pershing made Languasan his first objective.

Pershing's entire force, including reserves, numbered about twelve hundred men divided among two American companies and seven native ones. He sent the reliable Major George Shaw, the officer who won the Medal of Honor while serving under Pershing at the storming of Fort Pitacus, with Company M, Eighth U.S. Infantry, and the Fortieth Company of Philippine Scouts to seize Languasan. The Eighth Infantry

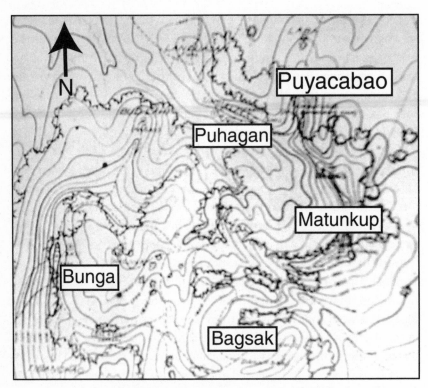

An overhead view of the five forts of Bud Bagsak.

was relatively new to the Philippines and included many inexperienced recruits. At daybreak they went forward while the mountain guns began shelling the cottas looming along the crater rim. Moving through the underbrush, the attackers could see little. But the veterans among them heard the familiar sounds of beating drums, ringing gongs, Moro battle chants, and the occasional discharge of a lantaka.

The defenders had failed to appreciate the tactical significance of Languasan. Consequently, they offered little resistance to Shaw's column, confining themselves to long-range potshots from the crater rim. Shaw occupied the knoll at noon and called for artillery. The ground was too steep for the pack mules, so the gunners had to carry the disassembled mountain howitzers the last five hundred yards to Languasan. Meanwhile, converging fire from the Moro positions intensified, so the regulars pulled out their trench shovels and began digging a protective earthwork. The Scouts had not been issued shovels, so they had to scrape the ground using mess kits and bayonets. Their lack of entrenching tools left them exposed to increasingly accurate Moro fire that killed two and wounded five, whereas the regulars suffered no casualties.

By now it was obvious that the three northernmost cottas overlooking the crater's open face provided mutually supporting fields of fire. If one could be captured, the others became vulnerable. Pershing knew that he could violate classic strategy and divide his forces in the face of the enemy because the Moros habitually chose a passive defense and would remain holed up in their fortifications. He sent Captain Nichols to assault Puyacabao and Matunkup. Just finding an accessible route to the crater rim proved daunting. While two companies of Philippine Scouts slowly worked their way upward, Nichols sent Captain George Charlton with his Fifty-first Moros to attack Matunkup. Matunkup perched on the edge of the crater rim atop a sheer cliff. A Moro defender recalled how the American shelling inflicted terrible losses on this exposed position: "We were in the main cotta of Bagsak, my father and I. But my uncle and brothers were in Matunkup. Toward noon my brother came up to us horribly torn, deaf, and almost blind. The jagged metal from shells had torn the flesh of his legs to shreds. He said the inside of the fort of Matunkup was roaring with exploding shells like a volcano. There was no air to breathe. Only dust and acrid powder smoke. My poor brother wanted to die but couldn't."[7]

Captain Taylor Nichols and his Moro Scouts.

Charlton's Moros gamely climbed up the slope while exposed to a fierce but mostly ineffectual fire. They reached a small plateau about one hundred feet beneath the cotta. From there, they had to make a vertical ascent using long tendrils of jungle vines to pull themselves upward hand over hand. From time to time they paused to hack toeholds with their machetes. With their hands occupied, the attackers were defenseless, so men leaned out from the cotta's parapet to hurl spears, barongs, and rocks at them. Now the attackers began taking losses until the Scout companies scaling the nearby cliff leading to Puyacabao saw their plight and paused to deliver long-range supporting fire. Although this fire inflicted few losses, it helped keep the defenders' heads down, thus allowing the Fifty-first Moros to continue their ascent. Once they gained the parapet, they were unstoppable. By 12:20 P.M. the "impregnable" Matunkup was in government hands at the cost of three killed and six wounded. One of the wounded Scouts lived because of Second Lieutenant Louis Mosher, who ran through fierce fire to within twenty yards of the Moro position. He picked up the badly wounded man and carried him to safety, thereby becoming the last of eighty-eight men to earn the Congressional Medal of Honor for combat in the Philippines during this era.

With Matunkup in friendly hands, Nichols changed his tactics for capturing Puyacabao. Rather than making a costly frontal attack, he led his men through the dense undergrowth on a flank move around the

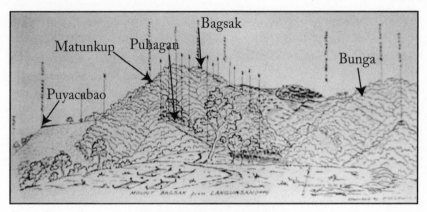

Bud Bagsak from Languasan.

cotta. His Scouts then descended into the crater between Puyacabao and Matunkup and emerged to attack Puyacabao from the rear. This attack surprised the defenders, who offered a feeble resistance even though Datu Amil was there to inspire them. At the cost of only five wounded, Puyacabao fell by 12:30. Although the attackers did not know it, a handful of Moros escaped to Puhagan, carrying with them Datu Amil, who was suffering from a bad shrapnel wound inflicted by the preliminary bombardment.

Having captured two cottas, Pershing suspended his offensive for the rest of the day. Everyone had been awake and on the move since the previous evening. It was time to consolidate a good day's work. Pershing anticipated a Moro counterattack against Languasan and authorized Shaw to withdraw if his position became untenable. Instead, Shaw formed a defensive laager with his infantry. Gunners unlimbered the two mountain howitzers inside the infantry circle, loaded with shrapnel, and set the fuses at zero in anticipation of point-blank fire. Until the moon rose at 2:00 A.M. the night was very dark and full of menace. Shaw recalled, "It was a very dangerous place as there were Moros all around and we did not know when they might take a notion to rush us."[8] He had his soldiers remain at 50 percent alert during the long but ultimately uneventful night.

To ensure Languasan's security, early in the morning of June 12 Pershing sent two companies of Philippine Scouts to reinforce Shaw, raising his strength to about three hundred men. Once they were in place, the two mountain howitzers opened fire against Puhagan. At a range of only two hundred yards the guns could not miss. Each shot chipped away at the stone walls, sending a lethal mix of rock and iron fragments throughout the interior. From the heights near the two captured cottas, marksmen targeted Puhagan's interior. Here died Datu Amil, although the Americans did not know it. Officers saw through their field glasses Amil's followers dressed in their colorful ceremonial clothing and heard accompanying music and chants. Major Shaw told his men to prepare: "They're going to charge. They've gotten themselves all dressed up to die."[9] Their ensuing banzai-like rushes accomplished nothing beyond providing another demonstration of fearless valor. Most of the attackers, including Datu Amil's son, who led one of the charges, died before they came within fifty yards of the American trench line. Only one attacker, Datu Jami, known in government circles as the biggest cattle thief on Jolo, got within fifteen yards of the American trenches. The defenders suffered few losses, but one was Captain Nichols. Although Shaw had warned him that there was a sharpshooter on Bagsak armed with a high-powered rifle, Nichols unwisely stood to see the oncoming Moros. This was the opportunity the marksman had been waiting for. His shot struck just below Nichols's eye, killing the officer instantly.

Having seen Puhagan reduced to rubble, Pershing considered how best to finish the job. With Puhagan silenced, he saw no need to risk losses by actually occupying the place. He had intended to advance from Matunkup toward Bagsak. The distance was only six hundred yards. However, the previous day a party of the Fifty-first Philippine Scouts had examined the route and discovered that there was no choice but to proceed along a one-man-wide trail that ran along the eastern crater rim. When they neared Bagsak they impetuously tried to rush the fortress. Everyone of the first ten who tried fell wounded or dead. When informed of this, Pershing switched his focus to the western rim and ordered Captain Patrick Moylan to take the Twenty-fourth and Thirty-first Scouts from Languasan and capture Bunga.

Moylan's scouts attacked Bunga by following two narrow hogback volcanic ridges. Again it was a tortuous, hand-over-hand crawl using vines to pull oneself upward. Luckily, Bunga's defenders had very few firearms, so it was a physical toil without much danger. Moreover, the defenders were clearly demoralized by the fall of the other presumably impregnable cottas and the death of Datu Amil. The Scouts captured

Bunga around 1:30 with the loss of only one killed, an unlucky soldier almost cut in half with a barong, and one wounded.

Meanwhile, Pershing, Collins, and a ten-man escort scouted Bagsak up close. Crawling on their hands and knees, the general and his men got within seventy-five yards of the huge fortress without detection. Pershing saw the Moros gazing across the crater, their entire attention focused on the battle for Bunga. He was so close that he could hear the Moros conversing. Collins remembered, "It was an extremely dangerous reconnaissance, and I have often thought since that a single volley from the Moros on Bagsak that day might have changed considerably America's part in the World War."[10] Pershing saw Bagsak's thick stone walls pierced with bamboo firing tubes. Had American riflemen occupied the deep firing trenches behind these walls, they would have commanded the steep slopes and held out as long as they had ammunition. Here only some of the defenders had firearms and Pershing knew that they could be defeated. But he was in no hurry. Careful preparation would save lives.

Accordingly, his command spent June 14 hand-hauling the mountain guns into position to provide fire support, bringing up extra ammunition, feeding the men decent hot meals, and preparing field hospitals. The weather had been especially hot with frequent showers. An overpowering stench from the dead at Puhagan prompted Shaw to send a detachment to bury the fallen Moros. It was only then that the Americans learned of the death of the rebellion's leader, Datu Amil. Also during the day, Collins, accompanied by Charlton's Moro Scouts, examined alternative routes of attack and found a useful jumping-off point about five hundred yards south of Bagsak. When Collins reported his find, Pershing thought that an advance from this direction might surprise the Moros. Since Charlton's unit already occupied the ground, they would lead the assault. Because of this decision, the last large battle of the Moro War pitted Moro versus Moro.

The Moros inside the main cotta mistook Pershing's cautious tactics as weakness. After each day that they held Bud Bagsak they told themselves that the Americans were growing discouraged. Their religious leaders assured the warriors that the Americans lacked the bowels to close with them and engage in hand-to-hand combat, that the huge cotta was impregnable, that Allah would intervene.

As soon as the Sunday morning fog of June 15, 1913, thinned, an

American mountain howitzer positioned near Bunga opened fire on Bud Bagsak. The range was only eight hundred yards. The target was huge. The intense shelling crumbled walls and collapsed the bomb-proofs, burying alive men, women, and children. Protected by this bombardment, Charlton's Moros began their advance at 9:00 A.M. The ground was so steep that it took them four and a half hours to climb five hundred yards. A Moro rifleman shooting from his firing trench recalled that the attackers were hard to hit at long range because they advanced in dispersed order and used the rocks and underbrush for concealment. The advance stalled when the artillery had to suspend its fire for fear of hitting friendly troops. Pershing sent another scout company to reinforce Charlton. The problem was not lack of numbers but rather the very skillfully designed defense.

Moro engineering had taken advantage of natural features to funnel the attackers into a narrow killing ground by building heavy bamboo fences that prevented anything except a frontal attack. With each step forward, the attackers' frontage narrowed, thus allowing the defenders to concentrate their fire. To cross the final one hundred yards the Scouts had to storm three successive trench lines, each faced with heavy logs. The Scouts began with a valiant charge that overran the first trench, but then their momentum was spent. Moro marksmen, taking advantage of their superior elevation, fired into the trench and pinned the attackers to their ground. Unable to maneuver because of the restrictive bamboo fences, the Moro Scouts had no choice but to huddle in the trench and absorb losses. Three of their comrades died and seven fell wounded.

Pershing saw the assault stall. He perceived that his effort to prevent American casualties had backfired. Captain Nichols's death at the hands of the Moro sharpshooter and a serious wound suffered by an American lieutenant had upset Pershing. He knew that these experienced Scout officers were invaluable and hard to replace. Consequently, when devising the final assault, he had tried to limit American losses by ordering his officers to command from the rear. This was a total reversal of their usual habit of leading from the front. It placed the burden of command on native noncommissioned officers. Confronting an extremely challenging tactical situation, these corporals and sergeants did well to capture the first trench but thereafter could do nothing more than hold the ground they had conquered. Displaying commendable flexibility, Pershing changed his approach. He ordered the white officers to go forward and assert command. Then, in a remarkable display of solidarity, the general joined them at the forefront of the danger zone. Revolver in hand, he and the other officers walked up and down the trench to help rally the troops and prepare them for what he guessed would ensue.

Pershing's knowledge of the Moro character informed him that when confronted by hesitation, the Moros would attack. Thirty minutes later came the expected counterattack as Moro warriors rushed forward, flinging barongs and hurling spears. The charge failed. It was a needless sacrifice of men who could have been more valuably used behind the secure stone walls of Bud Bagsak.[11]

The Scouts surged from their trench and pursued the retreating Moros. Some men tore apart the bamboo fence on their right in order to open a wider avenue of attack. They captured the second trench and pursued the retreating Moros to the third trench, located just beneath Bud Bagsak's wall. At 4:25 the attackers were within twenty-five feet of the objective. The Moros fought desperately, standing up to hurl spears at the men below. Nearby Scout riflemen opened fire, pinning the cotta's defenders behind its stone walls. Now all the defenders could do was blindly fling spears and barongs at the attackers. A spear struck one Scout fully in his chest, driving him to the ground. A comrade placed his foot on the wounded man and yanked the spear free.

A defender related: "Now the Americans were not three lengths of a coconut palm from us, firing from our old pits. Their cannon sprayed the top and inside of our fort constantly with metal so that we could not show our heads to shoot down on them. Yet our fire was so hot they dared not spring from their trenches for the final rush."[12]

At 5:00 P.M. the shelling stopped and Pershing ordered the final assault. The surviving Moros emerged from their holes to man the wall. A defender recounted, "I managed to stand on top of the wall of Bagsak and fire into the faces of the soldiers. I saw a man with red hair and fierce glaring blue eyes topple back and fall as my shot caught him in the stomach. Another soldier as he vaulted to the top of the wall was slashed in two pieces by one of our *barong*-men. I drew my *barong* and slashed at the head of another soldier, and then things turned black, I was falling."[13]

The attackers finally captured Bagsak. It had taken three and a half hours of bitter struggle to advance the final one hundred yards. Lieutenant James Collins was there at the end. Although he shared in the exultation of victory, it was tinged with sadness: "I doubt if there was a man on Bagsak at the finish who had not the greatest admiration for the enemy and the courageous stand he had made. The pity was that centuries of Moro traditions, prejudices, and superstitions made affairs of this sort not only necessary but inevitable."[14]

For Pershing, as his biographer noted, it was "the hardest battle of his life."[15] For the entire five-day campaign, one American officer and fourteen men were dead, twenty-five wounded. No one knew how many Moros had died, but Pershing estimated their killed at two to three hundred, while others guessed the number was more than five hundred. The slain included many women and children. The number of Moro wounded went unrecorded.

General Bell had often been skeptical of the Pershing way. Bell was part of the clique that resented Pershing's promotions outside of the established hierarchy and tended to agree with those who said that Pershing's command style as governor of Moro Province was driven by self-interest; as James Harbord put it, the future of Moro Province "is being hazarded more or less as a tail to the Pershing kite."[16] However, Bell managed to send a congratulatory telegram to Pershing on June 18, 1913, praising his men's "patience perseverance courage and admirable conduct."[17] Pershing, in turn, singled out the performance of the Moro Scouts. They had already achieved an exemplary record in tracking down Moro criminals. At Bud Bagsak they showed themselves equally capable in pitched battle.

Pershing's campaign planning had been superb. He prepared his plans in minute detail and in utter secrecy. His sense of terrain was excellent, his composure and courage splendid. Officers and men who witnessed Pershing's conduct collected affidavits to support his nomination for the Congressional Medal of Honor. When Pershing learned of this he wrote the adjutant general asking to be removed from consideration. He explained that he had gone forward to rally the firing line because it was necessary. He saw nothing exceptional in his actions.

BY 1913 THE American public had lost interest in Moroland. Thus, reports of another battle generated little public passion. The popular periodical the *Outlook* observed that readers were probably surprised to learn that another battle had taken place between Americans and Moros. It provided a very brief account, noting that the action was necessary so

Pershing could impose law and order, mentioned that American casualties were few, and that "the loss of the Moros is not known, but it is said that near the end of the fighting they almost literally threw themselves on the bayonets of the American soldiers, and that few escaped alive."[18]

In fact, the Battle of Bud Bagsak broke the back of armed Moro resistance to American rule. For fourteen years the Moros had fought the Americans as they had fought the Spaniards. But when it came to kris versus Krag, the kris could not win. All the Moros accomplished was to show yet again that they were not afraid to die. From the American viewpoint, the battle changed almost everything. Before, soldiers in the Jolo garrison slept on the floors of their barracks with mattresses stuffed against the windows to stop terrorist bullets. Henceforth, garrison life returned to how it had been during the Bliss era.

Nineteen thirteen proved to be the bloodiest year of the entire Moro War. Although Bud Bagsak ended mass resistance, it did not end the violence. The battle inflamed the Jolo Moros. Showing their amazing resilience in the face of repeated defeats, they resumed building cottas. The constabulary would come across cottas, dynamite them, and the next week find that a new cotta had appeared on the rubble. Four months after the battle another Moro band built a cotta atop another volcanic mountain not far from Bud Bagsak. The Philippine Scouts stormed the cotta in the last major battle of the Moro War, losing six killed and forty wounded amid heavy fighting. By the end of the year, U.S. combat troops had been withdrawn from the field and the constabulary assumed all patrol duties. Thus it fell to Moro constables led by American officers to enforce disarmament.

The constabulary received orders to seize every barong, kris, and kampilan they encountered during the course of a patrol. It proved bloody work. For hundreds of years the possession of an edged weapon had been a Moro symbol of manhood. The Moros could not help seeing Pershing's disarmament policy as a coordinated policy to unman them. A constabulary officer recalled: "It was a terrible thing to take the barong away from a Joloano Moro. You were taking away his visible masculine characteristic. You made him a woman and less than a woman. Most any Constabulary officer could kill a Moro and take his blade. Some officers did. It was all part of the day's work to them. When they met a Moro wearing a barong they called for the blade. If he resisted or started to run, they shot him and entered it in their report."[19]

Cotta victory.

Whereas constabulary officers without scruples had no problem killing Moros who refused to disarm, many officers found the work dis-
tasteful. Lieutenant Tiffany described how his patrol composed of Moro
constables would see a Moro carrying a blade with a carved mahogany
handle indicative of a fighting weapon. He would hail the Moro and patiently talk to him in an effort to convince him that the world was full of
real men who did not carry barongs. It was against the law and he must
give it up. Sometimes the Moro would. Sometimes he would decide that
life was not worth living without his barong and he would attack: "The
Moro soldiers would not be sorry for him as they shot him down. They
knew that he wanted to die. Sometimes he would cast himself upon the
bayonets. Being a Moro, he preferred to die on a blade. Yes, disarming
Moros was a sad and messy business."[20]

Back in August 1912, Pershing had proudly reported that since enforcing disarmament, "theft and robbery have been replaced by peace
and industry." Moros told him that for the first time they could leave
their livestock out at night with the assurance that the animals would
be there in the morning. Armed men no longer dominated the weak.
"Now that the barriers between the strong and the weak have been broken down, it is an easy matter to get information against Moro criminals." A tipping point had been reached because once the native
population began informing against the criminals, rounding them up

became much easier. Most important, Pershing reported that "human life is now considered of some value."[21]

In his final report, General Pershing summed up what had been accomplished in a decade of American rule. He observed that so far U.S. efforts had focused on suppressing crime, preventing injustice, establishing peaceful conditions, and maintaining supervisory control. Pershing concluded, "It remains for us now to hold all that we have gained and to substitute for a government by force something more in keeping with the changed conditions. Just what form this will take has not been altogether determined. In general, however, the tendency should be to educate Moros to govern according to our ideas of right and justice."[22]

Pershing's work in Moro Province was done. His hopes to command the Division of the Philippines had not been met. Instead, he would return to the United States to command a brigade in San Francisco, effectively a demotion. He was fifty-three years old, and it appeared that his career had again stalled. Still, he departed Mindanao with the respect of almost everyone who knew anything about his service. The civilian governor of the Philippines wrote, "You have restored peace and disarmed the turbulent population, promoted civilization and education, and as rapidly as possible substituted civilian for military control."[23] On December 15, 1913, General Pershing and his family boarded a steamer to return to the United States. The next day Frank W. Carpenter relieved Pershing and became the first civil governor of the Department of Mindanao and Sulu.

NINETEEN

A Forgotten War

Savage people, especially Mohammedans, whose religion accentuates their opposition to any control by Christians, can not be changed entirely in a few years, and the American people must not expect results to be accomplished in Mindanao, or elsewhere in the Philippines, in a few years, such as other nations operating under similar conditions have taken a century or more to accomplish.

—Tasker Bliss, 1906

Selective Memories

MANY AMERICAN OFFICERS RECALLED their experiences in the exotic islands of the Sulu Archipelago with a special nostalgia. Hugh Scott reflected that never before or after did he live a life of such intense immediacy. The outcome of his diplomatic confrontations with Moro datus, "when everything was set on a hair-trigger," provided unsurpassed excitement. Two decades after his service in Moroland he wrote, "What an extraordinary grand and glorious feeling it is to get one's self scared almost out of one's wits, yet in the end to escape by the skin of the teeth!"[1]

In 1915, Maureen Pickering's husband visited Mindanao and retraced his wife's trip to Camp Keithley. Eleven years earlier it had taken fifteen anxious hours for a mule-drawn ambulance to travel sixteen miles along a primitive corduroy road. Now the same trip was without peril and took only an hour by motor bus. The camp had moved from its mountaintop to the shore of Lake Lanao, and instead of grass huts, living quarters were made of wood. Outward appearances suggested that little else had changed except, crucially, the sense of ever-present danger. Families no longer slept with loaded guns on the bed stand. People circulated freely outside the camp perimeter without fear of sudden attack. Pickering sensed a land at peace.

Some officers visited the islands and found the effort to recover golden memories depressing. Sydney Cloman returned to the remote island of Bongao in 1915 to see his former duty station. Smallpox had killed off nearly all of his old Moro friends. Almost all signs of the civic improvement Cloman had overseen had disappeared. The fort his men had garrisoned had badly decayed. In sum, "the general appearance of the place was about what it was before the Americans came."[2]

In 1921 Leonard Wood returned to Mindanao and, in contrast to Cloman, found substantive change. He wrote in his diary that across from Datu Piang's house "is an electric light plant, a modern market and modern mosque . . . a change just about as great as one can imagine. The whole scene along the [Rio Grande] river made one feel as though one were witnessing the final act in long drama. The darkest and most dismal scenes finally end up with Right prevailing and everybody happy. The only thing is that the Moros . . . although they are getting on very well . . . are not happy."[3] His gloomy observation brings up a question: What had been accomplished by more than a decade of conflict?

When Americans arrived in Moroland, what they saw of Moro culture appalled them. They took the slavery, ferocious jurisprudence, and degradation of women they witnessed as obvious signs of a debased people. They did not perceive that there was a functioning Moro governmental organization based on Islamic principles. Instead of gradually introducing reforms and working through the traditional Moro political structure of datu council rule, the Americans impatiently chose direct rule. By military force they first abolished slavery and later disarmed the people while simultaneously imposing a Western-style civil society. Progressive Moro leaders tried to adapt. Their plaintive appeal in a petition to the U.S. government said, "The American laws are wise and show great learning about the principles and blessings of self-government. They are undoubtedly most beneficial to those people who can best understand them. The Moro hopes someday to understand them."[4] Most

Moros were not interested in adapting to infidel rule. Their belief in the sanctity of death in combat and the ignominy of surrender guaranteed that aggressive American punitive policies would lead to slaughter.

The Moros were an invaded people who fought with inferior weapons against a technologically far superior force. They pitted kris versus Krag, raised barongs beneath a shrapnel hail of modern artillery fire, and when all else failed, donned their finest clothes to die. Victor Hurley, who interviewed Moro and American war veterans, had no illusions about Moro savagery. Nonetheless, he condemned American conduct and concluded that the Americans were as guilty of imperial excess as the Spanish: "The Spaniard brought religion at the point of the arquebus. The American brought law to an inferior people at the point of the Krag."[5]

Given their material inferiority, the Moros' best hope to defeat the Americans was by adopting guerrilla warfare. They had one essential ingredient to wage successful guerrilla operations: a large pool of utterly devoted fighters. But they lacked almost everything else. They possessed neither safe havens within their lands nor foreign sanctuaries across a border. Time and again, U.S. infantry, Philippine Scouts, and the constabulary found ways to penetrate Mindanao's jungles and swamps, thereby demonstrating that anywhere the insurgents could go they could follow. On a larger scale, horses and steam power gave government forces superior strategic mobility and delivered the supplies to nourish a protracted campaign. The U.S. Navy, with its mosquito fleet of small gunboats, each crewed by thirty-five sailors and armed with a pair of three-pounder cannon and two Colt one-inch automatics, not only cleared pirates from the Sulu Seas but also effectively isolated the insurgents from outside help.

At times of intense stress the Moros massed inside a lakeshore cotta or in a mountain crater to await an American attack. Thus, the U.S. Army campaigns against the Moros generally culminated in a set piece attack against a heavily defended but well-defined static position. In contrast, the constabulary later confronted a Moro guerrilla campaign that proved much harder to defeat. Fortunately for the Americans, the Moros lacked a unifying leader who could have identified guerrilla warfare as the best way to engage the infidels. Consequently, the guerrillas operated in the absence of any coherent plan. They acted on impulse, presenting the constabulary with a nearly random series of hit-and-run attacks. Such attacks were frustrating and painful but never threatened to reverse the tide of government domination.

The most important reason the Moros failed was that their leaders never summoned latent nationalism, the idea of a unified Moro people. Instead, individual datus tried to benefit from the American presence in order to outcompete their rivals, sometimes by overtly assisting the Americans, other times by remaining neutral while gleefully watching the Americans destroy nearby settlements. Senior American leaders took advantage. While advising about strategy, Wood told Bliss that he should campaign into Buldung country without fear of Moros living in adjacent regions: "These sections are hostile, and never give each other any support. In fact, support of one band of Moros by another is practically unknown."[6]

Moro leaders rallied their people by offering resistance to foreign occupation but nothing more. They supported their call to battle with the assertion that the Americans were trying to impose Christianity. This assertion had to overcome two obstacles: the consistent American support for secular institutions, and the fact that few Moro leaders actually practiced devout Islam. Consequently, insurgent leaders also failed to summon religious fervor in their campaign against the Americans.

The exploits of two Moros, Datu Ali and Jikiri, vaulted them into positions of potential unifying leadership. Both were skilled, brave warrior chieftains. But at the end of the day, Jikiri was content to be a successful and famous pirate. Datu Ali was a much graver threat. He was able to hold in thrall an entire region on Mindanao. But his rule never spread far beyond familial ties. The intense rivalry among the hundreds of minor Moro leaders meant that there was no individual sultan or datu who was recognized as overlord.

In sum, the Moros fought at a tremendous disadvantage. Islandbound, they received no outside help. They had no sanctuaries where the Americans could not follow. They still used edged weapons at a time when modern firearms dominated. Nonetheless, they managed to sustain a fight for more than a decade.

In his memoirs, published in 1968, a year in which the raging conflict in Vietnam divided the nation, Benny Foulois observed that compared to the Vietnamese Communists, the Moros were not nearly so well organized and did not have nearly as competent military leaders.

Foulois pondered what had been learned during the American service in Moroland and what it implied for future counterinsurgencies: "We found that a few hundred natives living off their land and fighting for it could tie down thousands of American troops, have a serious impact on the economy of the United States, and provoke a segment of our population to take the view that what happens in the Far East is none of our business."[7]

THEN AND THEREAFTER, the decade-long war against the Moros was largely forgotten to Americans. A veteran of Wood's 1904 campaign returned home to receive his $16 mustering-out pay and little else. There were no bands to welcome him. It seemed like the people back home had forgotten all about the war. Subsequently, there was little interest in retelling the often ugly story of American military operations in Moro Province. In 1938, an officer submitted an article on chemical warfare to the *Military Engineer*. The writer made the case that had disabling gas been used at Bud Bagsak, victory could have come without loss to either side. The editor rejected the article, citing the chief of the Chemical Warfare Service, who wrote, "This discussion of these actions may revive public attention to military operations that might well remain forgotten."[8]

From 1903 to 1913, the average yearly strength of U.S. regular army troops in the Philippines Islands was twelve thousand men, while the average yearly strength of Philippine Scouts was five thousand. During one typical year in Moroland, there were fifty-two deaths, of which eighteen were due to gunshot wounds, three from edged weapons, five from drowning, and the balance due to various diseases, with dysentery leading the list. Overall, during the entire stretch of Moro campaigns, combat casualties were remarkably low. Only 107 regulars and 111 Philippine Scouts died in action or from mortal wounds, while 270 and 109, respectively, were wounded. The Philippine Constabulary suffered significantly higher losses. From 1901 to June 30, 1911, 104 officers and 1,602 enlisted men became casualties. Combat casualty totals underscore how much the Scouts and constabulary contributed to the benign assimilation of Moro Province. Non-battle-related casualties from disease and accidents—drowning being the most common accident in a combat theater comprising islands, rivers, lakes, and swamps—were appreciably higher than the deaths and incapacitations caused directly by battle.

Years after discharge, veterans of the Moro campaigns continued to suffer from disabling diseases including malaria. On the other side of the
ledger, estimates of Moro losses during the campaigns are pure guess-
work.

Compared to other American wars, recorded references to the Moro
campaigns are few. Regimental history and lore selectively preserve
memories of the conflict. For example, the coat of arms of the U.S. Fourth
Cavalry memorializes the first Battle of Bud Dajo with a green volcano
representing the mountain and an inverted kris symbolizing the Moro
defeat. Modern reference works for both the general reader and the specialist provide terse accounts of American victories and little about the
underlying context. In his otherwise excellent book about the Meuse-
Argonne, *To Conquer Hell*, historian Edward G. Lengel provides a two-
page biography of Pershing. While listing Pershing's duty stations and
accomplishments, Lengel writes that the general "helped to put down an
insurrection by the Moro Indians in 1903," and fails to mention his second tour as governor of Moro Province.[9] This type of error—in no way
were the Moros "Indians"—and omission is characteristic of modern
treatments of the Moro campaigns.

The terrorist attacks against the World Trade Center and the Penta-
gon on September 11, 2001, refocused the attention of military histori-
ans. Long-forgotten American counterinsurgency operations again
became relevant. Still, the Moro campaigns—with the participation of
juramentados, arguably the first American war against Islamic terrorists—
received scant attention, with the prize for understatement surely going
to Charles A. Byler, who in a 2005 article in *Military Review* entitled
"Pacifying the Moros" wrote, "The Army's experience with the Moros
demonstrates how religious and cultural differences between a local
people and the Americans sent to govern them can complicate efforts to
bring about pacification."[10]

SOMETIMES WARS ARE remembered because they witnessed a sea change
in weaponry—the triumph of the long bow versus the mounted knight,
the dominance of infantry defending trenches against a bayonet charge.
The Moro campaigns featured modest technological change but, for the
farsighted, clearly pointed toward the weapon that would dominate the
next war. The standard army handgun at the beginning of the Moro

campaigns was the .38-caliber revolver. Close-quarters combat against the Moros revealed the need for a handier pistol with greater stopping power. In 1911 the army adopted the .45-caliber Colt automatic pistol designed by John Browning. The famous Colt .45 remained the standard-issue sidearm for the U.S. military until 1985.

In 1866 the army had adopted the Gatling gun, a manually operated machine gun. During the Indian and Spanish-American Wars they had seen limited use but received favorable reviews. A battery of Gatling guns famously contributed to the American victory at the Battle of San Juan Hill. Gatling guns and other rapid-firing machine guns had accompanied various expeditions into Moroland and been used to slaughter the Moros at Bud Dajo. A trio of American wizard-inventors, Hiram Maxim, John Browning, and Isaac Lewis, played leading roles in developing the next generation of automatic machine guns. Many of the world's armies adopted weapons based on their designs. But until 1914, no one fully appreciated their impact on modern field tactics. The 1911 U.S. Infantry Drill Regulations described machine guns as an emergency weapon only. In keeping with this opinion, between 1898 and 1916 the U.S. Army received a paltry congressional authorization for machine gun procurement that allowed a mere four machine guns for each regular regiment and a handful for the National Guard. It permitted an annual allowance of one thousand rounds per gun, something on the order of five minutes' target practice per year. Moreover, as a commander of a machine gun company complained in 1916, the machine guns were prone to jamming and other mechanical failures: "If you had all four guns going at one time, it was a great triumph."[11] One year later, the American army under Pershing's command learned the true influence of the machine gun.

Experience and Commitment

A successful counterinsurgency requires deep understanding of the native people. Such knowledge can come only from experience. The most plaguing problem the United States confronted in Moroland was the untimely turnover of personnel who knew what they were doing. A Moro leader remained in power until defeated in battle or enfeebled by disease or old age. His American counterpart remained in power only through the duration of his tour of duty. Moro leaders who befriended Americans felt betrayed when the Americans departed.

Major Hugh Scott governed the most turbulent, headstrong Moros anywhere. Over time, his balance of force and tact persuaded the people of Jolo to trust him. Tasker Bliss lamented, "It is a great misfortune that this officer can not remain for years at Jolo and continue the work which he has so successfully conducted thus far."[12] Many Jolo natives agreed. As late as 1923, a Moro responded to a visiting American officer who mentioned that he knew Scott by following him to the dock. As the officer's ship left, he called out, "Tell General Scott, come back."[13]

Regardless of their weaknesses, the three men who served as governor of Moro Province were smart and observant. They all perceived the importance of personal acquaintance when dealing with the Moros. In 1906 Wood wrote, "Personal acquaintance counts tremendously with these people, and this is one of the many reasons why long tenure of office by civil officials is so desirable."[14] American officers who built successful relationships with the Moros did so because they forged personal bonds. When such a man summoned a Moro leader to a meeting, that leader promptly came. When a man like Bullard or Scott rotated back to the United States, it was extremely hard for his successor, whom the Moros did not know, to maintain the goodwill that had been acquired through long practice. In 1909, the governor-general of the Philippines, Cameron Forbes, complained, "The whole tendency of the American occupation has been to discredit the native rulers. The Americans have not provided anything in place of the native organization . . . The constantly changing personnel of the district government has made it impossible for any one of ability to become thoroughly acquainted with the habits and peculiarities of the Sulu people."[15] Forbes added that for centuries the Moros had been accustomed to a personal form of government, giving undying allegiance to a person, not to an abstract concept such as a government. A Moro saw rapidly changing personnel in the provincial and district government as equivalent to a rapidly changing government.

An experienced constabulary officer agreed: "It is safe to say that nine-tenths of the trouble in Mindanao has been due to the impermanence of officials; no sooner did an officer . . . get to know his Moro men and manners than military orders carried him to some other sphere of usefulness; and his successor came with no fund of stored-up experience upon which to draw."[16]

Pershing's solution to the problem was to replace military officials with civilians as soon as the violence had been sufficiently tamped down. He saw the main advantage of civil control as the "permanency of its officials," in contrast to military officers, who come with very short tenures. He made a rough calculation that the average tenure of army officers on civil duty in Moroland was one year, two months, which was "ridiculous and absurd."[17] It was insufficient time for the officers to learn the local environment and to establish bonds of trust with the native peoples.

Most Americans who had experience in the province believed that an American presence would be needed for another two or three generations before the Moros could be successfully integrated into Filipino society. Filipino nationalists strongly disagreed, and hoped that President Woodrow Wilson gave them a responsive ear in the White House.

Wilson summoned Hugh Scott to discuss the matter of Philippine independence. Scott attended the meeting with considerable trepidation. He had been told that Wilson did not like to hear any subordinate voice opposition to his policies. Scott asked himself, "Are you going to tell him the real truth or nothing but polite evasion that will please him?" Scott decided that duty required the truth.

When Wilson asked his attitude toward giving immediate independence to the Filipino, Scott replied he did not know any such person in the sense that Wilson used the word. "I know the Igorrote, the tribe which lives near the north end of Luzon, whose importance is measured by the number of human heads they have on their roof. Do you want to give independence to him?"

Wilson answered no, and Scott continued: "If you give it to him, the Tagalog would soon take it away from him, the Visayan and Macabebe from the Tagalog, and the Mohammedan Moro would take it away from them all. You will then have succeeded in destroying everything accomplished by the United States during the last twenty years."[18] In sum, Scott explained, there was no such person as a Filipino in the national sense; rather, there was a race of people who had neither a shared national language nor a national purpose. The Philippines as a whole were a collection of numerous tribes, many of whom had been at war with one another for centuries.

But the Democratic Party had no interest in the nuances of Filipino tribal organization. It demanded the Philippines accelerate toward self-government. Accordingly, when Frank W. Carpenter superseded

Pershing to become the first civilian governor of Moro Province, Carpenter supervised the takeover of local governing tasks by Filipinos, almost all of whom were Christian. However, after a decade of military suppression, the Moros knew that further resistance was futile. They realized that with independence coming, the Americans were their best allies against the Filipinos. A year after Pershing had left, a very upset Moro leader who at one time had been able to amicably negotiate face-to-face with Pershing made an unusual request of an American officer: "Please tell General Pershing that we Moros don't want Independence. We want the continuation of the American Government in Sulu. P.S. Write me a letter if the Filipinos going to get their Independence, so we can be ready to fight the Filipinos."[19]

The Wilson administration ignored Moro concerns. Sultan Jamal-ul Kiram II signed the Carpenter Agreement in 1915, which explicitly recognized the sovereignty of the United States. The agreement stripped the sultan of his governmental authority, which Article 9 of the Bates Agreement had acknowledged, and reduced him to "titular head of the Mohammedan Church in the Sulu Archipelago." Although the sultan had long been something of a figurehead, the Carpenter Agreement silenced once and for all the voice of the Moros' best-known leader.

Through it all the Americans continued the Spanish policy of encouraging Christians to move from their home islands in the north to Mindanao. From an American viewpoint this policy had great merit. It addressed the emerging problem of overpopulation in the north. American planners thought that the primitive Moros and other tribal groups would be improved by contact with the more industrious and technologically more savvy Christians. Moreover, this would be a moneymaking process for American companies since the migrants would be better able to exploit Mindanao's natural resources, particularly its pineapples, coconuts, and rubber. Planting Christian colonists in Mindanao would allow the central government in Manila to control the island. Lastly, over time a growing Christian population would end the problem of Moro dissidence by sheer weight of numbers as the Christians increasingly took control of the land and the economy.

The first step in what was essentially a legalized land grab occurred in 1903 when Moro common land holdings were declared void and designated public lands open to settlement by Christian immigrants. Subsequent laws in 1913 and 1919 gave Christian settlers and foreign

companies greater entitlements, while limiting the number of hectares
Moros could own. In this manner, U.S. companies, including B. F.
Goodrich, Del Monte, Goodyear, and Weyerhaeuser, acquired large tracts
of land on Mindanao.

In 1920, the United States transferred direct rule of Moroland to the
Philippine government. The Moros again protested, saying that America was abandoning them. Four years later, a Moro delegation wrote to
the U.S. Congress, "You have left us defenseless, and it is your duty to
protect us or to return to us the weapons you took from us, and which
we freely gave you, relying on your promise."[20]

In 1935 a group of Lake Lanao datus sent a letter to President Franklin D. Roosevelt informing him that they were like a "small child lost in
the thick forests who does not know where to go." They asked if it was
right that their parents, the United States, having taught the child "the
right thing to do," should then abandon that child "when the child can't
yet live out in this cold and cruel world."[21]

Just how cruel a world became apparent two years later when the Philippine army began an offensive against a Moro group who had fortified
their cottas and resisted authority. For one week infantry operations supported by trench mortars faltered when confronted by fierce Moros defending formidable fortifications tunneled into the side of a hill. Filipino
forces could not bring their superior firepower to bear. To get the attack
moving, three bombers took off from Manila to bomb the Moros. Aboard
one of the planes was the Philippine army chief of staff. In the past, the
Moros had suffered terribly from American artillery bombardment. Now,
for the first time in history, they endured an aerial bombardment.

The Question of Commitment

The history of counterinsurgency shows the vital role of national commitment to achieve victory. Early in the Vietnam War, an American general toured a newly pacified village. A Vietnamese government official
asked, "All of this has meaning only if you are going to stay. Are you going to stay?"[22] The Moro campaigns were no different. A Moro datu remarked to an American captain, "Spaniards have come and gone. They
have been followed by Americans—and, in time, why should they not go
too?"[23] Tasker Bliss well understood the issue: "Of course it is impossible

at the present stage of the game to expect these dattos to give very loyal and open assistance to the government. To them the government is a long way off and their enemies are close at hand. More than that, they do not know how long the government is going to remain there."[24]

About a decade before the United States turned its military attention to the Moro question, the Spanish general Don Julian González Panado observed: "The reduction of Mindanao is an undertaking which requires time, resources and perseverance. The complete dominion of this territory cannot be obtained by a single campaign, however decisive, nor is it feasible to change in a few months the social and political conditions of a heterogeneous populations composed of tribes and families of distinct civilization and religion." Panado held other pithy opinions regarding counterinsurgency operations linked to the notion of commitment. No operation should be launched that does not produce "definite results" because anything short of that encouraged the Moros to continue to resist. Panado also advised against invading Moro territory unless one intended to stay and had the ability firmly to hold out against Moro attacks.[25]

During his first tour of duty on Mindanao, Pershing studied Panado's notes. Although his first campaign violated some of Panado's principles—it was impossible for this campaign to aim at "definite results" at a time when the Americans were entering unexplored regions and knew neither the terrain nor the people—subsequently the Americans did adhere to these principles. The military governors of Moro Province—Wood, Bliss, and Pershing—and their ablest subordinates, Bullard and Scott, were keenly aware that when they sent American forces against the Moros they needed to win. Anything short of tactical victory would adversely impact future operations. All senior American leaders firmly adhered to the policy of establishing permanent outposts. Even before they had a good grasp of the Lake Lanao geography, the basic strategy was in place, featuring a two-pronged advance toward the lake, construction of fortified camps to defend the two lines of communication, and maintenance of bases abutting the most hostile territory in order to respond quickly to insurgent activity.

Whether in 1903 or 2010, Americans are not a patient people when it comes to foreign entanglements. During World War II, General George C. Marshall was always aware of the limitations of national patience. Referring to the protracted struggle that pitted Britain and its American colonists against the French, he observed that the American public would not tolerate another Seven Years' War. A senior American intelligence officer in Vietnam agreed. He believed that America's foremost weakness in waging war in Vietnam was inherent to democracies: the "incapacity to sustain a long, unfocused, inconclusive, and bloody war far from home, for unidentified or ill-defined national objectives."[26]

The war against the Moros was unique in American history. The combat phase required more than a decade-long commitment of American forces. The American public accepted this commitment in large measure because they were ignorant of what was taking place in faraway Moroland. American casualties were remarkably few, pitched battles infrequent. Consequently, in sharp contrast to most wars, there was neither a constant stream of American deaths to remind the public about the cost of war nor epic engagements to rivet the nation's attention. Had the Moros united behind a skillful war leader who summoned their potential nationalism and manifest religious zeal, it might have been otherwise.

Moroland and the "Long War"

By 1920 the American government exerted little influence over Moroland. And so Manila replaced Washington as the center of power from which decisions regulating Moro lives flowed. The transfer of power did little to change hundreds of years of animosity between the Christian majority and the Muslim minority. In 1964, a specialist in Philippine history observed that many Muslim Filipinos believed that they shared closer ties with Muslim Indonesia and Malaysia than with the Manila government. Indeed, some Moros still referred to the Philippine government as "the government of foreigners."[27]

The Philippine government dealt with its Moro problem in the same way as had the Spanish and the Americans: namely, it continued to encourage the movement of Catholic migrants into Moroland. By 1960 Mindanao's population had climbed to 5.6 million. Back in 1903, three quarters of the people had been Muslim. In 1960, three quarters were Christian.

Today Zamboanga, the "gem-like" post once occupied by American soldiers, promotes itself as a tourist destination by advertising its Spanish colonial heritage. True to its past as a Christianized beachhead on a hostile shore, Zamboanga calls itself the "little Spain" of the Philippines and "the city of flowers." Zamboanga's current city hall was built by Americans in 1907 to provide a newer headquarters for Tasker Bliss and later Jack Pershing. The American-built teachers' school, completed in 1925, today serves as a college. Modern Zamboanga is home to a mixed-race population and features Spanish and American architecture alongside traditional Moro houses perched on stilts above the water. In a stunning denial of history, Zamboanga's tourist website recalls American occupation: "The iron-fisted policy of General Wood had impact upon Muslim leaders. They took his word as law, thus an era of cooperation developed."[28]

Abu Sayyaf, the terrorist organization purportedly linked to Al Qaeda, has its refuge in Moroland. In 2002, U.S. Special Forces advisers helped Philippine forces drive Abu Sayyaf from the island of Basilan, the onetime haunt of the pirate Jikiri. Seven years later, armed men stormed a jail on southern Basilan and freed more than thirty inmates, many of whom were believed to be members of either Abu Sayyaf or the Moro Islamic Liberation Front. According to press reports, the jailbreak "underscored the lawlessness in a region tormented by bandits, private armies and insurgents."[29]

In 2003, when the Philippine army announced that it would participate in a joint exercise—called "Balikatan" (shoulder to shoulder)—with U.S. forces on Jolo, many people protested and said that the Philippine constitution prohibited it. A banner near the main port read, WE WILL NOT LET HISTORY REPEAT ITSELF! YANKEE BACK OFF. Jolo's radio station played traditional ballads, known as *kissa*, that combined current events with historical reflections. A kissa vocalist sang: "We heard the Americans are coming and we are getting ready. We are sharpening our swords to slaughter them when they come. Our ancestors are calling for revenge."[30] The voice could be heard in the poor neighborhoods, wafting above the port's dense cluster of ramshackle homes built on poles.

THE AMERICAN SUBJUGATION of the Moros brought to an end the conflicts that began with the sinking of the battleship *Maine*. One enormous, unintended strategic consequence of McKinley's decision to seize and hold the Philippines was committing the nation to a new role as a colonial power in the Far East. With the end of the Moro campaigns, the

Philippine garrison had two strategic objectives: defend the islands from foreign invasion and control the population. After Japan's dramatic victory over the Russians, that foreign invasion appeared most likely to come from Japan. The occupation of the Philippines moved America's first line of defense against Japan thousands of miles west, to the far side of the Pacific. Tokyo Bay was 1,867 miles from Manila Bay. San Francisco Bay was 6,997 miles from Manila Bay. Although basing ships at Pearl Harbor reduced the distance by some 1,700 miles, U.S. ships still had to steam almost three times as far compared to vessels departing Japanese home waters.

Certain things could be and were done to defend America's new imperium. Congress authorized further modernization and expansion of the U.S. Navy. By 1917 it ranked third in the world, behind only Great Britain and Germany. To reduce transit times so that the Atlantic fleet could reinforce the Pacific fleet as circumstances demanded, American engineers returned to the long-dreamed-of idea of building a canal across the Isthmus of Panama. The canal opened in 1914. But neither the expansion of the fleet nor the completion of the Panama Canal altered the fundamental fact that the Philippines were much closer to Tokyo Bay than San Francisco Bay was. Consequently, the American garrison in the Philippines remained highly vulnerable to Japanese attack. It would have to fend for itself for a prolonged time before any reinforcements arrived from the continental United States. This realization formed the basis of the American defensive strategy calling for a phased withdrawal into the Bataan Peninsula. American military leaders conducted exercises and war games to evaluate this strategy. On December 7, 1941, the Japanese delivered the final examination.

With the American military concentrating on defending the Philippines against a foreign aggressor, it fell to native troops to control the people. The Battle of Bud Bagsak had decisively answered the question whether to arm native troops. Whereas Pershing's first campaigns against the Lake Lanao Moros featured entirely American forces, his last campaign at Bud Bagsak involved two American companies and seven native ones. Moreover, Pershing believed that the Scouts had surpassed regular American soldiers as counterinsurgents. He thought that American troops had grown contemptuous of their foes and become complacent about routine security and careless with their field craft. This belief underpinned his recommendation that the U.S. Army depart. Thereafter, the finishing touches of benign assimilation in Moroland came not from the army but from the Scouts and constabulary.

American strategists understood that population control required scattering the available manpower throughout the islands. However, to defend against a Japanese invasion required the American garrison to concentrate. Fortunately for the American planners, the increasing skill of both the Philippine Scouts and the Philippine Constabulary made the strategic choice easier. The constabulary handled public order from its police posts in both urban and rural areas. Meanwhile, the Scouts, fresh from their stellar performance against the Moros, and the American regulars concentrated at strategic posts where they could train as intact units and rehearse conventional tactics designed to respond to invasion.

After World War 1 Congress approved the absorption of the Philippine Scouts into the regular U.S. Army. Back in 1913, Pershing had predicted that should war come, the Philippine people would loyally stand next to America. His prophecy came true the day the Japanese invaded the Philippines. Philippine Scout units fought with particular distinction until the end on Bataan and Corregidor. James Lawton Collins, who had served as Pershing's aide at Bud Bagsak, observed, "Pershing's achievements in pacifying the Moros and in building up a program of public works . . . was to a great extent responsible for the loyalty of the people to America when the test came."[31]

The Cradle of Leadership

THE MORO WAR PROVED A CRADLE OF leadership for many of the men who guided the United States Army through its first world war. Four Moro War veterans rose to the army's highest officer rank, chief of staff: Wood, Scott, Bliss, and Pershing.

Tasker H. Bliss

Bliss departed Mindanao for a short stint as commander of the Division of the Philippines and then returned to the United States to serve as interim president of the War College. A series of domestic commands followed until February 1915, when he became assistant chief of staff under Hugh Scott. In May 1917, one month after the United States entered the world war, he superseded Scott and became responsible for the army's rapid expansion. When Bliss reached mandatory retirement age, sixty-four, in December 1917, President Woodrow Wilson insisted that he continue on active duty. Bliss went to France and served as the chief U.S. representative on the Supreme War Council. Pershing believed Bliss to be an excellent choice for the "perplexing diplomatic questions" that threatened Allied harmony.[1] Bliss, in turn, supported Pershing's strong opposition to dividing American troops among French and British commands, even though his relationship with Pershing was merely polite at best. Thereafter, he initially advocated Allied intervention in Russia against the Bolsheviks but later reversed himself.

Bliss shared Wilson's views regarding the establishment of international institutions to preserve world peace. Thus, Wilson named him to the Paris Peace Conference in 1919. Following his return to the United States, Bliss energetically promoted the League of Nations and international disarmament in a series of speeches and articles. His last formal assignment was fitting: in 1920 he became governor of the Soldiers' Home in Washington, D.C., at that time an asylum for old and disabled veterans.

Robert L. Bullard

Bullard served in the army without distinction from the time he left Mindanao until America's entry into World War I. He led the First Infantry Division in the first U.S. offensive operation of the Great War, the combat at Cantigny on May 28, 1918. Promoted to corps command, Bullard led the III Corps during the Meuse-Argonne campaign, combining a single-minded focus on the objective with a ruthless disregard for casualties. Like Pershing, Bullard emphasized willpower over physical and mental barriers. He earned the moniker "Counterattack Bullard" for disregarding orders and instead conducting a successful counterattack. Pershing assigned Lieutenant General Bullard command of the newly created Second Army, a command he held until the end of the war. In spite of the doubts he confided to his diary back in 1903 about the ability of authorities to recognize his merit, Bullard had risen very far indeed.

James Lawton Collins

After a brilliant start at Bud Bagsak, the career of "Little Jim" Collins fizzled. He continued as Pershing's aide-de-camp during the Mexican Punitive Expedition and in France. Late in the war he gained a coveted combat posting as commander of a battalion of field artillery in the First Infantry Division. His military service extended through the Second World War when, at the rank of brigadier general, he commanded the Puerto Rico Division and a logistical base in Ohio. The exploits of his younger brother, Joseph "Lightning Joe" Collins, eclipsed his own career. He died in 1963. His two sons both had successful military careers. The younger, Michael

Collins, piloted the *Apollo 11* command module during the first lunar landing.

Hugh Drum

Following his harrowing introduction to combat in the ditch beneath the walls of Fort Pandapatan, Hugh Drum rose far in the ranks of the army, but not as far as he thought he deserved. He served on Pershing's staff on the Mexican border and showed administrative talents befitting a new style of professional army officer. Pershing recognized this and selected the now thirty-eight-year-old Captain Drum for his handpicked headquarters staff bound for France. Drum ascended to chief of staff of the First Army with the brevet rank of brigadier general. In September 1918, Drum—now universally known as "Drummie"—summoned Colonel George C. Marshall to his office and ordered Marshall to take responsibility for the massive repositioning of American forces to the Meuse-Argonne front in preparation for a war-ending offensive. Drum had no idea that this exceedingly difficult assignment would launch Marshall's amazing ascent, a rise that ultimately eclipsed Drum himself. After the war, Drum served as director of training at Fort Leavenworth, where he taught Pershing's doctrine of open warfare. He transferred to the War Department in Washington, where he renewed a wartime feud in a highly public, ugly campaign against Colonel Billy Mitchell over the status of the army's air force. In 1933 he became an assistant to Chief of Staff Douglas MacArthur, and his path toward the army's top position seemed clear. To his surprise, in 1939 Drum was passed over in favor of George C. Marshall. The problem was partially that Drum's management style was confrontational. But the real reason that Drum was not chosen was more basic: He was not Marshall. Promoted to lieutenant general as a sop for being passed over, Drum stood poised, in his own mind, to play a Pershing-like role as field commander when the United States entered World War II. Instead, he was bitterly disappointed when he was offered a post in China, the position Joe Stilwell eventually filled and one that Drum considered a backwater command. To decline a command as the nation entered the war did not endear him to authorities in either the army or the government. Drum was relegated to stateside assignments until his mandatory retirement in 1943.

Benjamin D. Foulois

Foulois returned from his second tour of duty in the Philippines in 1906 to attend the Infantry and Cavalry School. He became interested in the military potential of airpower. The next year he wrote "The Tactical and Strategical Value of Dirigible Balloon and Aerodynamical Flying Machines." Foulois shared the growing consensus that balloons and planes would have important reconnaissance and artillery-spotting roles in future wars. His perception of airpower's true potential placed him ahead of most when he boldly predicted great aerial battles between fleets of aircraft and the eventual replacement of horse cavalry by an air force.

Foulois, Frank P. Lahm, and Thomas E. Selfridge took the lead in developing the army's air force. Beginning in July 1908, Foulois made fifty-five ascents in free balloons and dirigibles. But it was the arrival of Orville Wright and his plane in August 1908 that changed Foulois's career. At Fort Myers, Virginia, Foulois beheld for the first time a heavier-than-air flight. On September 9, Wright selected his friend Frank Lahm to be his first passenger. Together they proceeded to break nine world records over the next week. Disaster struck on September 17 when a mechanical defect, a faulty propeller, caused the plane to crash, killing Selfridge and badly injuring Wright.

Pilot Benny Foulois manning the controls, 1912 maneuvers.

Undaunted, Wright returned to Fort Myers with a new plane in June 1909. Foulois served with the ground crew assembling the plane. With Lahm again a passenger, the plane flew for more than an hour and forty minutes, setting a world record for flight duration. President Taft was among the dignitaries to greet the fliers when they landed. Three days later, Foulois accompanied Wright for the first time on a speed test that set three world records: speed of 42.5 miles per hour, distance of ten miles, and altitude of four hundred feet. Wright's success prompted the army to order Lahm and Foulois to take pilot training. Over the ensuing months, Foulois learned to fly while suffering numerous rough land-ings and two crashes. As noted, when later asked how he had endured such dangers, he replied, "Anyone who lived through the fighting in the Philippines could live through anything."[2]

In 1910, Foulois took a plane to Fort Sam Houston to evaluate it for army service. Assisted by his correspondence with the Wright brothers, Foulois, by trial and error, improved his flying skills. By the summer of 1911, the entire military aviation capacity of the United States comprised one licensed balloonist, a small dirigible, three captive balloons, one air-plane, and one pilot, Benjamin Foulois. That year, he designed the first airplane radio receiver and carried out the first aerial reconnaissance flights. By 1916 he was in command of the First Aero Squadron, which participated in Pershing's Mexican Expedition. This impressive-sounding title in reality amounted to command of eight of the thirteen already ob-solete planes that constituted the nation's entire military air arm. Foulois thereafter accompanied Pershing to France. Pershing discovered that the newborn air force was an organization rife with professional jealousies and lacking experienced administrators. He eventually chose Foulois to command the entire army air service in France. Unlike the war's other notable aviation officer, Billy Mitchell, Foulois proved an excellent team player as he struggled with the myriad problems confronting the fledg-ling air service.

After the end of the war, Brigadier General Foulois served as assis-tant chief of the air corps. He found that budget battles in Washington could be just as difficult as air battles in France and ground combat against the Moros. The army air corps was often starved for funds. Many doubted its usefulness. He paid close attention to technical devel-opments in Europe, particularly in Germany, and concluded that the United States air service badly needed realistic training. So he and his staff conceived of an aerial exercise featuring every operational plane in the army's inventory. It would provide valuable operational practice and tremendous publicity to help justify the service's funding requirements. Critics predicted disaster and scores of pilots dying from accidents. Foulois ignored them. On May 10, 1931, airfields from New York to California launched the 672 pursuit, observation, attack, bombardment, and transport planes of the U.S. Army's First Provisional Air Division, the "greatest peacetime concentration of aircraft in U.S. history," toward Wright and Fairfield fields in Dayton, Ohio. Poor weather delayed the concentration. Three planes took off from Bolling Field, Washington, D.C., but two had to turn back because of dirty weather. Only the third plane, flown by the "bald-headed, pipe smoking," fifty-one-year-old Benny Foulois, landed at Dayton.[3] In typical fashion, Foulois had led by example. He received accolades from the press, politicians, and even President Franklin Roosevelt. What he most cherished was the receipt of the only award he ever received for flying while on active service, the 1931 Mackay Trophy for "the most meritorious flight of the year."

Foulois retired in 1935 at the rank of major general and chief of the army air corps. For the remainder of his life he keenly followed aviation developments. He worked on his memoirs in an office decorated with the weapons he had seized from Moros he had personally killed, including the kris wielded by a female warrior and the kampilan carried by the sultan of Taraca, "the finest piece of cutlery in my collection today."[4]

James G. Harbord

James G. Harbord's two stints of service as assistant commander of the Philippine Constabulary prepared him well for the future. During his second tour, 1910–13, he particularly impressed Pershing. In 1917 Pershing provisionally invited Harbord to serve as his chief of staff. Pershing had two other candidates in mind and asked Harbord for his assessment. Harbord was reluctant to reply. Pershing said, "Well, Harbord, if you are going over on my staff we must be damned frank with each other."[5] Harbord told Pershing that he could do a better job than the other two candidates. As chief of staff, Harbord demonstrated outstanding organizational qualities in addition to personnel management skills that got things done, talents that were famously to serve him well in his subsequent civilian life. Although very willing to criticize candidly Pershing's plans, once Pershing made a decision Harbord supported it with tenacious loyalty, a quality Pershing truly prized given the variety of competing interests, both American and international, surrounding his headquarters. Like all staff officers, Harbord was eager to prove himself as a combat commander. Unwilling to spare him but recognizing the justice of his claim, Pershing reluctantly allowed him to transfer to the fighting line to command the Fourth Marine Brigade for its counterattack into Belleau Wood on June 6, 1918, a combat during which the Marine Corps suffered fifty-two hundred casualties. He rose to command the Second Division in Bullard's III Corps. Much to Harbord's regret, Pershing reassigned him to relieve the thrombosis afflicting the vitally important but horribly inefficient Services of Supply. In this capacity, for the war's final four months Harbord controlled the American Expeditionary Force's logistical system. He displayed administrative and management skills that marked him as one of the emerging breed of officers, a leader capable of running large and complex bureaucratic organizations. Harbord's postwar career saw him apply this skill first as Pershing's deputy when Pershing was appointed chief of staff of the U.S. Army and then in the private sector. Harbord became president of the Radio Corporation of America in 1923. He joined a company on the cutting edge of enormous technological change. RCA had transmitted its first transatlantic message just three years earlier. For seven years he navigated the company through this new era with surpassing skill before becoming chairman of the board, a position he held until his death in 1947.

Frank Ross McCoy

After emerging from Wood's shadow with his successful hunt for Datu Ali, McCoy received a variety of important diplomatic assignments, thereby cementing his reputation as both a man of action and a military intellectual. He became a member of the General Staff in 1911 and a member of the American Expeditionary Force's General Staff when it went to France. In 1918 he wrote *Principles of Military Training* and commanded a combat brigade. After the war he served as chief of staff on the American mission to Armenia, where he again exhibited diplomatic skill in complex circumstances. He thereafter served as a troubleshooter sent to the world's diplomatic and military hot spots, including the Philippines again, Nicaragua during Sandino's insurgency, and China for an investigation of the Japanese invasion of Manchuria. After World War II he was chairman of the Far Eastern Commission, an international organization given the task of determining Japan's postwar fate. Because he exerted influence on the highest reaches of government from Theodore Roosevelt's administration through the Truman administration, McCoy well merited the moniker given to him by a modern biographer, "Diplomat in Khaki." Throughout his life he remained devotedly loyal to Leonard Wood and worked hard to rehabilitate Wood's reputation.

John J. Pershing

Following his return to the United States, Pershing enjoyed a brief period of happiness until August 1915, when a fire at the Pershing family home killed his beloved wife and three of his four children (his surviving son, and eventually two grandsons, all served in the U.S. Army). The fire changed Pershing. Although he remained bound by his sense of duty to the army, his life was joyless. Elevated to major general, Pershing remarked that "all the promotions in the world would make no difference now."[6] Pershing commanded the so-called punitive expedition against Pancho Villa. Although the expedition largely failed, by one of those strange alchemies that periodically transform the American public, "Black Jack" Pershing became a household name. On May 3, 1917, he received a telegram from his father-in-law, the influential chairman of the Senate's Military Affairs Committee, Senator Francis Warren, relaying a question from the secretary of war asking how fluent the general's French was. Stretching the truth considerably, Pershing replied that back in 1908 he had spent two months in France and spoke quite fluently.

This answer satisfied authorities in Washington. The army chief of staff, Hugh Scott, sent Pershing a coded for-your-eyes-alone message informing Pershing that the War Department was sending a small force to France as a down payment on the U.S. pledge to send a massive force once it had been organized. Scott told Pershing that he would command the entire force. Pershing interpreted this to mean that he would merely command the entire advance guard. Only after he arrived in Washington did Pershing learn the incredible news that he was to take command of the entire American Expeditionary Force. Pershing had been preferred over five other major generals with more seniority, including Leonard Wood, Hugh Scott, and Tasker Bliss. It was an awesome responsibility and Pershing knew it: "The thought of the responsibilities that this high position carried depressed me for a moment. Here in the face of a great war I had been placed in command of a theoretical army which had yet to be constituted, equipped, trained, and sent abroad. Still, there was no doubt in my mind . . . of my ability to do my part."[7]

Pershing set about assembling his staff, and his most important choices were men with whom he had worked in Moroland. Duty in France overwhelmed Pershing and his staff. His controversial insistence that the green American army fight as a national entity pleased politicians, patriots, and army officers while inflicting enormous, and arguably unnecessary, losses on the rank and file. Pershing's conduct of the first American large-scale offensives showed how far he had come from his days in Moro Province. Absent was the tobacco-chewing captain who had squatted on the ground to engage a chess-playing Moro datu in patient negotiation. In his place was a man who worked incredibly hard, endured immense fatigue, and withered under the strain, his Mexican tan fading to an unhealthy, ghostlike gray and his erect posture reduced to a rounded shoulder slump. Formerly the possessor of intelligent empathy, during the costly Meuse-Argonne offensive he demonstrated no understanding of the doughboys' trials, not comprehending why exhausted, poorly trained, and poorly equipped soldiers failed against barbed wire, machine gun fire, high explosives, shrapnel, and gas. His only response to high casualty lists was to sack subordinates and insist that with the proper offensive spirit the doughboys would win through. With the loss of his family, Pershing had sunk to a personal nadir, able to live only by the exercise of iron will. He thought that the same spirit could and should infuse the American Expeditionary Force and allow it to overcome all physical and mental barriers. When Pershing ascended to army group command he returned to the administrative and diplomatic sphere where he excelled. His former command, the First Army, fared much better after he left, a fact that underscored his mediocre, uncreative battlefield management.

On November 11, 1918, nine years to the day after Pershing had returned to Zamboanga for his second tour of duty in Moroland, Germany signed the armistice ending World War I. Congress recognized his distinguished wartime service by authorizing the president to name him general of the Armies of the United States, the highest possible rank for any serving officer and one never previously attained by anyone. In 1921 Pershing ascended to chief of staff. The following year, after Congress authorized the Distinguished Service Cross for Pershing's valor at Bud Bagsak, Pershing declined it, just as he had done when his officers began collecting affidavits for a Medal of Honor for the same battle. On his eightieth birthday, in 1940, President Franklin Roosevelt summoned Pershing to the White House and personally presented the cross to honor Pershing's actions twenty-seven years earlier. The citation read: "For extraordinary heroism in action against hostile, fanatical Moros."

Gumbay Piang

Gumbay Piang's father benefited from his ongoing cooperation with the Americans. In 1915 Datu Piang became the only Muslim member on Cotabato's provincial board. As part of the stated American policy of integrating Muslims into Philippine society, the next year the Americans appointed him to the National Assembly. He dominated the Cotabato Valley until his death in 1933, having fought against, collaborated with, and prospered from both the Spanish and the Americans, and having had eighteen wives and an estimated eighty-four children, including Gumbay.

Gumbay Piang never forgot his debt to Benny Foulois for rescuing him from a raging river current in the Cotabato Valley. He attended the American-administered Philippine Normal School in Manila and thereafter rose through the ranks of the Philippine bureaucracy to become supervisor of the Bureau of Education. The Japanese invasion of the Philippines found Piang serving on Mindanao as a captain in the Philippine Constabulary. In 1942, Piang organized a Moro guerrilla force to fight the Japanese, choosing a unit insignia of a bolo and a kris, a Christian weapon and a Moro weapon, thereby symbolizing united resistance against the Japanese. He sent a message to the United States explaining what he was about: "Am son of your friend the late Datu Piang of Mindanao and as war leader of the Moros I wish to reiterate to the great American President my people's pledge of loyalty to the Government of the United States. The 20,000 Moros enlisted as bolomen of the United States Army whom I command will fight to the last and die for America their country."[8] Thereafter, Piang and his Moro guerrillas hunted the Japanese throughout the Cotabato Valley with the same zeal they had hunted Americans forty years earlier. Piang personally wielded a saber given to him by Douglas MacArthur. When the war ended, Piang sent Admiral Nimitz a kris used by his father, Datu Piang, as thanks for Nimitz's role in liberating the Philippines.

An elementary school on Mindanao bears his name. In 2008 the school provided shelter to some of the more than forty-one thousand displaced residents of the renewed fighting between the Moro Islamic Liberation Front and Philippine government forces.

Hugh L. Scott

Following his departure from Jolo, Scott served as superintendent of West Point until 1910. Promoted to colonel in 1911, he commanded the Third U.S. Cavalry in Texas, where he dealt with lingering Indian troubles. He continued to follow events on Jolo and paid particular attention to his difficult friend Panglima Indinan. Until 1912, Indinan remained a powerful and influential leader. However, government authorities suspected him of participating in a cattle-rustling operation. When they sent Indinan to break up the gang, he had the leader killed to cover up his own involvement. During his subsequent trial, Indinan received a death sentence, commuted to life imprisonment because of his long record of service to the Americans. Partially due to Scott's influence, Indinan was eventually paroled and pardoned.

Promoted to brigadier general in 1913, Scott skillfully handled Navajo disturbances in Arizona, again exhibiting the special talents that had earned him renown among the Jolo Moros. He ascended to the pinnacle of command as chief of staff in 1914. He worked hard preparing the army for participation in World War I and was a driving force in persuading Congress to accept conscription. He retired from the military in 1919 and spent the next ten years on the Board of Indian Commissioners. He also served for ten years as chairman of the New Jersey State Highway Commission. His 1928 autobiography, *Some Memories of a Soldier*, remains a fine read.

Leonard Wood

General Wood realized his life's ambition in 1910 when he succeeded
J. Franklin Bell as army chief of staff. Bell had brought innovative brutality to the subjugation of the Philippine insurrectos. Wood had merely
brought brutality against the Moros. Both had earned the enmity of the
anti-imperialists and the respect of their military peers.

Wood also carried on with Bell's efforts to reform the General Staff.
The idea of managerial reform of the army arose from a combination of
European military developments and maturation of the American progressive movement. Created in 1903, the General Staff quickly became
mired in inconsequential paperwork. Shortly after Wood became chief
of staff, one of his aides proposed that Wood randomly select one hundred General Staff papers to assess how many dealt with significant issues. Wood obliged and discovered that the answer was none. One of
the samples carried the signatures of the acting secretary of war as well
as General Bell. Both men had approved the recommendation that no
toilet paper be issued!

Wood wanted the General Staff to escape from the burden of minu-
tiae and focus more on war planning. To accomplish this goal, Wood,
ably backed by Secretary of War Henry L. Stimson, pushed for a simpli-
fied bureaucracy with clear lines of authority. It proved daunting. Old-
line army officers objected to any diminution of their special turf. Over
the decades they had entrenched themselves within their various bureaus and little by little collected power. The heads of the various bureaus
used their unsurpassed knowledge of bureaucratic procedure to block
all changes. The head of the Office of the Adjutant General, Major General Fred C. Ainsworth, was their exemplar. A pompous, self-important,
scheming officer, Ainsworth particularly detested the General Staff, calling it the "General Stuff." He systematically opposed Wood's reforms.
Wood struck back by baiting Ainsworth until the old bureaucrat could
stand it no longer. Ainsworth wrote a long, detailed, incendiary protest
against one of Wood's minor reforms, and it proved his undoing. Referring to Wood and Stimson, he said it was most inadvisable to allow "in-
competent amateurs" to change long-standing army routines. By once
again bringing up Wood's unusual career path and lack of formal military
education, this charge stung Wood to the quick. Stimson threatened to
court-martial the offending officer. Ainsworth chose retirement instead.

The chairman of the Senate Military Affairs Committee, Wyoming senator Warren, who also happened to be Jack Pershing's father-in-law, was made of sterner stuff. With the army struggling to fund vital new weapons such as machine guns and aircraft, the General Staff proposed closing obsolete forts and bases that were no longer useful but cost large sums to maintain. The list of base closings included a Wyoming fort that was the second-largest in the army and a useful part of the Wyoming economy. Warren had never shied from conflict. He, like Wood, had received the Congressional Medal of Honor, only Warren earned his during intense Civil War combat. Warren used his considerable influence associated with long service in the Senate to mastermind a congressional attack against the General Staff, reducing it by one third to thirty officers, limiting its functions, and specifically barring Wood from continuing in office. Although President Taft managed to block this last measure, Wood and Stimson paid a heavy price for the failure to foresee political reaction to their base-closing plan. Their blunder delayed the ascendancy of the General Staff system, but their efforts made possible the eventual transfer of real power from the bureaus to the General Staff. In keeping with a man who tolerated no superior and wanted to stand at the top alone, Wood's efforts firmly established the chief of staff as the army's senior officer.

After retiring from the army in 1921, Wood served as governor general of the Philippines from 1921 to 1927. In 1927, he returned from Manila to seek medical attention for his brain tumor. He died on the operating table of a Boston hospital on August 7, 1927. Wood's devoted aide, Frank McCoy, sponsored a tablet to honor General Leonard Wood that adorns Memorial Church in Harvard Yard. It reads:

> *Soldier*
> *Saver of Lives*
> *Lover of Manly Sports*
> *Restorer of Provinces Abroad*
> *Forger of Sword and Shield*
> *at Home*

Acknowledgments

While working with Bloomsbury Press on my previous book about the history of counterinsurgency, *Jungle of Snakes*, I became aware of a little-known American war fought against Islamic insurgents that took place in the southern Philippines. Writing a book about an obscure topic is always a gamble. I thank Peter Ginna of Bloomsbury Press and my agent, Jeff Gerecke, for having the confidence to support this project. Peter's willingness to publish military history that informs readers about America's ongoing counterinsurgency operations gives hope to those of us who think that history still matters. Peter also had the good sense to have his invaluable assistant, Pete Beatty, deal with the challenge of working through problems with a sometimes cranky author. Pete also performed a careful first edit. Thanks, Pete, for your encouragement and positive attitude!

As I have previously noted, when researching a book a writer embarks on a journey that mixes thrilling discovery with face-reddening frustration. In spite of new technology that allows access to information in ways that seemed unimaginable just two or three books ago, at the end of the day, research still depends upon the contributions of dedicated librarians and archivists. I am profoundly appreciative of the help received at the Library of Congress and the National Archives.

The U.S. Army Heritage and Education Center in Carlisle, Pennsylvania, remains a fabulous resource. Their archival collection of papers, letters, and diaries provided insight into the minds of a generation of American warriors who confronted challenges akin to those faced by today's soldiers and marines. In one of those special, serendipitous moments, a cherished associate, Dr. Richard Sommers, came by to ask what I was about. A few hours later he returned with an obscure archival file containing a period newspaper account of the death of Datu Ali. Wow and thanks!

Here in my home state, the University of Virginia in Charlottesville, the Virginia Military Institute, and Washington and Lee University continue to provide useful resources. A special shout-out to John Jacob, archivist at the Washington and Lee law library, for his help with the Homer E. Grafton case. Patti Hobbs at the Springfield-Greene County Library, Missouri, provided wonderful background material on Missouri-native Grafton. The archivists at the University of Oregon kindly provided copies of the Charles Furlong Papers (brother of Leonard Furlong).

Robert A. Fulton proved exceptionally kind by giving permission to use some of the splendid photographs he has placed on a public access Web site, www.morolandhistory.com. He also advised me about the technology of the era's shoulder arms. Bob, thank you so very much.

I continue to benefit from outstanding editorial support from my soul mate and wife, Roberta. Her encouragement, combined with a sometimes stern reminder, "Try using English, please," will live with me always. Subsequently, the book benefited from Bloomsbury's diligent editorial improvements provided by copy editor Sue Warga and proofreader Bill Drennan. From the heart of the Bloomsbury engine room, Mike O'Connor kept the production machine advancing. And a grateful nod to my publicist, Sara Mercurio.

Thank you all.

James R. Arnold
Lexington, Virginia
2010

Notes

Chapter 1: A Place Called Moroland

1. Lt. Dew to the Commanding Officer Post of Davao, October 13, 1909 Subject File, Philippines, 1907–1912, Box 320, John J. Pershing Papers, Library of Congress, Washington, D.C.

2. C. C. Smith, "The Mindanao Moro," *U.S. Cavalry Journal* (October 1906), 298.

3. Article 1 in the English version stated, "The sovereignty of the United States over the whole Archipelago of Jolo and its dependencies, is declared and acknowledged." The Tausug version stated, "The support, aid and protection of the Jolo Island and Archipelago are in the American Nation." A similar translation error had occurred with the 1878 treaty signed between the sultan and the Spanish. How these errors occurred remains mysterious. Najeeb Saleeby, an American of Lebanese descent who was assigned to Mindanao and Sulu, later detected the translation flaws and charged Charlie Schück, son of a German businessman who worked for the Americans as a translator, for deliberately mistranslating the treaty. However, Schück was acquitted of all legal charges.

4. Entry of August 20, 1900, Diary of Field Service in the Philippines 1898–1901, Box 1, William August Kobbe Papers, U.S. Army Military History Institute, Carlisle, Pennsylvania.

5. "Conditions in Sulu Islands," *New York Times*, May 26, 1901, 5.

6. William Thaddeus Sexton, *Soldiers in the Philippines* (Washington, D.C.: Infantry Journal, 1944), 199–200.

7. Sydney A. Cloman, *Myself and a Few Moros* (Garden City, NY: Doubleday, Page, 1923), 116.

Chapter 2: First Contacts

1. "Notes on the Government of the Country Inhabited by Nonchristians in Mindanao and the Neighboring Islands," in U.S. War Department, *Annual Reports of the War Department for the Fiscal Year Ended June 30, 1902*, Vol. IX, Report of the Lieutenant-General Commanding the Army and Department Commanders (Washington, D.C.: Government Printing Office, 1902), 560.

2. Peter G. Gowing, *Mandate in Moroland: The American Government of Muslim Filipinos 1899–1920* (Quezon City: New Day, 1983), 130.

3. Sweet to Adjutant-General Department of Mindanao and Jolo, May 1, 1901, in U.S. War Department, *Annual Reports of the War Department for the Fiscal Year Ended June 30, 1901*, Report of the Lieutenant-General Commanding the Army, Part 4 (Washington, D.C.: Government Printing Office, 1901), 339.

4. Hugh Lennox Scott, *Some Memories of a Soldier* (New York: Century, 1928), 289.

5. Sydney A. Cloman, *Myself and a Few Moros* (Garden City, NY: Doubleday, Page, 1923), 130.

6. Ibid., 135.

7. Ibid., 135; U.S. War Department, *Annual Reports of the War Department for the Fiscal Year Ended June 30, 1900*, Report of the Lieutenant-General Commanding the Army, Part 3 (Washington, D.C.: Government Printing Office, 1900), 258.

8. Cloman, *Myself and a Few Moros*, 136.

9. Ibid.

10. Robert Bacon and James Brown Scott, eds., *Military and Colonial Policy of the United States: Addresses and Reports by Elihu Root* (Cambridge, MA: Harvard University Press, 1916), 320.

11. Baldwin to Pershing, November 30, 1898, Box 316, John J. Pershing Papers, Library of Congress, Washington, D.C.

12. Frank E. Vandiver, *Black Jack: The Life and Times of John J. Pershing* (College Station: Texas A&M University Press, 1977), 1:263. Vandiver cites Pershing's memoirs at the Library of Congress for this reconstructed conversation.

13. Entry of August 23, 1900, Diary of Field Service in the Philippines 1898–1901, Box 1, William August Kobbe Papers, U.S. Army Military History Institute, Carlisle, Pennsylvania.

14. George MacAdam, "The Life of General Pershing VI," *World's Work* 38 (May 1919): 88.

Chapter 3: The Battle of Bayan

1. James R. Arnold, *Jungle of Snakes: A Century of Counterinsurgency Warfare from the Philippines to Iraq* (New York: Bloomsbury Press, 2009), 55.

2. "To the Moros of Lake Lanao," April 13, 1902, in U.S. War Department, *Annual Reports of the War Department for the Fiscal Year Ended June 30, 1902*, Vol. IX, Report of the Lieutenant-General Commanding the Army and Department Commanders (Washington, D.C.: Government Printing Office, 1902), 485.

3. "Memorandum on the Philippine Campaign (1902–1903)," Box 11, Hugh A. Drum Papers, U.S. Army Military History Institute, Carlisle, Pennsylvania.

4. Roosevelt to Chaffee, May 5, 1902, in U.S. War Department. *Annual Reports of the War Department for the Fiscal Year Ended June 30, 1902*, Vol. I, Report of the Secretary of War and Reports of Bureau Chiefs (Washington, D.C.: Government Printing Office, 1903), 18.

5. Peter G. Gowing, *Mandate in Moroland: The American Government of Muslim Filipinos 1899–1920* (Quezon City: New Day, 1983), 87.

Chapter 4: The Rise of Jack Pershing

1. Sanger to Davis, May 13, 1902, in U.S. War Department, *Annual Reports of the War Department for the Fiscal Year Ended June 30, 1902*, Vol. IX, Report of the Lieutenant-General Commanding the Army and Department Commanders (Washington, D.C.: Government Printing Office, 1902), 491.

2. Davis to the Adjutant General, October 15, 1903, Box 369, John J. Pershing Papers, Library of Congress, Washington, D.C.

3. Benjamin D. Foulois, *From the Wright Brothers to the Astronauts: The Memoirs of Major General Benjamin D. Foulois* (New York: McGraw-Hill, 1968), 15.

4. Ibid., 27.

5. Ibid., 29.

6. Benjamin D. Foulois to mother, March 25, 1902, Box 3, Benjamin D. Foulois Papers, Library of Congress.

7. McCoy to Carpenter, December 2, 1903, Box 10, Frank McCoy Papers, Library of Congress.

8. Edward M. Coffman, *The Regulars: The American Army 1898–1941* (Cambridge, MA: Belknap Press, 2004), 44.

9. Peter G. Gowing, *Mandate in Moroland: The American Government of Muslim Filipinos 1899–1920* (Quezon City: New Day, 1983), 90.

10. Pershing to Davis, August 28, 1902, Box 317, Pershing Papers.

11. Field Orders No. 9, September 17, 1902, in U.S. War Department, *Annual Reports of the War Department for the Fiscal Year Ended June 30, 1903*, Vol. III, Reports of Division and Department Commanders (Washington, D.C.: Government Printing Office, 1903), 335.

12. Report of Captain John J. Pershing, October 15, 1902, in U.S. War

Department, *Annual Reports of the War Department for the Fiscal Year Ended June 30, 1903*, Vol. III, Reports of Division and Department Commanders (Washington, D.C.: Government Printing Office, 1903), 334.

13. Foulois, *From the Wright Brothers*, 31.
14. Ibid.
15. Davis to the Adjutant General, October 15, 1903, Box 369, Pershing Papers. Davis's report includes Pershing's report.
16. General Miles's Address to the Troops at Camp Vicars, November 15, 1902, Box 369, Pershing Papers.

Chapter 5: The Conquest Begins

1. Davis to Sumner, April 10, 1903, in U.S. War Department, *Annual Reports of the War Department for the Fiscal Year Ended June 30, 1903*, Vol. III, Reports of Division and Department Commanders (Washington, D.C.: Government Printing Office, 1903), 321.
2. A. Henry Savage Landor, *The Gems of the East* (New York: Harper & Brothers, 1904), 289.
3. U.S. War Department, *Annual Reports of the War Department for the Fiscal Year Ended June 30, 1903*, Vol. III, Reports of Division and Department Commanders (Washington, D.C.: Government Printing Office, 1903), 343.
4. Landor, *Gems of the East*, 296.
5. Camp Marahui, August 24, 1903, Diary Book 2, Robert Lee Bullard Papers, Library of Congress.
6. "Report of Captain John J. Pershing," May 15, 1903, in U.S. War Department, *Annual Reports of the War Department for the Fiscal Year Ended June 30, 1903*, Vol. III, Reports of Division and Department Commanders (Washington, D.C.: Government Printing Office, 1903), 348.
7. U.S. Army Center of Military History, "Medal of Honor Recipients: Philippine Insurrection," http://www.history.army.mil/html/moh/philippine.html.
8. Peter G. Gowing, *Mandate in Moroland: The American Government of Muslim Filipinos 1899–1920* (Quezon City: New Day, 1983), 93.
9. "Report of Major General George W. Davis, U.S. Army, Commanding Division of the Philippines," July 26, 1903, in U.S. War Department, *Annual Reports of the War Department for the Fiscal Year Ended June 30, 1903*, Vol. III, Reports of Division and Department Commanders (Washington, D.C.: Government Printing Office, 1903), 155.

Chapter 6: "A Model Administrator"

1. Jack McCallum, *Leonard Wood: Rough Rider, Surgeon, Architect of American Imperialism* (New York: New York University Press, 2006), 2.

2. Robert Lee Bullard, *Personalities and Reminiscences of the War* (Garden City, NY: Doubleday, Page, 1925), 9.

3. Edward Marshal, *The Story of the Rough Riders, 1st U.S. Volunteer Cavalry: The Regiment in Camp and on the Battle Field* (New York: G. W. Dillingham, 1899), 111.

4. McCallum, *Leonard Wood*, 118.

5. U.S. War Department, *Annual Reports of the War Department for the Fiscal Year Ended June 30, 1902*, Vol. I, Report of the Secretary of War and Reports of Bureau Chiefs (Washington, D.C.: Government Printing Office, 1903), 9.

6. William Harding Carter, *The Life of Lieutenant General Chaffee* (Chicago: University of Chicago Press, 1917), 172.

7. Theodore Roosevelt, "General Leonard Wood: A Model American Military Administrator," *Outlook* 61 (January 7, 1899), 19–23.

8. Hermann Hagedorn, *Leonard Wood: A Biography* (New York: Harper & Brothers, 1931), 2:22.

9. Wood to Roosevelt, September 22, 1903, Box 32, Leonard Wood Papers, Library of Congress, Washington, D.C.

Chapter 7: The New Governor Takes Charge

1. Edward M. Coffman, *The Regulars: The American Army 1898–1941* (Cambridge, MA: Belknap Press, 2004), 76.

2. Alternative propositions are described at http://www.zamboanga.net/Arts&CultureZamboangaHistory.htm.

3. The 1903 census estimate for all of Moro Province was 460,353, a number considered to be an underestimate. Gowing provides population estimates. See Peter G. Gowing, *Mandate in Moroland: The American Government of Muslim Filipinos 1899–1920* (Quezon City: New Day, 1983), 242–43.

4. McCoy to Carpenter, December 2, 1903, Box 10, Frank McCoy Papers, Library of Congress, Washington, D.C.

5. Camp Marahui, August 24, 1903, Diary Book 2, Robert Lee Bullard Papers, Library of Congress.

6. McCoy to Mrs. T. F. McCoy, August 16, 1903, Box 10, McCoy Papers.

7. Camp Marahui, August 24, 1903, Diary Book 2, Bullard Papers.

8. U.S. War Department, *Third Annual Report of Major General Leonard Wood Governor of the Moro Province From July 1, 1905 to April 16, 1906* (Washington, D.C.: Government Printing Office, 1906), 12.

9. Indeed, this was Major Owen Sweet's opinion. See "Sweet to Adjutant-General Department of Mindanao and Jolo," May 1, 1901, in U.S. War Department. *Annual Reports of the War Department for the Fiscal Year Ended June 30, 1901*, Report of the Lieutenant-General Commanding the Army, Part 4 (Washington, D.C.: Government Printing Office, 1901), 339.

10. Hugh Lennox Scott, *Some Memories of a Soldier* (New York: Century, 1928), 297.
11. Ibid., 298.
12. Ibid.
13. McCoy to Carpenter, December 2, 1903, Box 10, McCoy Papers.
14. Wood to Roosevelt, September 20, 1903, Box 32, Leonard Wood Papers, Library of Congress.
15. September 9, 1903, Diary Book 2, Bullard Papers.
16. This account is in Bullard's annotated copy of his article "The Caliber of the Revolver" in Box 9, Bullard Papers.
17. September 17, 1903, Diary Book 2, Bullard Papers.
18. October 8, 1903, Diary Book 2, Bullard Papers.
19. Wood to Strachey, January 6, 1903, Box 32, Wood Papers
20. Wood to Cockrell, September 11, 1903, Box 32, Wood Papers.
21. Wood to Taft, October 7, 1903, Box 32, Wood Papers.
22. Benjamin D. Foulois to mother, February 2, 1904, Benjamin D. Foulois Papers, Library of Congress.
23. Foulois to mother, February 2, 1904, Foulois Papers.
24. McCoy to Charles E. Magoon, October 17, 1903, Box 10, McCoy Papers.

Chapter 8: Leonard Wood Goes to War

1. November 29, 1903, Diary Book 2, Robert Lee Bullard Papers, Library of Congress.
2. Peter G. Gowing, *Mandate in Moroland: The American Government of Muslim Filipinos 1899–1920* (Quezon City: New Day, 1983), 158.
3. This account is in Bullard's annotated copy of his article "The Caliber of the Revolver" in Box 9, Bullard Papers.
4. This is often overlooked, but see Bullard's diary entry of December 26, 1903: "In the campaigning in Jolo there was considerable destruction of the country necessary to impress the natives. Many cottas were destroyed and many houses burned. Some women and children were unavoidably killed in battle as they mixed up with the men."
5. McCoy to Carpenter, December 2, 1903, Box 10, Frank McCoy Papers, Library of Congress.
6. Diary entry of November 16, 1903, Leonard Wood Papers, Library of Congress.
7. December 1, 1903, Diary Book 2, Bullard Papers.
8. Taft to Wood, December 8, 1903, Box 33, Wood Papers.
9. Jack McCallum, *Leonard Wood: Rough Rider, Surgeon, Architect of American Imperialism* (New York: New York University Press, 2006), 218.

10. December 26, 1903, Diary Book 2, Bullard Papers.

11. Pershing to Governor-General, November 1, 1913, "Status of the Sultan of Sulu" folder, Special Correspondence, Philippine Correspondence, Box 280, Pershing Papers.

12. December 31, 1903, Diary Book 2, Bullard Papers.

13. December 26, 1903, Diary Book 2, Bullard Papers.

14. Excerpts from Hamilton's diary are reprinted in A. B. Feuer, *Combat Diary: Episodes from the History of the Twenty-second Regiment, 1866–1905* (New York: Praeger, 1991), 160.

15. Feuer, 160.

Chapter 9: "Like Rats in a Trap"

1. Hermann Hagedorn, *Leonard Wood: A Biography* (New York: Harper & Brothers, 1931), 2:41.

2. McCoy to mother, December 3, 1903, Box 3 and March 5, 1904, Box 4, Frank McCoy Papers, Library of Congress.

3. Richard Barry, "The End of Datto Ali," *Collier's*, June 6, 1906, 18.

4. McCoy to mother, April 12, 1904, Box 4, McCoy Papers.

5. April 3, 1904, Diary, Wood Papers.

6. Oskaloosa Smith, *History of the Twenty-second United States Infantry, 1866–1922* (New York, 1922), 96.

7. McCoy to mother, April 12, 1904, Box 4, McCoy Papers.

8. Ibid.

9. "Report of Brigadier General George W. Davis," August 1, 1902, in U.S. War Department, *Annual Reports of the War Department for the Fiscal Year Ended June 30, 1902*, Vol. IX, Report of the Lieutenant-General Commanding the Army and Department Commanders (Washington, D.C.: Government Printing Office, 1902), 495.

10. McCoy to mother, April 12, 1904, Box 4, McCoy Papers.

11. Wood to Francis Greene, September 5, 1904, Folder 7, Box 35, Wood Papers.

12. April 7, 1904, Diary, Box 3, Wood Papers.

13. McCoy to mother, April 20, 1904, Box 4, McCoy Papers.

14. Ibid.

15. Benjamin D. Foulois, *From the Wright Brothers to the Astronauts: The Memoirs of Major General Benjamin D. Foulois* (New York: McGraw-Hill, 1968), 37.

16. Ibid., 38.

17. Maureen P. Mahin, *Life in the American Army from the Frontier Days to Army Distaff Hall* (Washington, D.C.: Baker-Webster, 1967), 106.

18. June 21, 1904, Diary Book 3, Robert Lee Bullard Papers, Library of Congress.

19. Wood to Roosevelt, September 20, 1903, Wood Papers.

Chapter 10: Eye of the Storm

1. William Thaddeus Sexton, *Soldiers in the Philippines* (Washington, D.C.: Infantry Journal, 1944), 200.

2. Hugh Scott, *Some Memories of a Soldier* (New York: Century, 1928), 314.

3. Ibid., 312.

4. Richard K. Kolb, "Campaign in Moroland: A War the World Forgot," *Army*, September 1983, 52.

5. See Charles T. Haven and Frank A. Belden, *A History of the Colt Revolver* (New York: William Morrow, 1940), 304, and James R. Arnold, *Jeff Davis's Own: Cavalry, Comanches, and the Battle for the Texas Frontier* (New York: John Wiley and Sons, 2000), 138–41.

6. This account is in Bullard's annotated copy of his article "The Caliber of the Revolver" in Box 9, Robert Lee Bullard Papers, Library of Congress, Washington, D.C.

7. U.S. War Department, *Third Annual Report of Major General Leonard Wood Governor of the Moro Province From July 1, 1905 to April 16, 1906* (Washington, D.C.: Government Printing Office, 1906), 7.

8. Hermann Hagedorn, *Leonard Wood: A Biography* (New York: Harper & Brothers, 1931), 2:49–50.

9. Wood to Grebel, October 25, 1904, Folder 7, Box 35, Leonard Wood Papers, Library of Congress.

10. Scott, *Some Memories*, 391.

11. McCoy to family, May 6, 1905, Box 1, Frank McCoy Papers, Library of Congress.

12. Benjamin D. Foulois, *From the Wright Brothers to the Astronauts: The Memoirs of Major General Benjamin D. Foulois* (New York: McGraw-Hill, 1968), 39.

13. Hagedorn, *Leonard Wood*, 2:60–61.

14. "Report Commanding Officer, Cotabato," June 4, 1902, in U.S. War Department, *Annual Reports of the War Department for the Fiscal Year Ended June 30, 1902*, Vol. IX, Report of the Lieutenant-General Commanding the Army and Department Commanders (Washington, DC: Government Printing Office, 1902), 528.

15. Richard Barry, "The End of Datto Ali," *Collier's*, June 6, 1906, 18.

16. Ali to Wood, July 14, 1904, English translation in Dispatch Book 5 (June–July 1904), Box 1, McCoy Papers.

17. Barry, "The End of Datto Ali," 18.

18. McCoy's report of this operation is in "McCoy to Military Secretary," Department of Mindanao, October 31, 1905, Box 11, McCoy Papers.

19. Barry, "The End of Datto Ali," 18.

20. Ibid., 17.

Chapter 11: Storm at Bud Dajo

1. Richard K. Kolb, "Campaign in Moroland: A War the World Forgot," *Army*, September 1983, 57.

2. Benjamin D. Foulois, *From the Wright Brothers to the Astronauts: The Memoirs of Major General Benjamin D. Foulois* (New York: McGraw-Hill, 1968), 17.

3. Edward M. Coffman, *The Regulars: The American Army 1898–1941* (Cambridge, MA: Belknap Press, 2004), 96.

4. Ibid.

5. Hugh Lennox Scott, *Some Memories of a Soldier* (New York: Century, 1928), 307.

6. Report of the Governor of the Moro Province, September 22, 1905, in U.S. War Department, *Annual Reports of the War Department for the Fiscal Year Ended June 30, 1905*, Vol. X, Report of the Philippine Commission, Part 1 (Washington, D.C.: Government Printing Office, 1905), 345.

7. Victor Hurley, *Jungle Patrol: The Story of the Philippine Constabulary* (New York: E. P. Dutton, 1938), 332.

8. Hermann Hagedorn, *Leonard Wood: A Biography* (New York: Harper & Brothers, 1931), 2:64.

9. Scott, *Some Memories*, 321.

10. Ibid., 308.

11. Ibid., 380.

12. Jack McCallum, *Leonard Wood: Rough Rider, Surgeon, Architect of American Imperialism* (New York: New York University Press, 2006), 228, citing "Transcript Sawajaan to Reeve," December 4, 1905, Wood Papers.

13. Stedje to Adjutant, February 1, 1906, Box 37, Wood Papers. Stedje was the firing range officer.

14. Reeves to Langhorne, March 1, 1906, Box 37, Wood Papers.

15. February 28, 1906, Diary, Box 3, Wood Papers.

16. Langhorne to Wood, February 9, 1906, Box 37, Wood Papers

17. A. J. Bacevich, *Diplomat in Khaki: Major General Frank Ross McCoy and American Foreign Policy, 1898–1949* (Lawrence: University Press of Kansas, 1989), 37.

18. Wood to Duncan, March 2, 1906, in "Report of Engagement with Moro Enemy on Bud-Dajo, Island of Jolo, March 5th, 6th, 7th, and 8th, 1906," Col. J. W. Duncan, 6th Inf. Commanding, Folder "Battle of Bud-Dajo 1906," Box 278, John J. Pershing Papers, Library of Congress.

19. McCoy to family, March 10, 1906, Box 4, McCoy Papers, Library of Congress.

20. Wood to President, May 14, 1906, Box 37, Wood Papers.

21. "Report of Engagement with Moro Enemy on Bud-Dajo, Island of Jolo, March 5th, 6th, 7th, and 8th, 1906," Col. J. W. Duncan, 6th Inf. Commanding, Folder "Battle of Bud-Dajo 1906," Box 278, Pershing Papers. Pershing used Duncan's report while planning his own operations on Jolo in 1911.

22. John R. White, *Bullets and Bolos: Fifteen Years in the Philippine Islands* (New York: Century 1928), 304.

23. Ibid., 308.

24. "Report of Engagement with Moro Enemy on Bud-Dajo, Island of Jolo, March 5th, 6th, 7th, and 8th, 1906," Col. J. W. Duncan, 6th Inf. Commanding, Folder "Battle of Bud-Dajo 1906," Box 278, Pershing Papers.

25. White, *Bullets and Bolos,* 309.

26. Lawton's note is appended in Diary of Events, Major General Leonard Wood, February 1, 1906–December 31, 1906, Box 3, Wood Papers.

27. Langhorne claims that Lawton asked him for tactical advice and that he came up with the notion of the flanking move. Lawton makes no mention of this purported advice. It is hard to image that an officer who had never seen the ground would have the decisive voice in this situation. For Langhorne's depiction see his "Notes on Bud Dajo Expedition," Diary of Events, Major General Leonard Wood, February 1, 1906–December 31, 1906, Box 3, Wood Papers.

28. Wood was in an awkward command relationship. Having been appointed to head the entire Department of the Philippines, he had retained his position as civil governor of Moro Province while naming Bliss as military governor of Moro Province.

29. Report of Captain Edward P. Lawton, Philippines Miscellaneous Material, Box 217, Wood Papers.

30. Ibid.

31. Brian McAllister Linn, *Guardians of Empire: The U.S. Army and the Pacific 1902–1940* (Chapel Hill: University of North Carolina Press, 1997), 39.

32. McCoy to family, March 10, 1906, Box 4, McCoy Papers.

Chapter 12: The End of the Storm

1. McCallum and Bacevich claim losses as eighteen killed and fifty-two wounded, citing Wood's telegram to Andrews on March 9. However, Wood's telegram ignores minor casualties. See Wood to Andrews, March 9, 1906, Diary of Events, Major General Leonard Wood, February 1,

1906–December 31, 1906, Box 3, Leonard Wood Papers, Library of Congress, Washington, D.C.

2. March 7, 1906, Diary of Events, Major General Leonard Wood February 1, 1906–December 31, 1906, Box 3, Wood Papers.

3. Miller to McCoy, March 12, 1906, General Correspondence, March–April 1906, Box 11, Frank McCoy Papers, Library of Congress.

4. March 31, 1906, Diary Book 3, Box 1, Robert Lee Bullard Papers, Library of Congress.

5. Donald Smythe, "Pershing and the Disarmament of the Moros," *Pacific Historical Review* 31, 3 (August 1962): 250.

6. Roosevelt to Wood, March 10, 1906, Diary of Events, Major General Leonard Wood, February 1, 1906–December 31, 1906, Box 3, Wood Papers.

7. John Morgan Gates, *"Schoolbooks and Krags": The United States Army in the Philippines, 1898–1902* (Westport, CT: Greenwood Press, 1973), 173.

8. "Comments on the Moro Massacre," March 12, 1906, in Jim Zwick, ed., *Mark Twain's Weapons of Satire: Anti-Imperialist Writings on the Philippine-American War* (Syracuse, NY: Syracuse University Press, 1992), 172.

9. Hermann Hagedorn, *Leonard Wood: A Biography* (New York: Harper & Brothers, 1931), 2:66.

10. Taft to Wood, March 12, 1906, Diary of Events, Major General Leonard Wood, February 1, 1906–December 31, 1906, Box 3, Wood Papers.

11. Wood to War Department, March 13, 1906, Box 37, Wood Papers.

12. See "Engagement at Mt. Dajo: Message from the President of the United States," March 15, 1906, in 59th Congress, 1st session, House Document 622.

13. Ide to Secretary of War, March 20, 1906, Box 37, Wood Papers.

14. Diary entries of March 16 and 17, 1906, in Diary of Events, Major General Leonard Wood, February 1, 1906–December 31, 1906, Box 3, Wood Papers.

15. Ide to Taft, March 20, 1906, Diary of Events, Major General Leonard Wood, February 1, 1906–December 31, 1906, Box 3, Wood Papers.

16. *New York Times*, March 20, 1906.

17. "The Battle in Jolo," *Outlook* 82 (March 17, 1906): 582–83.

18. Jack McCallum, *Leonard Wood: Rough Rider, Surgeon, Architect of American Imperialism* (New York: New York University Press, 2006), 230.

19. From transcript of meeting on Sabah, April 13, 1906, Box 3, Wood Papers.

20. *The Correspondence of W. E. B. Du Bois: Volume I Selections, 1877–1934*, ed. Herbert Aptheker (Amherst: University of Massachusetts Press, 1973), 136.

21. Report Philippines Division, U.S. War Department, *Annual Reports of the War Department for the Fiscal Year Ended June 30, 1906*, Vol. III, Reports of

Division and Department Commanders (Washington, D.C.: Government Printing Office, 1906), 211.

22. U.S. War Department, *Third Annual Report of Major General Leonard Wood Governor of the Moro Province From July 1, 1905 to April 16, 1906* (Washington, D.C.: Government Printing Office, 1906), 13; and Report Department of Mindanao, April 12, 1906, in Report Philippines Division, U.S. War Department, *Annual Reports of the War Department for the Fiscal Year Ended June 30, 1906*, Vol. III, Reports of Division and Department Commanders (Washington, D.C.: Government Printing Office, 1906), 279.

23. "Report of the Governor-General of the Philippine Islands for the Fiscal Year 1906 and Other Stated Periods," in U.S. War Department, *Annual Reports of the War Department for the Fiscal Year Ended June 30, 1906*, Vol. VII, Part 1, Report of the Philippine Commission (Washington, D.C.: Government Printing Office, 1907), 85.

24. U.S. War Department, *Third Annual Report of Major General Leonard Wood Governor of the Moro Province from July 1, 1905 to April 16, 1906* (Washington, D.C.: Government Printing Office, 1906), 14.

25. "Report of the Governor-General of the Philippine Islands for the Fiscal Year 1905 and Other Stated Periods," in U.S. War Department, *Annual Reports of the War Department for the Fiscal Year Ended June 30, 1905*, Vol. X, Part 1, Report of the Philippine Commission (Washington, D.C.: Government Printing Office, 1907), 85.

Chapter 13: Tasker Bliss and the Return to Benign Assimilation

1. Hugh Lennox Scott, *Some Memories of a Soldier* (New York: Century, 1928), 322.

2. Ibid., 400.

3. Ibid., 376.

4. Frederick Palmer, *Bliss, Peacemaker: The Life and Letters of General Tasker Howard Bliss* (New York: Dodd, Mead, 1934), 19.

5. Bliss to wife, July 9, 1906, Box 22, Tasker Howard Bliss Papers, U.S. Army Military History Institute, Carlisle, Pennsylvania.

6. U.S. War Department, *The Annual Report of the Governor of the Moro Province for the Fiscal Year Ended June 30, 1907* (Manila: Bureau of Printing, 1907), 29.

7. U.S. War Department, *The Annual Report of the Governor of the Moro Province for the Fiscal Year Ended June 30, 1907* (Manila: Bureau of Printing, 1907), 23.

8. Wood to Bliss, July 17, 1906, in Official Correspondence, Folder 61, Box 15, Tasker Howard Bliss Papers, Library of Congress, Washington, D.C.

9. Palmer, *Bliss*, 92.

10. During the entire three days, four Americans died and twenty were wounded.

Chapter 14: The Problems of Pacification

1. Edward M. Coffman, *The Regulars: The American Army 1898–1941* (Cambridge, MA: Belknap Press, 2004), 165.

2. "Report Philippines Division," in U.S. War Department, *Annual Reports of the War Department for the Fiscal Year Ended June 30, 1906*, Vol. III, Reports of Division and Department Commanders (Washington, D.C.: Government Printing Office, 1906), 208.

3. Charles D. Rhodes, "The Utilization of Native Troops in Our Foreign Possessions," *Journal of the Military Service Institution of the United States* 30, 15 (January 1902): 9.

4. Coffman, *The Regulars*, 86.

5. "Report Philippines Division," in U.S. War Department, *Annual Reports of the War Department for the Fiscal Year Ended June 30, 1906*, Vol. III, Reports of Division and Department Commanders (Washington, D.C.: Government Printing Office, 1906), 213.

6. Coffman, *The Regulars*, 50.

7. "Report Philippines Division," in U.S. War Department, *Annual Reports of the War Department for the Fiscal Year Ended June 30, 1906*, Vol. III, Reports of Division and Department Commanders (Washington, D.C.: Government Printing Office, 1906), 214.

8. "The United States Versus Homer Grafton," http://www.lawphil.net/jud juris/juri1906/apr1906/gr_l-2400_1906.html.

9. The 62nd Article of War granted military courts the power to try officers and soldiers in time of peace for any noncapital offense that the civil law declared to be a crime against the public.

10. "The United States Versus Homer Grafton," http://www.lawphil.net/jud juris/juri1906/apr1906/gr_l-2400_1906.html.

11. Ibid.

12. Ibid.

13. "Report Philippines Division," in U.S. War Department, *Annual Reports of the War Department for the Fiscal Year Ended June 30, 1906*, Vol. III, Reports of Division and Department Commanders (Washington, D.C.: Government Printing Office, 1906), 220.

14. "Report of Field Operations, Leyte, Colonel F. A. Smith, 8th Infantry, December 10, 1906 to June 10, 1907," in Folder 11, Box 217, Leonard Wood Papers, Library of Congress, Washington, D.C.

15. "206 US 333 Homer Grafton Versus United States," http://openjurist
    .org/206/us/333.
16. *United States v. Dixon* (91-1231), 509 U.S. 688 (1993).

Chapter 15: "Sponge Cake, Coffee, Cigars"
1. "Agricultural Fair a Great Success," *Mindanao Herald*, February 16, 1907, 1.
2. "Bliss to Wife," May 1, 1907, Box 22, Tasker Howard Bliss Papers, U.S.
   Army Military History Institute, Carlisle, Pennsylvania.
3. Edward M. Coffman, *The Regulars: The American Army 1898–1941* (Cambridge, MA: Belknap Press, 2004), 76.
4. Maureen P. Mahin, *Life in the American Army from the Frontier Days to
   Army Distaff Hall* (Washington, D.C.: Baker-Webster, 1967), 99.
5. Ibid., 104.
6. "Report Department of Mindanao, April 12, 1906," in U.S. War Department. Report Philippines Division, *Annual Reports of the War Department
   for the Fiscal Year Ended June 30, 1906*, Vol. III, Reports of Division and
   Department Commanders (Washington, D.C.: Government Printing
   Office, 1906), 288.
7. Coffman, *The Regulars*, 77.
8. John R. White, *Bullets and Bolos: Fifteen Years in the Philippine Islands*
   (New York: Century, 1928), 233.
9. Mahin, *Life in the American Army*, 103.
10. Diary of Second Lieutenant George C. Lawrason, in John H. Nankivell,
    *The History of the Twenty-Fifth Infantry Regiment United States Infantry
    1869–1926* (Fort Collins, CO: Old Army Press, 1972), 131.
11. Schück to Scott, February 6, 1909, in Hugh Lennox Scott, *Some Memories
    of a Soldier* (New York: Century, 1928), 401.
12. "Report Department of Mindanao, April 12, 1906," in U.S. War Depart-
    ment, Report Philippines Division, *Annual Reports of the War Depart-
    ment for the Fiscal Year Ended June 30, 1906*, Vol. III, Reports of Division
    and Department Commanders (Washington, D.C.: Government Printing
    Office, 1906), 314.

Chapter 16: Jungle Patrols
1. Brian McAllister Linn, *Guardians of Empire: The U.S. Army and the Pacific
   1902–1940* (Chapel Hill: University of North Carolina Press, 1997), 40.
2. Victor Hurley, *Jungle Patrol: The Story of the Philippine Constabulary* (New
   York: E. P. Dutton, 1938), 167.
3. "Being a Constable Among the Moros," *Boston Evening Transcript*, July 19,
   1913, 36.
4. Furlong to Fred Stockbridge, Malaybalay, March 22, 1910, Box 7, Folder 2,

Charles Furlong Papers, Special Collections and University Archives, University of Oregon.

5. Hurley, *Jungle Patrol*, 287.

6. Victor Hurley, *Swish of the Kris: The Story of the Moros* (New York: E. P. Dutton, 1936), 212.

7. "Report Philippines Division," U.S. War Department, *Annual Reports of the War Department for the Fiscal Year Ended June 30, 1906*, Vol. III, Reports of Division and Department Commanders (Washington, D.C.: Government Printing Office, 1906), 212.

8. "Report of the Governor-General," U.S. War Department. *Annual Reports of the War Department for the Fiscal Year Ended June 30, 1906*, Vol. VII, Part 1, Report of the Philippine Commission (Washington, D.C.: Government Printing Office, 1907), 87.

9. Among much correspondence on the subject, see Lieutenant Allen Wallace, Philippine Scouts to Bliss, January 13, 1907, Box 59, Tasker H. Bliss Papers, Library of Congress, Washington, D.C.

10. Bliss to Wood, January 14, 1907, Box 59, Bliss Papers, Library of Congress.

11. Bliss to wife, July 9, 1906, Box 22, Tasker Howard Bliss Papers, U.S. Army Military History Institute, Carlisle, Pennsylvania.

12. Frederick Palmer, *Bliss, Peacemaker: The Life and Letters of General Tasker Howard Bliss* (New York: Dodd, Mead, 1934), 92.

Chapter 17: The Return of John Pershing

1. George MacAdam, "The Life of General Pershing VI," *World's Work* 38 (May 1919): 97.

2. Ibid., 98.

3. The number is variously cited as 835 and 862, with Vandiver claiming 909. See Frank E. Vandiver, *Black Jack: The Life and Times of John J. Pershing* (College Station: Texas A&M University Press, 1977), 1:390.

4. Ibid., 456.

5. Ibid., 477.

6. Robert Ginsburgh, "Pershing as His Orderlies Knew Him," *American Legion Monthly* 5, 4 (October 1928): 11.

7. Vandiver, *Black Jack*, 477.

8. Governor of Moro Province, Folder 1, Box 370, Pershing Papers.

9. Ginsburgh, "Pershing." 9.

10. Ibid., 10.

11. MacAdam, "The Life of General Pershing VI," 101.

12. Pershing to Bell, April 2, 1911, Box 370, Pershing Papers.

13. Memorandum for General Pershing from Captain Humphreys, January 14, 1911, Box 370, Pershing Papers.

14. Pershing to Bell, April 22, 1911, Box 370, Pershing Papers.

15. Stuart Creighton Miller, *"Benevolent Assimilation": The American Conquest of the Philippines, 1899–1903* (New Haven, CT: Yale University Press, 1982), 260.

16. Pershing to Bell, April 22, 1911, Box 370, Pershing Papers.

17. Pershing to Warren, February 9, 1912, Box 370, Pershing Papers.

18. Annual Report of the Governor of the Moro Province for the Year Ending June 30, 1912, page 11, Box 371, Pershing Papers. For full text, see Executive Order No. 24, Zamboanga, Mindanao, September 8, 1911, also in Box 371.

19. Pershing to Bell, December 16, 1911, Box 370, Pershing Papers.

20. "Extracts From the Diary of Lieutenant Boswell Regarding the Investment and Surrender of Dajo," Box 371, Pershing Papers.

21. Vandiver, *Black Jack*, 541.

22. Victor Hurley, *Jungle Patrol: The Story of the Philippine Constabulary* (New York: E. P. Dutton, 1938), 316.

23. Ibid., 317.

24. Ibid., 319.

Chapter 18: Bud Bagsak: The Last Battle

1. Victor Hurley, *Jungle Patrol: The Story of the Philippine Constabulary* (New York: E. P. Dutton, 1938), 333.

2. Donald Smythe, *Guerrilla Warrior: The Early Life of John J. Pershing* (New York: Charles Scribner's Sons, 1973), 186.

3. Pershing to Forbes, February 28, 1913, Box 76, Pershing Papers.

4. James Collins is not to be confused with his younger brother Joseph Lawton, the "Lightning Joe" of World War II fame.

5. James L. Collins, "The Battle of Bud Bagsak and the Part Played by the Mountain Guns Therein," *Field Artillery Journal* XV (November–December 1925): 561.

6. The orders read "Headquarters Jolo Field Forces, Bun Bun, 1 A.M." See Pershing to Adjutant General, October 15, 1913, Box 371, Pershing Papers. However, Vandiver writes that the *Wright* did not make landfall until 3:30 A.M., suggesting perhaps that the orders were written aboard the *Wright* and not at Bun Bun. See Frank E. Vandiver, *Black Jack: The Life and Times of John J. Pershing* (College Station: Texas A&M University Press, 1977), 1:560.

7. Hurley, *Jungle Patrol*, 333.

8. Donald Smythe, "Pershing and Counterinsurgency," *Military Review* 46 (September 1966): 90.

9. Ibid.

10. Collins, "The Battle of Bud Bagsak," 566.

11. For details see Bell to Adjutant General, July 3, 1913, Box 178, Pershing Papers.

12. Hurley, *Jungle Patrol*, 335.

13. Ibid., 335–36.

14. Collins, "The Battle of Bud Bagsak," 569.

15. Vandiver, *Black Jack*, 567.

16. Smythe, *Guerrilla Warrior*, 157.

17. Bell to Pershing, June 18, 1913, Box 278, Pershing Papers.

18. "A Battle with Moros," *Outlook* 104 (June 21, 1913): 355.

19. Hurley, *Jungle Patrol*, 340.

20. Ibid., 341.

21. Pershing to Bell, August 23, 1912, Box 370, Pershing Papers.

22. Ibid.

23. George MacAdam, "The Life of General Pershing VI," *World's Work* 38 (May 1919): 103.

Chapter 19: A Forgotten War

1. Hugh Lennox Scott, *Some Memories of a Soldier* (New York: Century, 1928), 292.

2. Sydney A. Cloman, *Myself and a Few Moros* (Garden City, NY: Doubleday, Page, 1923), 38.

3. Hermann Hagedorn, *Leonard Wood: A Biography* (New York: Harper & Brothers, 1931), 2:392.

4. "A Review of the Moro Petition, Its Origin, Scope and Purpose, And How Its Object May Be Realized in Aid of the American System of Control," in Najeeb M. Saleeby, *The Moro Problem: An Academic Discussion of the History and Solution of the Problem of the Government of the Moros of the Philippine Islands* (Manila, 1913), 5.

5. Victor Hurley, *Swish of the Kris: The Story of the Moros* (New York: E. P. Dutton, 1936), 175.

6. Wood to Bliss, July 17, 1906, Official Correspondence, folder 61, Box 15, Tasker H. Bliss Papers, Library of Congress, Washington, D.C.

7. Benjamin D. Foulois, *From the Wright Brothers to the Astronauts: The Memoirs of Major General Benjamin D. Foulois* (New York: McGraw-Hill, 1968), 41.

8. Donald Smythe, *Guerrilla Warrior: The Early Life of John J. Pershing* (New York: Charles Scribner's Sons, 1973), 203.

9. Edward G. Lengel, *To Conquer Hell: The Meuse-Argonne, 1918* (New York: Henry Holt, 2008), 13.

10. Charles A. Byler, "Pacifying the Moros: American Military Government in the Southern Philippines, 1899–1913," *Military Review* (May–June 2005): 41.

11. Edward M. Coffman, *The Regulars: The American Army 1898–1941* (Cambridge, MA: Belknap Press, 2004), 162.

12. "Reports of Provincial Governors," U.S. War Department, *Annual Reports of the War Department for the Fiscal Year Ended June 30, 1906*, Vol. VII, Part I, Report of the Philippine Commission (Washington, D.C.: Government Printing Office, 1907), 345.

13. Coffman, *The Regulars*, 46.

14. "Reports of Provincial Governors," U.S. War Department, *Annual Reports of the War Department for the Fiscal Year Ended June 30, 1906*, Vol. VII, Part I, Report of the Philippine Commission (Washington, D.C.: Government Printing Office, 1907), 351.

15. Forbes to Barrows, September 24, 1909, Box 320, John J. Pershing Papers, Library of Congress.

16. John R. White, *Bullets and Bolos: Fifteen Years in the Philippine Islands* (New York: Century, 1928), 216.

17. Pershing to Harbord, November 3, 1913, in file "Constabulary Notes," Box 278, Pershing Papers.

18. Scott, *Some Memories*, 484–85.

19. Tulawie to Gordon, Jolo, December 24, 1914, Box 37, Pershing Papers.

20. Mehol K. Sadain, "Sulu Treaties," Yuchengco Museum, Makati City, September 20, 2008, http://www.yuchengcomuseum.org/programs.

21. Peter G. Gowing, *Mandate in Moroland: The American Government of Muslim Filipinos 1899–1920* (Quezon City: New Day, 1983), 315.

22. Victor H. Krulak, *First to Fight: An Inside View of the U.S. Marine Corps* (Annapolis: Naval Institute Press, 1984), 185.

23. A. B. Feuer, *Combat Diary: Episodes from the History of the Twenty-second Regiment, 1866–1905* (New York: Praeger, 1991), 159.

24. Bliss to Pershing, September 27, 1909, Box 370, Pershing Papers.

25. "Notes in Regard to Mindanao by Don Julian González Panado," Philippine Correspondence, Box 279, Pershing Papers.

26. Phillip B. Davidson, *Vietnam at War* (Novato, CA: Presidio, 1988), 798.

27. F. Delor Angeles, "The Moro Wars," in Peter G. Gowing and Robert D. McAmis, eds., *The Muslim Filipinos* (Manila: Solidarida, 1974), 31.

28. "City of Zamboanga," http://www.zamboanga.net/Arts&CultureZamboangaHistory2.htm.

29. Patrick Barta, "Jailbreak in Philippines," *Wall Street Journal*, December 14, 2009, A10.

30. Orlando de Guzman, "Reporter's Diary. Songs of Resistance: History Repeats Itself," www.pbs.org/frontlineworld/stories/philippines/guzman02.html.

31. Smythe, *Guerrilla Warrior*, 183.

Afteword: The Cradle of Leadership

1. John J. Pershing, *My Experiences in the World War* (New York: Frederick A. Stokes, 1931), 2:190.

2. Edward M. Coffman, *The Regulars: The American Army 1898–1941* (Cambridge, MA: Belknap Press, 2004), 165.

3. "National Affairs: Great Green Snake," *Time*, May 25, 1931.

4. Benjamin D. Foulois, *From the Wright Brothers to the Astronauts: The Memoirs of Major General Benjamin D. Foulois* (New York: McGraw-Hill, 1968), 38.

5. Charles Penrose, *James G. Harbord* (New York: Newcomen Society, 1956), 15.

6. Edward G. Lengel, *To Conquer Hell: The Meuse-Argonne, 1918* (New York: Henry Holt, 2008), 14.

7. Pershing, *My Experiences in the World War*, 1:18.

8. Piang to Stimson, February 22, 1942, http://www.fdrlibrary.marist.edu/psf/box5/a60z02.html.

Bibliography

Books

Aptheker, Herbert, ed. *The Correspondence of W. E. B. Du Bois: Volume I Selections, 1877–1934*. Amherst: University of Massachusetts Press, 1973.

Arnold, James R. *Jungle of Snakes: A Century of Counterinsurgency Warfare from the Philippines to Iraq*. New York: Bloomsbury Press, 2009.

"Attack by United States Troops on Mount Dajo, March 26, 1906." 59th Congress, 1st Session, Senate Doc. 289. Washington, DC: Government Printing Office, 1906.

Bacevich, A. J. *Diplomat in Khaki: Major General Frank Ross McCoy and American Foreign Policy, 1898–1949*. Lawrence: University Press of Kansas, 1989.

Bacon, Robert, and James Scott Brown, eds. *Military and Colonial Policy of the United States: Addresses and Reports by Elihu Root*. Cambridge, MA: Harvard University Press, 1916.

Bryan, William Jennings. *The Memoirs of William Jennings Bryan*. Philadelphia: John C. Winston, 1925.

Bullard, Robert Lee. *Personalities and Reminiscences of the War*. Garden City, NY: Doubleday, Page, 1925.

Carter, William Harding. *The Life of Lieutenant General Chaffee*. Chicago: University of Chicago Press, 1917.

Cloman, Sydney A. *Myself and a Few Moros*. Garden City, NY: Doubleday, Page, 1923.

Coffman, Edward M. *The Regulars: The American Army 1898–1941*. Cambridge, MA: Belknap Press, 2004.

"Engagement at Mt. Dajo: Message from the President of the United States, March 15, 1906." 59th Congress, 1st Session, House Doc. 622. Washington, D.C.: Government Printing Office, 1906.

Feuer, A. B. *Combat Diary: Episodes from the History of the Twenty-Second Regiment, 1866–1905*. New York: Praeger, 1991.

Foulois, Benjamin D. *From the Wright Brothers to the Astronauts: The Memoirs of Major General Benjamin D. Foulois.* New York: McGraw-Hill, 1968.

Gates, John Morgan. *"Schoolbooks and Krags": The United States Army in the Philippines, 1898–1902.* Westport, CT: Greenwood Press, 1973.

Gowing, Peter G. *Mandate in Moroland: The American Government of Muslim Filipinos 1899–1920.* Quezon City: New Day, 1983.

Gowing, Peter G., and Robert D. McAmis, eds. *The Muslim Filipinos.* Manila: Solidarida, 1974.

Hagedorn, Hermann. *Leonard Wood: A Biography.* 2 vols. New York: Harper & Brothers, 1931.

Hunt, George A. *The History of the Twenty-seventh Infantry.* Honolulu: Honolulu Star Bulletin, 1931.

Hurley, Victor. *Jungle Patrol: The Story of the Philippine Constabulary.* New York: E. P. Dutton, 1938.

———. *Swish of the Kris: The Story of the Moros.* New York: E. P. Dutton, 1936.

Krulak, Victor H. *First to Fight: An Inside View of the U.S. Marine Corps.* Annapolis: Naval Institute Press, 1984.

Landor, A. Henry Savage. *The Gems of the East.* New York: Harper & Brothers, 1904.

Lane, Jack C. *Armed Progressive: General Leonard Wood.* San Rafael, CA: Presidio Press, 1978.

Lengel, Edward G. *To Conquer Hell: The Meuse-Argonne, 1918.* New York: Henry Holt, 2008.

Linn, Brian McAllister. "Foreshadowing the War in Iraq: The U.S. War in the Philippines, 1899–1902." In *Warriors and Scholars: A Modern War Reader,* ed. Peter B. Lane and Ronald E. Marcello, pp. 254–73. Denton: University of North Texas Press, 2005.

———. *The Philippine War: 1899–1902.* Lawrence: University Press of Kansas, 2000.

———. *Guardians of Empire: The U.S. Army and the Pacific 1902–1940.* Chapel Hill: University of North Carolina Press, 1997.

Mahin, Maureen P. *Life in the American Army from the Frontier Days to Army Distaff Hall.* Washington, D.C.: Baker-Webster, 1967.

Man, W. K. Che. *Muslim Separatism: The Moros of Southern Philippines and the Malays of Southern Thailand.* Oxford, UK: Oxford University Press, 1990.

Manual for the Philippine Constabulary, 1915. Manila: Philippine Constabulary, 1915.

Marshal, Edward. *The Story of the Rough Riders, 1st U.S. Volunteer Cavalry: The Regiment in Camp and on the Battle Field.* New York: G. W. Dillingham, 1899.

Matloff, Maurice, ed. *American Military History*. Washington, D.C.: U.S. Army Office of the Chief of Military History, 1969.

McCallum, Jack. *Leonard Wood: Rough Rider, Surgeon, Architect of American Imperialism*. New York: New York University Press, 2006.

McCoy, Alfred W. *Policing America's Empire: The United States, the Philippines, and the Rise of the Surveillance State*. Madison: University of Wisconsin Press, 2009.

McIver, George Willcox. *A Life of Duty: The Autobiography of George Willcox McIver, 1858–1948*. Charleston, SC: History Press, 2006.

Miller, Stuart Creighton. *"Benevolent Assimilation": The American Conquest of the Philippines, 1899–1903*. New Haven, CT: Yale University Press, 1982.

Millet, Allan R. *The General: Robert L. Bullard and Officership in the United States Army 1881–1925*. Westport, CT: Greenwood Press, 1975.

Nankivell, John H. *The History of the Twenty-fifth Infantry Regiment United States Infantry 1869–1926*. Fort Collins, CO: Old Army Press, 1972.

Palmer, Frederick. *Bliss, Peacemaker: The Life and Letters of General Tasker Howard Bliss*. New York: Dodd, Mead, 1934.

Penrose, Charles. *James G. Harbord*. New York: Newcomen Society, 1956.

Pershing, John J. *My Experiences in the World War*. 2 vols. New York: Frederick A. Stokes, 1931.

Potter, David. *Sailing the Sulu Seas: Belles and Bandits in the Philippines*. New York: E. P. Dutton, 1940.

Rice, George D. *Photographs of the Battle of Bacolod*. Manila, 1903.

Saleeby, Najeeb M. *The Moro Problem: An Academic Discussion of the History and Solution of the Problem of the Government of the Moros of the Philippine Islands*. Manila, 1913.

Scott, Hugh Lennox. *Some Memories of a Soldier*. New York: Century, 1928.

Sexton, William Thaddeus. *Soldiers in the Philippines*. Washington, D.C.: Infantry Journal, 1944.

Smith, Oskaloosa, et al. *History of the Twenty-second United States Infantry, 1866–1922*. New York, 1922.

Smythe, Donald. *Guerrilla Warrior: The Early Life of John J. Pershing*. New York: Charles Scribner's Sons, 1973.

The Statutes at Large of the United States of America from March 1897 to March 1899 and Recent Treaties, Conventions, Executive Proclamations, and The Concurrent Resolutions of the Two Houses of Congress. Vol. XXX. Washington, D.C.: Government Printing Office, 1899.

U.S. War Department. *Annual Reports of the War Department for the Fiscal Year Ended June 30, 1900*. Report of the Lieutenant-General Commanding the Army. Part 3. Washington, D.C.: Government Printing Office, 1900.

————. *Annual Reports of the War Department for the Fiscal Year Ended June 30, 1901*. Report of the Lieutenant-General Commanding the Army. Part 4. Washington, D.C.: Government Printing Office, 1901.

————. *Annual Reports of the War Department for the Fiscal Year Ended June 30, 1902*. Vol. IX. Report of the Lieutenant-General Commanding the Army and Department Commanders. Washington, D.C.: Government Printing Office, 1902.

————. *Annual Reports of the War Department for the Fiscal Year Ended June 30, 1902*. Vol. I. Report of the Secretary of War and Reports of Bureau Chiefs. Washington, D.C.: Government Printing Office, 1903.

————. *Annual Reports of the War Department for the Fiscal Year Ended June 30, 1903*. Vol. III. Reports of Division and Department Commanders. Washington, D.C.: Government Printing Office, 1903.

————. *Annual Reports of the War Department for the Fiscal Year Ended June 30, 1905*. Vol. X. Report of the Philippine Commission, Part 1. Washington, D.C.: Government Printing Office, 1905.

————. *Third Annual Report of Major General Leonard Wood Governor of the Moro Province from July 1, 1905 to April 16, 1906. Brigadier General Tasker H. Bliss from April 16, 1906 to August 27, 1906*. Washington, D.C.: Government Printing Office, 1906.

————. *Annual Reports of the War Department for the Fiscal Year Ended June 30, 1906*. Vol. III. Reports of Division and Department Commanders. Washington, D.C.: Government Printing Office, 1906.

————. *Annual Reports of the War Department for the Fiscal Year Ended June 30, 1906*. Vol. VII, Part 1. Report of the Philippine Commission. Washington, D.C.: Government Printing Office, 1907.

————. *The Annual Report of the Governor of the Moro Province for the Fiscal Year Ended June 30, 1907*. Manila: Bureau of Printing, 1907.

————. *Annual Reports, 1908*. Vol. VII, Part 1. Report of the Philippine Commission. Washington, D.C.: Government Printing Office, 1909.

Vandiver, Frank E. *Black Jack: The Life and Times of John J. Pershing*. 2 vols. College Station: Texas A&M University Press, 1977.

White, John R. *Bullets and Bolos: Fifteen Years in the Philippine Islands*. New York: Century, 1928.

Zwick, Jim, ed. *Mark Twain's Weapons of Satire: Anti-Imperialist Writings on the Philippine-American War*. Syracuse, NY: Syracuse University Press, 1992.

Articles

"Agricultural Fair a Great Success." *Mindanao Herald*, February 16, 1907.

"American Abrogates Treaty With Moros." *New York Times*, March 15, 1904.

Bacevich, Andrew J., Jr. "Disagreeable Work: Pacifying the Moros, 1903–1906." *Military Review* 62, 6 (June 1982): 49–61.

Barry, Richard. "The End of Datto Ali." *Collier's*, June 6, 1906, 17–18.

Barta, Patrick. "Jailbreak in Philippines." *Wall Street Journal*, December 14, 2009.

"A Battle with Moros." *Outlook* 104 (June 21, 1913): 355.

"The Battle in Jolo." *Outlook* 82 (March 17, 1906): 582–83.

"Being a Constable Among the Moros." *Boston Evening Transcript*, July 19, 1913, 36.

Bullard, Robert L. "Preparing Our Moros for Government." *Atlantic Monthly* 97 (March 1906): 385–94.

———. "Road Building Among the Moros." *Atlantic Monthly* 92 (December 1903): 818–26.

Byler, Charles A. "Pacifying the Moros: American Military Government in the Southern Philippines, 1899–1913." *Military Review* (May–June 2005): 41–45.

Collins, James L. "The Battle of Bud Bagsak and the Part Played by the Mountain Guns Therein." *Field Artillery Journal* 15 (November–December 1925): 559–70.

"Conditions in Sulu Islands." *New York Times*, May 26, 1901.

Deady, Timothy K. "Lessons from a Successful Counterinsurgency: The Philippines, 1899–1902." *Parameters* 35, 1 (Spring 2005): 53–68.

Fleming, Thomas J. "Pershing's Island War." *American Heritage* (August 1968): 32–35, 101–4.

Ginsburgh, Robert. "Pershing as His Orderlies Knew Him." *American Legion Monthly* 5, 4 (October 1928): 9–11, 64–68.

Jones, Seth G. "Going Local: The Key to Afghanistan." *Wall Street Journal*, August 8–9, 2009.

Kolb, Richard K. "Campaign in Moroland: A War the World Forgot." *Army*, September 1983, 50–53, 56–59.

Landor, A. Henry Savage. "Experience in the Philippines." *Harper's Weekly*, May 14, 1904, 760–62.

"Lawyer Defends Soldier: Tells Supreme Court Justices Record Is One They Might Envy." *Washington Post*, March 20, 1907.

MacAdam, George. "The Life of General Pershing VI." *World's Work* 38 (May 1919): 86–101.

"National Affairs: Great Green Snake." *Time*, May 25, 1931.

Onishi, Norimitsu. "Curbed in Island Towns, Islamists in Philippines Take to Forests." *New York Times*, September 26, 2009.

Rhodes, Charles D. "The Utilization of Native Troops in Our Foreign Possessions." *Journal of the Military Service Institution of the United States* 30, 115 (January 1902): 1–21.

Roosevelt, Theodore. "General Leonard Wood: A Model American Military Administrator." *Outlook* 61 (January 7, 1899): 19–23.

Smith, C. C. "The Mindanao Moro." *U.S. Cavalry Journal* 27, 62 (October 1906): 287–308.

Smythe, Donald. "Pershing and Counterinsurgency." *Military Review* 46 (September 1966): 85–92.

———. "Pershing and the Disarmament of the Moros." *Pacific Historical Review* 31, 3 (August 1962): 241–56.

Wright, Tom. "Hidden Links Bolster Southeast Asian Militants." *Wall Street Journal*, August 28, 2009.

Worcester, Dean C. "The Non-Christian People of the Philippine Islands." *National Geographic* 24 (November 1913): 1158–256.

Dissertation

Johnson, Elliott L. "The Military Experiences of General Hugh A. Drum from 1898–1918." University of Wisconsin, 1975. Ann Arbor: University Microfilms, 1976.

Internet Sources

"City of Zamboanga." http://www.zamboanga.net/Arts&CultureZamboanga History2.htm.

De Guzman, Orlando. "Reporter's Diary. Songs of Resistance: History Repeats Itself." www.pbs.org/frontlineworld/stories/philippines/guzman02.html.

"Piang to Stimson, February 22, 1942." http://www.fdrlibrary.marist.edu/psf/box5/a60z02.html.

Sadain, Mehol K. "Sulu Treaties." Yuchengco Museum, Makati City, September 20, 2008. http://www.yuchengcomuseum.org/programs.

"206 US 333 Homer Grafton Versus United States." http://openjurist.org/206/us/333.

"Uncle Sam, the Moros, and the Moro Campaigns: A Pictorial History from 1899 to 1920." http://morolandhistory.com.

U.S. Army Center of Military History. "Medal of Honor Recipients: Philippine Insurrection." http://www.history.army.mil/html/moh/philippine.html.

"The United States versus Homer Grafton." http://www.lawphil.net/judjuris/juri1906/apr1906/gr_l-2400_1906.html.

Archival Sources

Library of Congress, Washington, D.C.
    Tasker Howard Bliss Papers
    Robert Lee Bullard Papers
    Benjamin D. Foulois Papers

Frank McCoy Papers
John J. Pershing Papers
Hugh Scott Papers
Leonard Wood Papers
U.S. Army Military History Institute, Carlisle, Pennsylvania
Tasker Howard Bliss Papers
Hugh A. Drum Papers
John P. Finley Papers
William August Kobbe Papers
Regimental histories: 6th Infantry, 27th Infantry, 28th Infantry, 4th
Regiment U.S. Cavalry
Spanish-American War Veterans Survey
University of Oregon Libraries
Charles Furlong Papers

Index

A NOTE ON THE AUTHOR

James R. Arnold is the author of more than twenty books, including *Jungle of Snakes: A Century of Counterinsurgency Warfare from the Philippines to Iraq*; *The First Domino: Eisenhower, the Military, and America's Intervention in Vietnam*; *Presidents Under Fire: Commanders in Chief in Victory and Defeat*; *Jeff Davis's Own: Cavalry, Comanches, and the Battle for the Texas Frontier*; and *Crisis in the Snows: Russia Confronts Napoleon, the Eylau Campaign 1806–1807*. He lives on a farm near Lexington, Virginia.